ADVICE TO
WAR
PRESIDENTS

ADVICE TO
WAR
PRESIDENTS

A REMEDIAL COURSE
IN STATECRAFT

ANGELO M. CODEVILLA

BASIC
BOOKS

A Member of the Perseus Books Group
New York

Books published by Basic Books are available at special discounts for bulk purchases in the United States by corporations, institutions, and other organizations. For more information, please contact the Special Markets Department at the Perseus Books Group, 2300 Chestnut Street, Suite 200, Philadelphia, PA 19103, or call (800) 810-4145, ext. 5000, or e-mail special.markets@perseusbooks.com.

Designed by Trish Wilkinson
Set in 12-point Adobe Garamond

Library of Congress Cataloging-in-Publication Data

Codevilla, Angelo, 1943-
    Advice to war presidents : a remedial course in statecraft / Angelo M. Codevilla.
        p.   cm.
    Includes index.
    ISBN 978-0-465-00483-6 (alk. paper)
    1. United States—Foreign relations—Philosophy. 2. United States—Foreign relations—21st century. 3. United States—Foreign relations—20th century. 4. War (Philosophy) I. Title.
JZ1480.C64 2008
327.73—dc22   2008035933

10 9 8 7 6 5 4 3 2 1

To the memory of Bryan Wells,
whose heart beats within me since May 20, 2004

Forgive them, for they know not
what they do.

—JESUS, LUKE 23:24

CONTENTS

PREFACE

Can't anybody here play this game?
—CASEY STENGEL

This book outlines the essentials of international affairs—diplomacy, alliances, war, economic statecraft, intelligence, and prestige (nowadays called *"soft power"*)—by contrasting them with the too convenient constructs current in American discourse. I treat the G. W. Bush Administration's incompetence in foreign policy as resulting from just another mixture of our twentieth-century statesmen's factions and faults.[1] Drawing examples from 1914 to today, I show how our statesmen have substituted imagination for the realities of statecraft. What I say may strike many as novel, because common sense about diplomacy, war, and statecraft is uncommon nowadays. When our statesmen call for new ideas, they generally want fresh excuses for conventional wisdom. I offer none here.

THE BOTTOM LINE

The century that began in 1914 and has yet to end has been a time of continuous war, more or less hot. The cooler 1920s and 1990s incubated the more intense disorders that followed. Presidents and their advisers have thrown America's mighty weight around the world's balances.

America's armed forces won nearly all their battles, and America's Soviet enemy died of its congenital disorders. But the American people found themselves ever less secure as our statesmen lost peace after peace. Losing the peace your country fought for means you lost the war. Nothing you can say, no status or credentials, can relieve you of that. Losing wars while winning battles is hard and rare. Yet American presidents and their advisers have managed to do just that for nearly a century. This requires explanation. This book is about dissecting ruinous counsel about war and peace. In the course of clearing rubbish, I hope to uncover sound principles and distill them into advice for future war presidents.

Modern American incompetence about war and peace has deep roots. As our century opened, Woodrow Wilson disdained the straightforward task of keeping Germany from dominating our seas as well as Europe's land and instead sacrificed 117,000 Americans to the chimera of ending all wars. In the process, he spawned a language about foreign affairs that has never ceased to confuse. Nor have post–World War I arrangements ceased to kill. Franklin Roosevelt refused to rearm as Nazi Germany and imperial Japan rose. He spoke in soporific generalities until after France had fallen. Then, after the attack on Pearl Harbor on December 7, 1941, Roosevelt out-Wilsoned Wilson by telling Americans that the victory of something called the United Nations (UN) would forever cleanse the world of "ancient evils, ancient ills." He placed America's eggs in Stalin's basket and kept them there after the danger had become the Soviet Union's rise, not its fall. Only in Japan did America gain the peace our arms had won, because Douglas MacArthur—a throwback to the statesmanship of common sense—kept Washington's wise men and the Soviets at bay in Tokyo. But in Korea, rid of MacArthur's simple idea of victory, Washington sent 50,000 Americans to die in a "police action" by which President Truman intended "to avoid a wider war." John Kennedy, Lyndon Johnson, and Richard Nixon sacrificed another 50,000 Americans in Vietnam believing, as Lyndon Johnson said, "there is no victory in Vietnam, for anyone." (The North Vietnamese soldier who drove his tank through the US embassy gate in Saigon in 1975 thought differently.) Thus did the "best and brightest" statesmen of the age lose America that war.

Twenty years later, as the Soviet monster was self-destructing, George Bush I did his best to keep it alive. In 1991 Bush I also sent troops to the Persian Gulf. Like Franklin Roosevelt, he did so for the sake of what he imagined was a "New World Order." Yet like Roosevelt he spawned the opposite. Nor was America at peace under Bush and Clinton even where its troops were not fighting, because our government was advising, aiding, or just hectoring inconclusively in all the world's quarrels. Bush II, for his part, met the ensuing terror and disorders by declaring war on nobody in particular, explaining in 2005 that America had to make the entire world "free" as a precondition of preserving its own freedom. Peace suffered as well as freedom. Even Woodrow Wilson would have gasped.

So must common sense. Our century's Americans have had to fight too much and gotten so little peace because presidents and their advisers have run the business of war and peace in disregard of basic skills, and have done so in a language foreign to reality. In international affairs, as in anything else, Vince Lombardi's teaching holds true: The difference between winners and losers lies in basic skills, like blocking and tackling. Theodore Roosevelt stated those fundamentals succinctly: "Speak softly and carry a big stick." The following pages show how the illusions that make up today's "mainstream thinking" foul up diplomacy, economics, wars, intelligence, and prestige (or soft power)—the international equivalents of blocking and tackling. They are written as a primer for presidents who may wish to fire failed coaches and get back to basics.

DRAMATIS PERSONAE

The US foreign policy establishment has remained recognizably itself for most of a century. Its leaders in 2010 trace their intellectual, social, and career lineages to the ideas, men, and foundations of Wilson's time a century ago. It is no exaggeration, for example, to say that Elihu Root (early century) begat Henry Stimson (early to midcentury), who begat McGeorge Bundy (late mid), who begat Anthony Lake (late twentieth to twenty-first). The American people have been unhappy with their work: disillusioned by the Great War's results, angry and suspicious about why World War II ended with most of the world in the hands of enemies, mad as hell about Korea and Vietnam, and puzzled by their nation's impotence in the face of terrorists. But after each debacle, the makers of our foreign policies have closed ranks, and America's universities, foundations, and media have continued to accredit them. This establishment has marginalized discussion of its failures because, despite divisions on details, its main components have cast discussion of international affairs in the language and assumptions of the early twentieth century's Progressive movement. All of this century's presidents have surrounded themselves with various mixtures of what today we call Liberal Internationalists, Realists, and Neoconservatives—"schools" that have far more in common than separates them.

"Liberal Internationalists" such as the late Arthur Schlesinger Jr., believing that mankind's problems have technocratic solutions, want to put America's muscle at the service of international institutions. They want to make the world look like the European Union, where experts ensure a modicum of prosperity and a maximum of leisure by making political differences irrelevant and banishing thoughts of God. For them, as for Wilson, America has no interest distinct from that of mankind. They suppose that all peoples want the same things and should get them through liberal recipes, administered by an international community of persons like themselves, and financed by the US treasury. Thus Harvard's Stanley Hoffman proposed a "world steering committee."[2] You may imagine that in addition to himself he would have placed on it Anthony Lake, a liberal perennial from the 1960s, National Security Adviser to President Clinton in the 1990s, and to President Barack Obama in 2009, who defined himself as "neo-Wilsonian."[3] Placing US troops under UN command was a hallmark of his and Clinton's tenure.

Others, such as Joshua Muravchik, labeled "Neoconservatives," want to shape foreigners according to the US national interest.[4] This emphasis on the national interest would seem to set them apart from Liberals and Wilson. But the difference is superficial because for them that interest lies largely in transforming the world's regimes into democracies, which, once accomplished, is supposed to make foreign nations and their interests more and more alike, more and more like us, less and less foreign. They see democracy itself as the spontaneous harbinger of the very peace and progress and obviation of politics that Liberal Internationalists want to engineer. Their vision of modernity is as secular and materialistic as that of other Progressives. As for peace, while Neoconservatives maintain that regimes can be mortal enemies, they agree with Liberal Internationalists that peoples themselves cannot be. Neoconservatives are somewhat more willing to use force than Liberals, but they share a distaste for the traditional distinction between war and peace.

For "Realists" in big business and in the foreign affairs bureaucracies such as James Baker and Brent Scowcroft, enlightened self-interest rules the world—even when it does not. Whereas Liberals and Neoconservatives believe that administration and democracy, respectively, must lead the world to peace and prosperity—and to nations' behaving as the United States would like—Realists are confident that all this will inevitably happen as governments adjust their interests. For them then, mankind's chief common interest is moderation, because it makes possible all necessary adjustments. As Liberals think that all *well administered* peoples are alike and Neoconservatives that all *democrats* are alike, Realists think that all *"moderates"* are essentially alike. To promote moderation, they are just as eager as Liberals and Neoconservatives to banish considerations of right and wrong, of honor, as well as ancient traditions and passions. Whereas the others disbelieve in war out of their own visions of progress, Realists disbelieve in war because they imagine that all must find it as inconvenient as they do. Hence for them the acme of success is getting along with foreign governments—and the more troublesome, the greater the need to get along. The signature of American Realist foreign policy has been deference to Russia's, China's, and the Arab world's regimes.

Far from being diverse, this establishment is unanimous on the essentials: All its parts want to reform, to teach, to stabilize—somehow to *better*—the world, to remake it in their image of America: secular, peaceful, orderly, emancipated, and cosmopolitan. Moreover, each imagines that the rest of mankind shares their own twist on those concepts. Each wants America to "lead the world" by identifying its interests and values with those of mankind. Believing that mankind's desire for peaceful pleasant living overrides its divisions into civilizations and nations, each faction of the establishment is confident that the old rules of statecraft are irrelevant to our time. Because these elites are committed to spreading peace and prosperity even as they wield the instruments of coercion, they would not force their visions onto the world. Hence they all combine big words and plentiful carrots with small sticks.

But note: This joint vision of the world is as narrow and peculiar as that of the remotest Tibetan lamasery.

REALITY

Our statesmen's formulae cannot grasp the world. Imagining that administration can substitute for politics (as if politics could be banished from the distribution of goods) has not prevented the Liberal Internationalists' creatures—the UN, the international lending institutions, the European Union itself—from being covens of corruption. In some cases Liberal projects, far from submerging ancient quarrels, have stoked them instead—as two generations' multibillion-dollar ventures in Palestinian affairs surely did. In Europe, Liberal statecraft has enervated the continent in the face of blackmail from Russia on energy and from the Middle East on immigration, and tries to make America ashamed of being otherwise.

The Neoconservative dream that democracy might make people good was dispelled by the converse reality: Democracy is what any people make it. Various peoples have freely and fairly chosen murderous governments and, indeed, have taken joy in murdering and degrading. Democracy must mirror the demos, and as the Nazi years showed, perverse regimes can lead even previously civilized people to support slaughter.

The Realist bet on "moderation"—the apolitical division of mankind into "moderates" and "extremists"—has obscured substantive questions of what anyone is moderate or extreme *about*. It has led to moderation in the pursuit of America's interests in the hope of thereby coaxing "extremists" into "moderation," to promoting moderation for its own sake, and to making to terrorists the kinds of concessions the Realists once made to the Soviets. America's enemies have found it just as easy to decipher the logic of "Realism" as to exploit the logic of our establishment's bets on Liberal administration and Neoconservative democracy.

The world transcends these Progressives' imagination. Our establishment offends foreigners by telling them not to care about the things they care about. Typically, a Washington insider described the clashes between

Islam's Sunni and Shia as "kindergarten stuff they should get over." But that "stuff" is what they are about. Worse, fascination with others' quarrels diverted attention from America's interests.

The very words in which American Progressives' values are expressed are meaningless to most human beings. No amount of wishing can abstract from fact that we are one variety or another of Sinotic or North African or Negroid or European, break the molds in which our civilizations cast us, cancel the categories that our religions have stamped on our minds, make tasteful things that have revolted us since childhood, lessen our tribal aversions and affections, or reduce the relevance of the regimes in which we live. Our statesmen deny the relevance of differences—of other peoples' loves and hates, calculations and intrigues—treating all as if they were not foreign at all, confusing the human race with *homo economicus californianus*. But you must keep in mind that foreign relations are about dealing with foreigners—people whose identities and agendas are inalienably their own. Because this has ever been so, the art of international affairs developed as it did over millennia. Problem is, our establishment has largely set aside that art and created another to fit its own image.

When our statesmen have come a cropper operating by the rules and language of their collective imagination, they have not asked whether they should perhaps go back to fundamentals—understanding foreigners as they understand themselves, *diplomacy* and *war* as dictionaries define them and as history has embodied them. Rather, following Wilson's example, they have blamed their failures on the American people's narrow-minded reticence to follow their leaders patiently "for the long haul." While admitting imperfection, they have given themselves passing grades. But war gives only two grades: A and F.

FUNDAMENTALS

Aristotle taught that just as a farmer's actions must be judged by how well he produces grain or fruit, victory is the natural purpose of war, and peace is the fruit of victory. Hence the statesman must ask, Is *this* the kind of peace we want? Does *this* action actually produce *that*? Speeches, "positions" about international affairs, and military expeditions must not be confused with statecraft any more than tractors, work, and wishes are to be confused with farming, or muscles and mouth with football.

The practical art of statesmanship, then, especially in war, consists of measuring the ends sought with the means necessary to achieve them. Twentieth-century American elites, however, have committed our country to the grandest of ends but have not measured them against the means necessary to achieve them—ends hazily imagined, and means they might not have used even if they had them. Instead of scaling up means or scaling down ends, they invented vocabularies to describe a fantasy in which the means with which they felt comfortable would suffice to remake the world. This meant abandoning the wisdom concerning peace, war, diplomacy, intelligence, prestige, and economics accumulated in our civilization over millennia. In the new, unprecedented world they imagined, any given instance of peace was not the product of a particular victory and arrangement of power but rather the absence of conflict. Diplomacy was not a set of tools but a substitute for force. Intelligence was not a matter of a few hidden details but a magic wand to uncover the secret to effortless success. Prestige was a reputation, not for being effective but for being pleasant. Wealth was not one of many elements of power but everyone's overriding purpose.

To be other than sorcerers' apprentices, American statesmen had better deal with reality as described in dictionaries. This book does not impose its own categories. It looks at international affairs as the interaction of individuals and groups who are what they are, want what they want, and do what they do. It is about the consequences of forgetting common-sense definitions: that diplomacy is mere communication, that international intercourse requires a positive imbalance of means over ends, that allies are available in inverse proportion to the need for them, and that war is the avenue to peace via the gateway of the enemy's death or submission.

The book's advice to American presidents in this continuing century of war is, above all, to keep it simple: to come down from rhetorical highs, to use words according to their ordinary meanings, and sharply to distinguish war from peace, lest they give us violence without end.

INTRODUCTION
A Remedial Primer

Fine things are hard.
— ARISTOTLE

This book is a primer on the tools of statecraft. For many years I taught a course at Boston University on how states may use prestige, diplomacy, economics, subversion, and force to serve their ends.[1] The course meant to introduce students to the tools of statecraft. Knowing what the tools can and cannot do, what handling and mishandling them means, is essential to practicing any art. The course consisted largely of putting students in contact with historic instances in which statesmen had used the tools correctly. But all too often, the thoughts and actions of current and recent American statesmen imposed themselves as negative counterpoints. Reasonably, students would ask: "Why do our leaders mess up so regularly?" This question led naturally to another: "Don't our top people know the basics of their jobs?" And since the question seemed to contain its own answer, it led to a more fruitful one: "What is the very least that anyone—President, legislator, adviser, or publicist— should know who handles or influences the handling of statecraft's deadly tools?"

This book is an answer to that question. It is a *primer* on wartime statecraft—neither definitive nor exhaustive. Just the basics. It is needed because our statesmen's errors are not ones of detail but rather proceed precisely from misunderstanding the basics. It is meant for people who are already acquainted with international affairs, often very well acquainted with well-accepted definitions of diplomacy and other instruments and with the standard recipes for using them, but who wonder why the recipes so often don't work. So this longtime professor set about explaining where current recipes come from and comparing them with the old standards in the field.

To explain each of statecraft's tools, the book treats them singly. And since statecraft is a practical art, the explanations consist largely of historical examples. But exemplary international events invariably involve many factors. That is why the book deals with exemplary events, e.g., the Peloponnesian war and the Cuban Missile Crisis several times, each time extracting the lessons they contain about a specific tool. So the diplomacy chapter mines the Cuban Missile Crisis' lessons for diplomacy while the intelligence chapter looks at the same incident from the standpoint of intelligence, and so forth. In the same way, the book describes the similarities and differences among the several "schools" of twentieth-century American statesmen as they manifest themselves in diplomacy, war, etc. It treats the same events several times, but from different perspectives.

This book does not recommend policies. Presidents and citizens are awash in White Papers stuffed with recipes for every imaginable problem. Nearly all are written in a language loaded with assumptions that are strange to reality. Rather, the book invites the reader to think of war and peace in terms that carry their ordinary, common-sense meaning. Thus it sheds light on the major intellectual benchmarks by which this century's Presidents and some of our most influential citizens gauge international affairs. It shows that these benchmarks, these axioms, these recipes, are not written in the stars, that it is not absolutely necessary for statesmen to behave as ours have during the last century. Indeed this primer argues that the art of statecraft and its tools set very different intellectual benchmarks.

To grasp anew the perennial instruments of statecraft we begin by examining the language, the words in which our statesmen have done our business since Wilson's time—terms that refer to things that exist only in their vocabulary, such as "collective security." Others, like "diplomacy," carry meanings different from those of standard dictionaries. Then, examining the axioms of their mentality, e.g., that mankind shares "universal human aspirations," we see that these have lethal consequences for whoever might try living by them. Thus having understood the materials out of which twentieth-century statesmen forged their tools, we look at those tools themselves. We grasp how they manage to confuse their own preferences for how nations should behave with the prestige that makes the difference when human passions clash. We see the practical consequences of regarding the medium of communication that is diplomacy as possessing thaumaturgic value apart from the substance of the messages conveyed. The same mentality leads them to regard money as a substitute for force rather than as its product. We note that the different ways in which they use the word "war" similarly ignore the reality that war really involves killing and cowing lots of people lest we lose our peace and our lives. We see in our statesmen's reverence for ever-more "intelligence" eagerness for putting off decisions, avoiding responsibility, and escaping hard choices. Finally, the same distaste for deciding who the enemy is and how to deal with him explains our government's passion for security—meaning for policing the general public as if all were equally likely to be enemies. By contrast, classic texts and America's experience teach that true security comes not from militarized policing but from civil society making sharp choices about friends and enemies.

Twentieth-century statesmen and academics vie to describe the problems of wartime statecraft as bewilderingly complex. But precisely because they are complex, the art of statecraft consists of simplifying them. Only if the statesman's axioms are congruent with reality, only when his objectives are clear and feasible, when he knows what each tool in his kit can and cannot do is he then able to orchestrate them. So, since the statesman's task is to arrange disparate elements and forces to produce his desired result, his maxim should be: "Keep it simple!"

CHAPTER 1

USE THE DICTIONARY

If language is not correct then what is said is not what is meant. If what is said is not what is meant, then what ought to be done remains undone. If this remains undone, then morals and acts deteriorate. If morals and acts deteriorate, justice will go astray. If justice goes astray, the people will stand about in helpless confusion. Hence, there must be no arbitrariness in what is said. This matters above everything.
— CONFUCIUS

Calling things by their name, using words according to their ordinary meaning, anchors the mind to reality. But when reality is bitter, when the things that are differ from what we wish, we sugarcoat them with euphemisms or put our wishes' names on them. Thus hoping to transform our surroundings, we fool ourselves. Since the turn of the twentieth century, generations of American statesmen have so detested war's bloody realities, mankind's miseries and divisions, have been so confident of their capacity to cure them, that they have described them with words that presume cures. *Each abstraction or euphemism distorts an unpleasant fact of life, makes impossible things seem possible, unmanageable ones seem manageable. The sum of them shields our statesmen's axioms against common sense.* Language that falsifies international life alienates our statesmen from the arts of statecraft.[1]

America's Founders wrote of statecraft in a language that was cold, precise, discriminating, and moralizing—a language that reflected basic choices between war and peace, life and death, freedom and slavery, honor and cowardice, fear and interest. In *The Federalist #6,* Alexander Hamilton wrote that "men are ambitious, vindictive, and rapacious. . . . The causes of hostility between nations are innumerable." He reminded his readers, to whom it was "generally known," that much of Europe's contemporary turmoil was due to common human failings, including "the bigotry of one female, the petulancies of another and the cabals of a third." His point was: "Have we not seen enough of the fallacy and extravagance of those idle theories which have amused us with an exemption from the imperfections, the weaknesses and the evils incident to societies of every shape?" Moreover, America's Founders felt acutely the fragility of America's own moral character. That character was certainly George Washington's paramount concern, as he stressed in his letters to Congress from the fighting fronts, in his first Inaugural Address, and in his Farewell Address. Bluntly, the Founders referred to North African potentates as pirates and pests, and discussed dispassionately the costs and benefits of bribing or annihilating them. Reading our statesmen's words from Washington to William Seward you get used to moral judgments mixed with arguments over ends and means. You see no euphemisms, and get the sense that these statesmen thought about foreign affairs in continuing conversation with the ancients and with the basic texts of the craft.

But by 1900, America's leaders talked heady talk. Though they traveled more than had the Founders, their words reflected narrower, more parochial minds. Fewer are the references to history. The distinctions between America and the rest of the world are less sharp and principled. Their references to morality, though perhaps more abundant than ever, are shallower. By 1900, our statesmen had been deeply affected by the ease with which so much land had come into the Republic's possession, and by how Europe and Japan had seemingly heeded their counsel regarding the Western Hemisphere, China, Morocco, and international law. It seemed inevitable that law would rule the world, and that they would write it. World War I occasioned even headier talk.

But only in speech did our statesmen slip reality's leash. Some of their words refer to things that exist only in their imagination. And while others may be found in the dictionary, our statesmen's usage stuffs them with ersatz meaning. When Woodrow Wilson first spoke this language, the American people found it strange. Thus *The New Republic* editorialized: "Moral enthusiasm is what he gives us, redeemed only by the most abstract references to living. . . . When you have cleaned your morality into a collection of abstract nouns, you have something that is clean and white. But what else have you?"[2] Nevertheless, by the 1920s, abstraction from reality had become the rule in American political discourse. Herbert Hoover's and Franklin D. Roosevelt's rhetoric was more abstractly Wilsonian than Wilson's. Such talk remains the common currency of prestige journals as well as of TV commentary and Presidential campaigns in our time.

In sum, because our statesmen had developed a very peculiar mindset, they developed what amounts to a tribal language, meaningful only to themselves. A thick dictionary would be needed to retranslate it into English. As we peruse the elements of statecraft, we will see countless evasive verbal maneuvers, many peculiar to narrow historical circumstances. Here I break down the moves of some notable verbal gymnastics.

THE INTERNATIONAL COMMUNITY

Today's fantasy of an *"international community,"* within which all mankind supposedly lives by common standards, evolved from the *reality of modern international law,* which originated in the 1648 treaties of Westphalia. But these treaties in fact denied any common standard. By agreeing to Westphalia the Holy Roman Emperor, the kings of Spain, France, and Sweden, the Dutch Republics, the Swiss federation and German princes acknowledged that they no longer had in common the Christian canon law that had ruled relations among them since the days of Charlemagne. Asserting their *sovereignty,* they promised thenceforth not to interfere in each others' internal affairs, and to abide by their promises. Modern international law is neither more nor less than the sum of those promises—namely, treaties, conventions, agreements, customs, etc. In practice, the promisers keep promises as long as they find it convenient to do so, and to the extent that the promisees make it inconvenient not to do so. Each and every nation is *equal only in its sovereign right* to judge for itself what it owes and is owed.

That is why the "nations" never had much in "common," in the dictionary sense that husbands and wives have property and children in common. As John Quincy Adams taught, sovereigns' interests may be parallel—but are never common. Nor does any amount of intercourse commonality make. The noises coming from our statesmen about *what the international community* demands from Iran, North Korea, Sudan, etc., hardly obscure the fact that antagonism—not commonality—reigns on such matters, that the world's major governments pursue policies often diametrically opposed.

Because *sovereign autonomy is the essence of international law,* serious persons do not imagine that its proceedings can prevent states from harming or even annihilating one another. Much less should one expect today's states, which arguably have less in common than the world's polities have had since the Dark Ages, to pursue common goods, much less to safeguard one another at risk to themselves. Thus in 1795, when the "international community" consisted only of a few European Christian kings, they calmly eliminated Poland from the map by dividing it between Prussia, Russia, and Austria. In 1914, when most of Europe's sovereigns were related to one another, they began the Great War that set the tone for our bloody time.

As this was about to happen, turn-of-the-twentieth-century Progressives were imagining that this "community," which included all Christian peoples, would ensure peace and justice to all its members and extend it to the rest of mankind. In 1910, Nicholas Murray Butler, first head of the Carnegie Endowment for International Peace, wrote:

> To suppose that men and women into whose intellectual and moral instruction and upbuilding have gone the glories of the world's philosophy and art and poetry and religion, into whose lives have been poured for two thousand years the precepts and the inspiration of the Christian religion, over whose daily conduct have been thrown since the days of Draco and of Solon the restraints of law and of consideration for the rights and property of others—to suppose that these men and women when gathered together in groups called nations . . . are to fly at each others' throats to burn, to

ravage, to kill, in the hope of somehow establishing thereby truth and right and justice is to suppose the universe to be stood upon its apex.[3]

Thus determined to bring order, justice, peace, and unity out of the violent injustice of relations among sovereign nations, Progressives invented a series of institutions with names that made their task seem possible, if not already achieved. Former Secretary of State Elihu Root got the 1912 Nobel Peace Prize for having fostered 113 bilateral treaties of "compulsory arbitration." What might such a thing be? Arbitration is real enough. From time immemorial, governments and individuals have chosen to submit some of their disputes to the judgment of third-party arbiters. But *compulsory* arbitration is nonsense because states heed arbiters' adverse decisions only when they don't find them too inconvenient. "Compulsion" can be inflicted on any state only by force. Treaties, including ones that promise to abide by arbitration, are promises that the parties may or may not choose to observe or enforce. Hence the notion of *compelling* arbitration is self-contradictory.

After compulsory arbitration had failed to prevent the Great War, Progressives upped the ante by imagining the 1914 "League to Enforce Peace" and its successor, the 1919 "League of Nations." *League*? To what were the Nations supposed to be leaguing, meaning tying or binding, themselves? What forces, what ligaments, were to do the tying? Woodrow Wilson argued that though the 1919 settlement had not settled the nations' claims and fears, it had established the League, which would resolve them and ensure the peace.[4] On the basis of the League, American and British statesmen brokered the birth of unnatural entities, from Danzig to the Danube, from Prague to Palestine, from Istria to Iraq. But who would fight to sustain Poland and Czechoslovakia? Whose force would keep Yugoslavia and Iraq united, safeguard the Polish Corridor, or let Lebanon live? The Nations nominally leagued together by the Versailles settlement lacked common will to enforce it, because the settlement had neither settled the claims of each nor given anyone a stake in upholding anyone else's claims. What sense is there in subscribing to ambitious arrangements while abstracting from the issues that make them ambitious, and forswearing force to settle them? Unprecedented pledges of common purpose involved more nations with less in common than before. It was as if the foundations' very flimsiness led its architects to pile heavy burdens upon them.[5]

Why then did each nation sign the Treaty of Versailles? None signed up to fight for others. Perhaps a few Czechs or Poles imagined that Britain and France would fight for them in the League's name. But Frenchmen and Britons were not about to die for Danzig or the Sudetenland. Some war-weary Europeans might have imagined that the Americans would fight their battles. But for many Americans, the League was a collective self-denial of violence by which they meant to shame potential violators into forbearance. For others it was a collective act of faith that the satisfied and meek might dissuade the aggrieved and the bold with talk and money.

MEMBERS OF THE COMMUNITY

Because the Treaty's Anglo American drafters wanted the League to include all "civilized" peoples, they had to include as members the Nations defeated and dismembered in the Great War, hoping that these nations would not use that membership to challenge its results. Also, in homage to the ideology that the general progress of civilization was homogenizing all peoples, they made Ethiopia and Japan the first non-European members of the community. And by labeling Europe's colonies "League mandates," they expressed faith that, eventually, non-European civilizations would add whatever commitment to the League's hopes that the European members lacked. In sum, the League consisted of foggy hopes.

World War II blew the fog away. By 1939, never mind 1945, the Leagued nations' antagonisms dwarfed their pre-Leagued ones. To shield minds from this red-hot fact, Progressives invented words even denser and farther from reality: No longer were the Nations merely Leagued together. Now they would be *United*—meaning literally that whereas they had been many and disparate once upon a time, now they were becoming a single one. *E pluribus unum.* But united around what, for what, kept by what? The UN's charter says that "we the peoples" of the nations are "determined," meaning both resolute and foreordained, to "save succeeding generations from the scourge of war . . . to unite our strength to maintain international peace and security . . . to ensure . . . that armed force shall not be used, save in the *common interest* . . . to take effective *collective measures* for the prevention and removal of threats to the peace, and for the suppression of acts of aggression or other breaches of the peace." To accomplish all that, the signatories pledged: "All members shall *refrain in their international relations from the threat or use of force against the territorial integrity or political independence of any state*" (emphasis mine).

Thus the UN charter dealt with the contradictions that had discredited the League by grasping all their horns simultaneously. The preamble's first words are counterfactual: The world's *peoples* had not conceived the UN, and the member *governments* had mutually incompatible objectives in mind for it. The member nations renounced war, but retained the right to self-defense, and the right to define the meaning thereof in their own interest. So because only some of the members' interests may concur (though for disparate reasons) while others will run counter, the notion of *collective* measures on the whole's behalf is nonsense—because *no collectivity exists*. Moreover, by abjuring acts against the independence or territorial integrity of any member state, the UN's framers denied the reality that defending peace—anybody's peace, really—would most likely require undoing the independence, territorial integrity, or regime of whichever nation (now disunited?) might have broken that peace.

Aware of these realities in 1945, the members of the Security Council secured themselves against each other even as they were pledging to provide security for all. They officially recognized each others' "sovereign equality" even as they acceded to Stalin's blatantly unequal demand to seat Byelorussia and Ukraine as sovereign nations, though no one—least of all Stalin—pretended they were. Yet that fiction was no bigger than the affirmation that membership in this "unity" was open only to "peace loving" states: Since the Communists considered that the "Imperialists'" very existence was a threat to peace, and vice versa, neither considered the other "peace loving." Consequently they would spend a half-century preparing to annihilate each another.

But the UN's "peace loving" qualification for membership—even had it been taken seriously—was a comedown from the League of Nations' requirement that its members be "civilized." That in turn had been a comedown from our statesmen's original position: that *Christian, Protestant civilization* was creating a peaceful community by transcending human differences. After the Great War had discredited their version of Christian civilization our statesmen hoped harder than ever for that transcendence, but now on the basis of hope itself. Disappointments only speeded their defining decency down.[6] The community's first non-Christian member, Japan, used its first act—partnership in the Washington Treaties of 1921— to secure naval primacy in the Western Pacific, therewith to rape China and get a head start on World War II. After our statesmen fought that war against the formerly Christian and civilized Germans, they dropped the very concept of civilization from the list of qualifications for membership. They could not do otherwise, since they yearned for the Soviet Union to be one of the UN's five pillars. So essential was the USSR to the dream of an all-powerful international community that the UN's framers disregarded that it proclaimed enmity to all "present day" civilization. For the dream's sake, the community had to include especially those who denied the very notion of commonality. And so de facto the only qualification for membership became government power, stripped of any ethical or political content.

By 1993, the logic of defining the community to include those most troublesome to it led the UN General Assembly to drop even state power as a qualification, as it honored one Yasser Arafat—leader of a band that bombed school buses and murdered ambassadors as well as ordinary folk—as if he were the head of a peace-loving state. They created the Palestinian Authority (PA) and gave him full power over it, hoping this might moderate him. Hence, "moderation"—or at least the hope of moderation—became the final pretend-criterion for membership. But moderation compared to what? The standard of measurement turned out to be hope driven by fear.

By the 1960s, this logic-transmogrifying the equality of international law into the pretense that all nations are really actually equal—led to a language that obscured distinctions between mankind's best and worst. "Uncivilized" became "underdeveloped," and then "developing."[7] But while Singapore, Taiwan, and South Korea developed, Africa and the Middle East spiraled deeper into misery—moral as well as material. Our statesmen brandished the word "racist" to banish from their minds and from public discourse the fact that what they called governments were really gangs that looted once flourishing places, and that tribal logic ruled life in most of the former colonies. But having agreed that Moscow's Stalin was "peace loving," our statesmen found it no great leap to regard as civilized such cannibal regimes as Idi Amin's in Uganda, to listen to Saudis lecturing Americans about religious toleration, or to accept that the "international community" should choose Libya and Sudan to define its standard of "human rights" for the UN. Hence in March 2008 the UN Human Rights Commission released a report according to which "acts committed in the course of war of national liberation against colonialism, apartheid, or military occupation"—of which Israel's "Judaization" of Jerusalem is the object example—must not be called "terrorism."

Arguably the most significant word in that language was the label "producers." Truly, the Swiss produce watches, the Japanese produce Toyotas, and the Germans Volkswagens. And although foreign companies manage much of Africa's exports, nevertheless, Cameroonians, say, really are *producers* of cocoa beans because they work the fields. But, *pace* our statesmen, the Arab sheiks who collect rent on oil produced by American engineers with South Asian labor are not oil *producers* in the sense that Norwegians are oil producers. By what definition are the sheiks *producers* or *owners*?

Sovereignty is the only attribute that the kings and sheiks share with the Norwegians that entitle them to the titles of owners and producers of oil. The men of Versailles, 1919, were pleased to pretend that the desert tribesmen of the fallen Ottoman Empire were sovereign, and hence possessed of absolute prerogative over "their" territory, just like the signatories of Westphalia. From the 1920s to the 1960s, while the oil companies paid royalties to keep these "royals" in palaces, neither side imagined that this sovereignty might override the companies' ownership of leases and lands, as well as of everything else having to do with the oil. That ownership was based not only on the commonsense Lockean (and even Marxian) criterion that mixing your labor with something makes you its owner but also on contracts. By the 1960s, however, our statesmen's use of the term "oil-producing countries" showed that they had come to believe their own fiction, that the theoretical sovereignty they had granted the Arabs and Iranians meant that these were somehow *producing* oil and that this overrode all other sources of right.

Precision about sovereignty is in order. In international law, sovereignty is bound up with the recognition thereof—a legal act of will. One state's recognition of another in law, *de jure,* may proceed from and consist of little but the desire that the state recognized as sovereign should exist. But recognition *de jure* creates sovereignty only in the minds of the recognizers. It may encourage others who agree, but it adds nothing to anyone's power. On the other hand, recognition of sovereignty may abstract entirely from whether anybody thinks a government should or should not exist, and relate exclusively to the *fact* that the government is exercising and can be expected to exercise sovereign control over a territory and its people in the face of foreseeable challenges—recognition *de facto.*[8]

In what sense, then, should we deem the oil-producing states *sovereign*? The Amazon's primitive tribes exercise sovereign control over themselves in the deepest jungle only until people with guns come to take the trees. Then they disappear along with the trees. By contrast, Iran and Norway are sovereign in fact because each is a functioning society with functional citizens. If deprived of recognition, their sovereignty would lack only recognition because the Norwegian people (and the Persians too) would continue to exist even if they were deprived of national institutions, just as Poland continued to exist after it was partitioned out of legal existence in 1795. But it may be said of Saudi Arabia and the Gulf States that their sovereignty consists of recognition alone. A majority of Kuwait's residents are not Kuwaitis. In the Emirates, three-fourths are foreigners. In these places, as in Saudi Arabia, the foreigners do the work. The local potentates and their subjects have no more capacity physically to control the oil fields than they have to work them. These so-called nations exist only through money that the native potentates receive, which they receive solely because our statesmen recognized them as sovereign over the oil. Were our statesmen to withdraw the recognition and the money, were they to treat the potentates as bandits, these men could do little about it. Nothing would be left of their sovereignty. To recognize things that exist only by virtue of your recognition is to mesmerize yourself.

In 1973, the governments of the Persian Gulf took this sovereignty literally. They raised the price of oil from less than $2 per barrel to over

$10, and our statesmen became collectors of the massive taxes the sheiks were imposing on the rest of the world. By 2008, they and the financiers who speculated on their actions had raised the price to over $140, causing discomfort to most of mankind and starvation to some. Nevertheless, our statesmen assumed that mankind would suffer injury indefinitely for the sake of respecting rights that dysfunctional governments cannot defend physically any more than intellectually. It would be truly novel if billions of productive people longed to suffer at the hands of a relative handful for the sake of misapplied language.

What came, then, of hypostatizing the terms "international community" and "equality"? Our statesmen got used to pretending that the perfumed representatives of smelly regimes were other than Communists, despots, tin-pot dictators, parasites, savages, desert bandits, and terrorists. Through fanciful language they evaded pondering who is trying to do what to whom at any given time, what is more or less just, who might fight for what, and what their own responsibility may be for securing our interest.

WAR, SECURITY, ALLIANCE, AND PURPOSE

Though war and politics are two aspects of the same reality, our statesmen's language has treated them as if they were opposites. Woodrow Wilson's contemporaries marveled at how he had invented words for things no one had ever seen to banish the very language that describes nations' conflicts and concurrences, wars and alliances. To Wilson we owe, among many other terms, "community of power" and "collective security." By making up terms implying that distinct bodies politic would combine to produce things that statesmanship had drawn out of single ones heretofore, he posited a statesmanship that transcends the difference between the singular and the plural, the particular and the universal. But individual bodies politic are distinct precisely because the planet's many peoples are at odds over who should have power over what. Wars are the exercise of power to gain power. Presuming to prevent them by combining all sides' contrasting objectives and tools of conflict reverses the sense of words and of reality. And so does the notion of securing people who fear one another by inventing words that pretend that they really want to protect each other. In short, Wilson taught his successors to deal with wars by pretending they don't have sides.

Wilson thought alliances were causes of conflict, not manifestations or tools thereof. Take away the alliances and you take away the conflicts. If no nation allies *with* another, then none can ally *against* another, right? Hence we can engineer peace by banishing alliances. Making peace that way seems a lot easier than resolving contrary claims by compromise, by balancing power, or by the triumph of some over others. Thus because by Wilson's pretend-logic alliances and guarantees start wars by directing the energies of some against others, he refused France's request for an alliance against Germany's resurgence, or even for a US guarantee of France's security.

That these deadly purposes and energies existed all by themselves seems not to have occurred to him. The League was supposed to foster peace because it was not an alliance but an "association" for mutual security on behalf of all, directed against none. Organizing international relations so apolitically was necessary and proper in the age of democracy because peoples supposedly had no political animosities against one another. But abstracting from the reality of who wants what, and of who is in whose way, stops no aggressors and cripples only your mind.

Franklin D. Roosevelt had to perform even greater linguistic feats. In October 1937 Japan was raping China, and Germany was about to swallow Austria and extinguish Czechoslovakia while waging proxy war in Spain against the Soviet Union. Franklin Roosevelt's speeches dealt with these things without using proper names—never "Germany," or "Japan," not "Hitler" or "Stalin." Rather, he labeled war and preparations for it the manifestation of a "disease" that called for "quarantine." He defined abstractly, impersonally, and pseudoclinically a problem that consisted of real people and their purposes. He defined America's interest in terms of an amorphous "peace." But whose peace? At the cost of what war? He refused to ask Congress and the American people to rearm, or to fortify Guam, the Philippines, and Hawaii. Even after Roosevelt had engaged America's armed forces, his words avoided engaging the political problems of the war. Nor is there evidence that he engaged them in the privacy of his mind. On January 2, 1942, he labeled World War II's alliance with Britain and Russia a universal "unity"—not for any ordinary purpose, but for transcending the very nature of the international order. That would take winning. But his demand for "unconditional surrender" masked evasion of what, precisely, America needed to win for itself in Europe and Asia. What it would take to win these concrete goods, and how it were best done, lay outside Roosevelt's language, and presumably his mind.[9]

After 1945, Roosevelt's successors could no longer deny that America had to confront the Soviet Union's enmity and that it needed the help of other nations. Nevertheless, Secretary of State Dean Acheson assured the Senate Foreign Relations Committee that, no, the North Atlantic Treaty Organization (NATO) was not really an alliance. It was not directed at any nation, just as the Marshall Plan was open to any nation. In our statesmen's lexicon, these arrangements were the antithesis of alliances, politically neutral arrangements opposed only to whomever might commit aggression. Whom did Acheson fool by glossing over the obvious fact that NATO and the Marshall Plan were meant to "keep the Russians out, the Americans in, and the Germans down?"[10] Moreover, calling the European countries of the late 1940s "allies" rather than "protectorates" represented more hope than reality. Yes, they were allies in that they shared America's objectives. But they were protectorates simply because they lacked the physical and above all the moral wherewithal to contribute significantly to their own defense. In our time, however, most Western European states are neither allies nor protectorates because their leading citizens see America as the world's most dangerous nation. Since the 1970s, their role in counsel has been to urge America to join them in appeasing common enemies, and to act as a brake on America. Using the word "Alliance" hides these harsh realities.

The bottom-line question about alliances must be "who's willing to do what, and why?" But that question is meaningful only to the extent that you relate it to what *we* are after. Alas, since Versailles 1919, our statesmen have abstracted from these essentials. The nonsense of *collective security* contains within it the further illusion that nations will place themselves in danger, or even go to war even though they have no particular interest in doing so, and hence that there is something abnormal about alliances or coalitions of the willing—as if anyone had ever seen coalitions of the unwilling.[11] Just as important, our statesmen's thinking about America's objectives has been addled by the commitment to maintain the "independence and territorial integrity" of the nations and nonnations designated by the Versailles settlement or defined by membership in the UN, embodied in the word "stability." "Instability" is American longhand for "bad."

And yet change is the law of life. Of all the objectives you can imagine, *stability* is the only one that makes no sense because it is substantively empty and utterly impossible. Our statesmen don't reject change per se, only such change that results from force rather than agreement. But such change happens every day, and our statesmen's occasional commitment of American blood and treasure against it has not, does not, and cannot stop it. "Stability" hinders only our asking of any given conflict: "What, exactly is that to us? What dog in that fight is ours, if any? What does it take to make it come out our way, and is that worth the trouble?"

By the 1960s, the Kennedy Administration was describing its relationship with Latin America as an "Alliance For Progress." While such language made some people feel above mortal struggles, it hid the fact that real interests were being brokered, some agendas favored, and others opposed. In short, such language makes it difficult to understand who is doing what to whom, who's on whose side, and why, and to figure out what is best for us.

WEAPONS

In our statesmen's language—but there alone—weapons are not the tools of opposing political wills but rather the causes of strife against which all can make common cause. Common sense says that the most important things about any weapon are the direction in which it is pointing and the intentions of the person wielding it. But because our Progressives are bent on denying the relevance of human differences, eager to avoid placing blame but wishing rather to indict impersonal, value-free causes for the world's troubles, they invented the notion that weapons themselves—inanimate objects though they be—are evil. At the turn of the twentieth century, as European peoples were preparing their minds to slaughter one another, Progressives such as Stanford's David Starr Jordan were writing that arms manufacturers were manufacturing international quarrels: "The war scares with Germany and Japan are made up for a purpose by foolish and wicked men . . . to exploit these scares is a crime against decency."[12] The price of one battleship, he lamented, would run Stanford University for a year. Despite the Great War, Progressives insisted that the populations who were waging it wanted nothing to do with it, that the weapons themselves caused war by stoking *irrational fears*. Thucydides had written that "fear"—reasonable expectation of specific enemy acts—was a prime cause of war. But the Progressives thought of "fear" as an irrational, generalized passion induced by the presence of arms, regardless of who held them and why. They forgot that men had slaughtered with rudimentary weapons, and with none at all.

So before, during, and since the Great War, "disarmament" has been on all proper lips. In practice, "disarmament" came to mean that governments would trade carefully hedged promises to limit certain kinds of weapons. But why sweat the details if not for advantage? To admit this question is to acknowledge that pretending to disarm is part of preparing for war. As the US Senate was about to establish the Arms Control and Disarmament Agency in 1961, Senator Richard Russell asked what sense it made to disarm while arming or to arm while disarming. Senator Hubert Humphrey chastised his question by calling disarmament part of the quest for "the holy grail of peace." What might that be?

The salient fact about "disarmament" is how simplemindedly Americans have taken it. Secretary of State Charles Evans Hughes and his successors let the Washington Treaties of 1921, amended in 1930—within whose provisions they knew the Germans and Japanese were arming—cover their own determination to disarm America as much as possible. Walter Lippmann summed it up in 1943: "The disarmament movement" had been "tragically successful in disarming the nations that believed in disarmament."

Thereafter, "disarmament" morphed into "arms control." The apolitical idea behind it was unchanged: If nations agree to restrain their armaments just a little, the process may eclipse the reasons why they armed in the first place. Your motives were supposed to be the same as their motives. The "mechanism" was to let negotiated restrictions on certain categories of arms "lead" the nations to harmony. How finely worded arms control provisions are supposed to do that is a mystery. For example, part of the US-Soviet Strategic Arms Limitation Treaty (Salt II) of 1979 provided that some Soviet Backfire-class bombers capable of reaching the United States without refueling should carry "Functionally Related Observable Differences" to distinguish them from others not counted under the treaty because they were presumably incapable of doing so. (By Freudian coincidence, the acronym was FRODS.) No one ventured to explain why the operationally meaningless addition of FRODS should have moved the Soviets to refrain from using any of these bombers for the purposes they could serve best. The Americans were content to let their imaginary language substitute for reality.

THE PSEUDOSCIENCE OF DEFENSE POLICY

Beginning in the 1950s, putting the conflict between the United States and the Soviet Union into the language of academic political science and game theory schematized international relations and obscured its substantive content. Thus Nobel laureate Thomas Schelling led a generation of academics to discuss "conflict behavior as a bargaining process . . . a dynamic process of mutual accommodation."[13] Schelling claimed to have written "a study of conscious, intelligent, sophisticated conflict behavior—of successful behavior . . . behavior in a conflict-winning sense."[14] Embedded in his language was the notion that "in addition to divergence of interest over the variables in dispute, there is a powerful *common interest* in reaching an outcome that is not enormously destructive of values to both sides"[15] (emphasis mine). Driving this verbal homogenization and depoliticization was the very political purpose of minimizing the differences between the United States and the Soviet Union in American political discourse. Schelling and the young Henry Kissinger argued *sotto voce* that the Soviets' aims were as limited as their own—not essentially different.[16] By embedding in the language the assumption that all countries are essentially interchangeable, driven by the same incentives and disincentives, that they operate on the basis of agreed rules, they made it difficult for those in America who wanted victory over the Soviet Union rather than accommodation to counter with arguments from the real world.

In this pseudoscience of conflict, the purposes for which the United States and the Soviet Union armed did not matter any more than did their capacities or their character. The United States and the Soviet Union were simply each other's obverse, as interchangeable as pieces on a game board. They and all other nations were engaged in competition and were assumed to be driven by what the "adversary" did. The only explanation for any action was "reaction" to what the other side was doing. Hence arms programs did not reflect military purposes that in turn reflected political ones, but were merely reactions to the other side's reaction to your previous reaction . . . *ad infinitum*. Such *arms races* could spiral or escalate upward or downward, regardless of intentions, objectives, capabilities. Each side's will, its fears, were assumed to be symmetrical.

By the 1960s, the politically meaningful terms "enemy," "war," and "victory" were replaced by "competitor," "conflict," and "prevailing." The latter morphed into "exit strategy." And as we will see, the Kennedy Administration replaced "strategy" with "Crisis Management." Whereas strategy implies a substantive goal, crisis management abstracts from purpose and avoids considering the consequences of whatever one does to avoid "escalation." Escalation is to be feared because violence itself is bad, hence more violence is worse than less, and the violence that you or the other side use is due to impersonal, apolitical forces beyond your or anybody else's control. Such language hides the fact that conducting war on any given level is to the advantage of some and the disadvantage of others.

THE DEADLY LANGUAGE OF PEACE

Allergic to using proper nouns to describe their objectives and the obstacles thereto, averse to war but eager to shape the world, our statesmen pinned labels on their *armed missions* that imply they are not war but peace. Yet the soldiers who suffered and died in the "humanitarian interventions" and "peacekeeping" efforts in places like Somalia and Yugoslavia wondered as reasonably as the ones who had been sent to Korea for a "police action" a half-century earlier why what they were doing felt so much like war. So should we, and ask as well: "What can such words possibly mean?"

When earthquakes, typhoons, tsunamis, droughts, and floods kill, impoverish, and bereave, our civilization (and ours alone) teaches that we should relieve our fellow man's sufferings with food, clothing, medicine, tools, and money. Strictly speaking, *humanitarian intervention* means mitigating human suffering—the ravages of nature, or of a past war regardless of political allegiances or conflicts. Since neither donors nor recipients are supposed to be acting politically, the mission is inherently nonmilitary. Guns are useless against tsunamis, mosquitoes, or mud. So why carry guns when you should be carrying food and shovels? But alas, most of mankind's suffering happens because of men, not nature, during and because of political conflicts. And when nature ravages, human predators make things worse. As Hobbes noted, man is man's worst predator: *Homo homini lupus*. Consequently, should you be serious about alleviating humanitarian disasters caused or worsened by humans, why carry food? First bring the guns to kill the killers and ravagers. Only when the sides are no longer contending will the food and stuff be other than stakes and fuel for them. But our statesmen know that humanitarian missions are not strictly, or even mainly, against nature because, under the label "humanitarian intervention," they have sent troops into places ravaged primarily by human savagery. Half-pretending to ignore ongoing conflicts, they also pretended not to choose sides.

But the logic of war prevails over pretense. When US troops landed in Somalia in December 1992 for operation "restore hope," President George H. W. Bush may actually have believed that "our mission has a limited objective—to open the supply routes, to get the food moving, and to prepare the way for a UN peacekeeping force to keep it moving." Yet he and his Administration knew that Somalia's troubles were sociopolitical rather than natural, that Somalia's warring factions were the cause of the country's famine, and that each had used the previous UN food aid to its advantage.[17] But because our statesmen believe that good government is inherently nonpolitical, they saw no contradiction between their desire to reform Somalia's sociopolitical dysfunction and their disavowal of any intention to *"dictate political outcomes."*

The incoming Bill Clinton Administration was explicit in its pretense that setting up local governments and police forces was a nonpolitical mission. But to whom would these institutions belong? Over whose dead bodies would they be established? These are quintessentially political questions. The US-UN's official mission was to *disarm the factions, reconcile them, and to reform the economy*. Perhaps our statesmen imagined that Somalia's factions would submit jointly, or that they would present an easy target by resisting uniformly. At any rate they truly had no intention to make war on anybody, despite having brought guns.

Our statesmen's language had disabled them from understanding that the parties to any war will vie with one another to turn any third party against the other. That is precisely what one Ali Mahdi did in Mogadishu— got the US troops into a fight with his rival, Mohammed Hussein Aideed. By May 1993, the "humanitarian intervention" had devolved into a war against Aideed—a war for which our statesmen were unprepared and the winning of which made no sense for US or Somali interests. They had not meant to make such a war or any war and, when they found themselves making it, thought better of it.

The term "humanitarian intervention" veils the reality that much of mankind lives in ways that shock American consciences, that our Progressives think of themselves as the world's saviors, that they are eager to use America's resources to "reform" others; hence that while they wish that needy foreigners would consent to their benign imperialism they are willing to exercise colonial power. But they don't know how much violence that takes and are unwilling to use more than "police violence," much less to wage war in the dictionary sense of the term. Yet ruling people without their consent *is* war.

The term "peacekeeping" is only a slightly less flimsy veil over this reality's harshest aspect: that various peoples wage wars that shock and sometimes endanger Americans, that our statesmen are unwilling to spectate as such wars take their course, that they would like to end them but cannot bring themselves either to join a side or to crush both. Hence they send, or support sending, troops to stand between warring parties without shooting at either. Such "peacekeeping" offers our statesmen the illusion of settling wars with only the show of force rather than the reality thereof. Pretending that the issues of the war are less important than pausing the fighting enables the illusion. Seldom do they ask, "Less important to whom?" "Whose agenda does the pause serve?" Because they do not ask, and because the essence of peacekeeping is the peacekeepers' determination not to wage war, such "peacekeepers" are really hostages to the warring party likeliest to shoot at them, shields behind which the most willful of the parties prepares for the next round.

Like "disarmament," "peacekeeping" abstracts from the essence of war, the political differences between the parties to it, by assuming that the parties have resolved or are in the process of resolving those differences enough to keep the peace. But if peace or the inclination thereto really existed between two parties, what need would there be for third parties to keep it? And since the issues between the two parties are not resolved, how can "peacekeepers" help resolve them? Insofar as they further one side's agenda, they are the other side's enemies. If they cannot resolve the issues to all sides' satisfaction and impose their own solution, are they willing to fight whichever side breaks the peace? And if they are not, what use are they? To the extent they incline in either party's direction, the "peacekeepers" become cobelligerents. And to some extent, they must, and do, become just that, whether consciously or not. Just as "disarmament" disarmed those who believed in it, to the advantage of those who armed, peacekeeping pacifies those who want peace more than advantage, to the advantage of those who take advantage of the peacekeepers to make war. Words may abstract from political conflict. They cannot make it go away.

As the Arabs of Sudan's northern desert oppressed and slaughtered the tribes of the south beginning in the 1990s, and in the southwestern province of Darfur a decade later, our statesmen joined their European counterparts in calling it genocide, as they had called similar events in the dying Yugoslavia and in Rwanda. In Sudan, as in these and other places, they decided to send peacekeepers. Our statesmen thought it best that the peacekeeping troops for Sudan should be gathered and sent by the African Union to forestall criticism that white Europeans were reimposing colonial rule on blacks. Because the peacekeepers were not sent to kill the killers, they became mere *spectators of genocide* as the killers went on killing. This outraged public and official opinion in Europe and America and led to UN resolutions approving the dispatch to Sudan of peacekeepers from the UN. But the UN's majority, led by its Islamic Conference, stipulated that the peacekeeping force would have to be acceptable to the government of Sudan—precisely to the people waging the genocide.

Unsurprisingly, the UN set conditions on the composition and mandate of the peacekeeping force that ensured it would do nothing to displease Sudan. The Euro-Americans know that the words they use to describe this instance of peacekeeping veil the fact that a substantial part of the UN's membership supported, while the UN's majority did not oppose, precisely the genocide they condemn. So, not to displease the Islamic Conference, our statesmen joined the UN in condemning the genocide while pretending not to know who was doing it. They acknowledged the existence of conflict between the government of Sudan and its people, but not that Sudan's government set some tribes to murdering others. The language in which they have dealt with this reality serves above all the pretense that there is an international community of peace-loving states, that through this community enlightened statesmen are stemming savagery, and that they are doing it without stigmatizing anyone, without bloodshed—that they are sophisticated, unlike their racist, militarist forebears who either let the savages ravage each other or subjugated them. If only it were so.

Russia, however, used "peacekeeping" in a way that mocked the Western usage and the Westerners who use it. When the Soviet Union's constituent parts declared their independence in 1991, Russia's troops took over the Abkhazian and South Ossetian parts of Georgia and the Transnistrian part of Moldova in the name of these regions' minorities. These troops, which the Russians called their "peacekeepers," defeated the Moldovans and Georgians and established Russia's peace in the regions, over the objections and dead bodies of their opponents. Our statesmen dared not disturb that peace.

LANGUAGE AND IGNORANCE

Using familiar terms loosely to describe things with which we are not familiar, and which do not apply to them, gets us lost in a fog of our own making. For example, the term "Islamofascism," used to describe strongly anti-Western movements in the Muslim world, betrays ignorance of those movements as well as of Islam and Fascism. Despite having become longhand for "bad," the word "fascism" really does refer to the political movement that ruled Italy between 1922 and 1943. It was an aggressively secular, socialist, nationalist movement that organized society in a corporatist way and stressed modernization. It was a public, mass phenomenon—not the affair of conspirators, much less of backward-looking religious zealots. Because Fascism had zero to do with racism, Mussolini's late dalliance with anti-Semitism was uncongenial to most of the party and incomprehensible to his country. In sum, Mussolini's fascism was a wholly European thing, comprehensible only by persons whose language, like Mussolini's, comprehends the intellectual categories of philosophers such as G.W.F. Hegel and Henri Bergson.

The closest thing to a *fascist* movement in the Islamic world is the Ba'ath party of Syria and Iraq. The Arabs who founded it imitated Fascism's aggressive rejection of religion, its nationalism and socialism. They were especially attracted to Nazi racism. Egypt's and similar secular regimes also have some kinship to fascism. And indeed the Arab world's secular regimes expressed themselves largely in European terms—until Iran's Islamic revolution led them to adopt Islamic words. But the term "Islamofascism" refers not to these secular regimes but to the Muslim Brotherhood and its offshoots, to the Wahabi sect, to Iran's Islamic Republic, and to "radical Islam" in general—movements that are blood enemies of the secular regimes in the Muslim world that bear any resemblance to fascism. The Islamists' intellectual currency, though addled by Marxism, is that of the Islamic tradition, and neither their structure nor their economic organization bear any resemblance to fascism. So while their relationship with Islam is disputable, their extraneousness to fascism is self-evident. Moreover, the term "Islamofascism" obscures the fact that secular *and* religious movements *and* governments alike sponsor and incite terrorism against America, that tyranny in the Muslim world is ubiquitous, and that it bears little resemblance to any European reality.

In sum, these and countless other terms do not alter reality—only their user's minds. Like narcotics, they change your capacity to perceive and deal with reality. Under their influence, you may stagger about the international scene believing you cut a fine figure, expecting deference, but impotent. When thwarted, your fellow addicts are likelier to tempt you into deeper dependency on intellectual hallucinogens than to counsel taking reality cold turkey. But sobriety's precondition is using words according to their ordinary meaning.

CHAPTER 2

//////////////////////

WATCH YOUR AXIOMS

A world I would know perfectly because I would
have been its author.
> —RENÉ DESCARTES

Like all professions, statesmanship lives by its axioms—the bedrock assumptions that color what it sees and by which it considers or rejects
what it hears and judges the propriety and feasibility of what it does.

Twentieth-century American statesmen framed the axioms of their
profession in words meaningful only to themselves, and then assumed
that these words mean the same things to all men. Heartened by America's very size and success, believing that "all men are created equal" but
not understanding what that means, proud that America is the *novus ordo
seculorum* and imagining themselves its agents, our statesmen redefined
their art. No longer would they pursue America's interest vis-à-vis others'
by measuring its reach against its grasp, ensuring a surplus of force over
rhetoric. Instead, they imagined they could pursue the undifferentiated
good of all humanity. Hence they set America's course by such synthetic
stars as "the interests of mankind," "the march of history," and relied on
the supposedly irresistible "force of world opinion." By such *omphalosko-
pia* they set strategies for diplomacy and wars for three generations, wasting able statesmen's time and valiant warriors' lives. The result, winning

battles and losing peace, has drawn down the well of the American people's good will and diminished their faith in America's cause.

A reasonable response to professional failures is to examine the commonplaces of professional discourse. Yet their very commonality has so embedded the axioms of American statesmanship in our minds that they are little changed in 2010 from their initial formulations circa 1900.

DUTY AND INTEREST

Arguing the case for taking Cuba from Spain in his 1898 war message to Congress, President William McKinley said:

> The grounds may be briefly summarized as follows: First, in the cause of humanity and to put an end to the barbarities, bloodshed, starvation, and horrible miseries now existing there, and which the parties of the conflict are either unable or unwilling to stop or mitigate. It is no answer to say that this is in another country, belonging to another nation, and is therefore none of our business. It is specially our duty for it is right at our door.[1]

The US government agreed to intervene in Cuba only after a national debate (culminating in passage of the Foraker Amendment), the outcome of which was agreement never to annex the island. Yet soon thereafter, the US government narrowly agreed to annex the Philippines—much farther from our shores than Cuba. Justifying this to "great applause" President McKinley said, "The war was no more invited by us than the questions which are laid at our door by its results. Now as then we will do our *duty*. Uplifting the Filipinos will take time, but we must work patiently"[2] (emphasis mine).

The notion that Americans have the *duty* to alleviate other peoples' lot, to improve them, had grown in the last quarter of the nineteenth century and became axiomatic in the twentieth. Happy that America had ended slavery and created the wealthiest society on earth, attractive to millions of immigrants, William Seward, Abraham Lincoln's Secretary of State, enjoyed repeating the verses "Our nation with united interests blest, / Not now content to poise shall sway the rest." By this he meant only that America would draw others to its ways. But the 1880s' most popular book, Josiah Strong's *Our Country,* said that America had been "divinely commissioned" to be its "brothers' keeper."

All this is to say that Americans were not immune to the temptations of Europeans who believed they were bearing "the white man's burden" of civilizing backward peoples. In 1900, Senator Albert Beveridge of Indiana was riding a wave of elite opinion when he argued that "self government and internal development had been the dominant notes of our first century; administration and the development of other lands will be the dominant note of our second century. . . . Cain was the first to violate the divine law of human action which makes us our brother's keeper. . . . The Declaration of Independence does not forbid us to do our part in the regeneration of the world. If it did, the Declaration would be wrong."[3] In short, old maxims of statesmanship were . . . just old. Beveridge and similarly minded people did not refute the Founders' point that self-government is the only legitimate government. They just cast it aside.

Ever since, our statesmen have assumed that if we don't try to resolve others' quarrels, tell them how to live, mind their business by force to some extent, then we are shirking our duty. That is because, supposedly *our government has a duty not just to the American people, but to all mankind.* That duty erases the difference between our business and other peoples' business. Whereas the statesmen of America's first century thought it normal to make war, but only to safeguard our honor and advance our interests, their twentieth-century successors doubted their right to make war, but are sure that we have the right to interfere in others' affairs so long as it is in what we believe is their interest. Thus *Time* magazine rejoiced that "the Iraq war has spelled the end of muscular moralism in US foreign policy," and proposed that America apply its moral fervor to "less blunt instruments to reshape the world."[4] Maximum of interference, minimum of force and moral content. That's the contemporary axiom.

On planet Earth, however, other people resent you for presuming to tell them how to live—for minding their business instead of your own. If you think you can "reshape the world" by lecturing, hectoring, bribing, and perhaps doing a little shooting, but not enough to really kill or cower those who have their own ideas of how to live, their own moral code, you are drinking your own Kool-Aid. Humanity is not clay, and you are not the potter. Moreover, whence comes the notion of a duty to mind others' business? Jesus' bidding to imitate the "good Samaritan" who took care of a helpless victim does not warrant you to force your favors on unwilling clients. Nor is it legitimate to read God's dismissal of Cain's excuse "am I my brother's keeper?" as commanding Cain to improve his brother's life: Rather, God was condemning Cain for murdering his brother. Nor does the presumption of duty to superintend your brother come from any human authority. In 1817, John Quincy Adams explained why America had no right to interfere in the wars between Spain and its colonists: "By what right could [we] take sides, who in this case of civil war had constituted us the judges which of the parties has the righteous cause? Then by an inquiry what the cause of the South Americans is and whether it really be as their partisans allege, the same as our own cause?"[5] As Adams implies, it is all too easy to mistake other people's business as congruent to ours and then to confuse the two.

Circumstances may make somebody else's war vital to us, in which case it becomes our business to pursue that war for *our* purposes, not theirs. Our government's particular duty is to be the American people's fiduciary agent for the conduct of America's business. This is the only duty it has the right and power to fulfill. Hence the axiom of an American *duty* to superintend mankind either implies submerging and hence shortchanging American interests, or it implies pursuit of American interests while arrogating to ourselves imperial prerogative over others' interests. In either case, the presumption of a general duty in the name of improving the world is pure hubris, obscures real differences between our interests and others', and is harmful to both.

The axiom of universal duty leans on the equally false but appealing axiom that *all peoples' interests are ultimately identical, or at least compatible.* Would not all benefit from peace, from turning energies to securing clean water and building sewers, to producing food and medicine, to educating the young and employing adults, to caring for the sick and the aged, to producing and trading freely rather than beggaring neighbors? Should not all put aside their antagonisms and grudges, as well as attachments to prejudices that stand in the way of improving life for all? Moreover, all peoples are interdependent, ever more so as better means of communications have brought us all closer together. Hence the pursuit of ethnic, religious, or national interests to the detriment of others is counterproductive. You and I know all that. And for a century our statesmen have assumed that the rest of mankind feels it as well, and needs only our help to act accordingly. Alas, they do not feel it.

In fact our century's history has been that of ethnoreligious separation and people-to-people strife. Prior to World War I, most peoples in Europe, Eurasia, the Middle East, and the Indian subcontinent lived in ethnically and religiously mixed empires. Muslims and Hindus lived side by side from Bengal to the Khyber Pass. Sunni, Shia, and Jews lived peaceably together from the Maghreb to Mesopotamia, while Germans lived from the Volga to Bohemia. In the Danube Valley, Magyars mingled with Romanians while Greeks and Turks intermingled in Thrace. In Africa, British, French, Belgian, Boer, and Portuguese colonists had imposed peace among the countless tribes: Luo and Kikuyu, Zulu and Xhosa, Hausa, Fulani, and Ibo. But in our century some 12 million Germans had to flee for their lives or were expelled from Eastern Europe, where Czechs, Slovaks, Poles, Ukrainians, Hungarians, Romanians, Macedonians, Russians, Serbs, Croats, Bosniaks, and Kosovars played out deadly dramas of ethnic cleansing. Jews were eliminated from Central and Eastern Europe, and all of the Middle East except Israel. Christianity has been largely purged from its Near Eastern cradle. Near a million Muslims and Hindus died as Pakistan was formed out of India and then split ethnically between the Bengali East and the Pushtun West. The Muslim world, far from uniting the Umma, poised for war between Sunni and Shia. In Africa—East and West, North and South—tribal conflict now rules, where it is not overruled by religious war. Bloody separation is the order of the day in Iraq. In Germany, Turkey's President told his countrymen, who make up a growing 6 percent of the population, that it would be treason for them to assimilate with Germans. Without admonition, the growing Muslim minorities in the rest of Western Europe demand that the local majorities adjust to them and look forward to oppressive majority status themselves.

Only American statesmen think it strange that human beings' resentments, rapacity, and lust for primacy—collective even more than individual—override desires for peace and productivity. Because our statesmen assume that the tendency to cut off one's nose to spite another's face abides only in a few leaders rather than in broad populations, they are constantly surprised when the foreign leaders whom they sponsor in the hope that they will transcend their peoples' conflicts rather than resolve them by war (e.g., in Israel and among Palestinians) end up disavowed by their peoples—and then that those peoples end up blaming America for their troubles. They ought to know better than to pretend to stand on a plane from which they can raise others above their conflicts. Rather, they should look to winning our own.

Were our statesmen to look closer, they would find that they are not immune to humanity's partisan logic. For most of our century, American and other Western Progressives have set aside the elementary lessons of liberal economics in favor of elaborate economic protectionisms that give them power and benefit their political constituencies in minute detail. That is why, although the volume of world trade currently dwarfs that of a century earlier, the complex rules of the European Union, the North American Free Trade Area, the General Agreement on Tariffs and Trade, and the World Trade Organization let goods and people move less freely than before 1914, when peacetime passports were unknown, migration was free, tariffs were transparent, and trade was settled by a gold standard beyond manipulation. Nor are American Progressives strangers to political prejudices, grudges, and partialities. The foreign commitments they make on America's behalf reflect their own domestic political identities and enmities.

That statesmen feel affinity to foreigners they imagine resemble themselves has ever been unremarkable. Remarkably, however, our statesmen inserted the American people in the midst of humanity's countless quarrels on behalf of persons and interests—Kirkuk must not be Kurdish, Fatah must rule Palestine, *this* government in Baghdad or Basra is acceptable to us, *that* one is not—that make sense only to them. Inherently partisan in foreign lands, such causes are divisive of America as well. It follows that the greater the volume of things alleged to be in America's interest, the more they must augment America's internecine strife—the opposite of America's interest.

INTEREST AND POWER

What about, then, the axiom that *America's interests and influence reach to every corner of the world?* Its truth was self-evident even to America's Founding Generation. But there is a world of difference between our Founders' and our current statesmen's understanding of that interest: For the former it was to secure respect, and commercial and cultural relations for America so that Americans could live at home as they wished and travel safely in the world's farthest reaches. By contrast, today's statesmen define America's interest practically in terms of their capacity to influence events abroad, at some price to Americans' domestic freedom and despite Americans' decreasing safety abroad. Whereas once our statesmen were interested in minimizing how the world affected America, now they are interested either in maximizing America's capacity to affect the world or in adjusting America to foreigners' demands.[6]

From George Washington through Theodore Roosevelt, American statesmanship tried to safeguard America from foreign interference, first by not taking part in foreigners' struggles—by not, in J. Q. Adams's words in his address on July 4, 1821, entering "the lists as parties to [any] cause other than our own" lest she "involve herself in all the wars of interest and intrigue, of individual avarice, envy and ambition which assume the colors and usurp the standard of freedom." While American traders and missionaries were pursuing interests in the Amazon, the Yangtze, and the Indus, never mind in Europe, and even as the US government was taking possession of America's "outworks," Hawaii, the Panama Canal Zone, and Puerto Rico, the US government defined success in foreign affairs in terms most clearly explained by John Quincy Adams in 1823: In matters purely European (or Asian), Americans might have feelings but no official opinion. In wars upon the sea—mankind's common possession—he said, "We have indeed a direct and important interest of our own." Our interest in the islands close to us is greater yet, and in Cuba it is "little inferior to that which binds the different members of this Union together."[7]

The operational principle, what is nearest is dearest, underlined the basic distinction between our national interest and others'. Americans would stretch national influence to cover the interests that radiated from home. But because the size and importance of those interests were inversely related to the distance from their source, there was a natural balance between America's national interest, influence, and power.

But no amount of influence, no amount of power, could balance the twentieth-century conception of the American national interest. Merely asking what it would take to "make the world safe for democracy" (whatever that might mean), to establish "freedom," to make the world unsafe for "religious extremism," or to uphold Franklin Roosevelt's commitment to banish "ancient evils, ancient ills" makes you realize that no earthly power could do such things and that any that could try would have to be monstrous. Our statesmen have not felt the need to imagine such a power because they have believed that the United States of America would not be pursuing these cosmic objectives alone or in the face of opposition. Rather, beginning with Elihu Root, David Starr Jordan, Nicholas Murray Butler, and Woodrow Wilson, followed by presidents and hacks, they have half-assumed, half-pretended, that mankind is already moving to do all such things and that America's interest and duty are to just help it along. Woodrow Wilson's request of Americans to "add their authority and power to the authority and force of other nations to guarantee peace and justice throughout the world" is the template of countless appeals to join gatherings of mankind that exist only in our statesmen's minds.[8]

Thus when the American people find themselves alone bearing the burden of what they were told was mankind's cause—as they were during the post-2003 occupation of Iraq—they have tended to feel that other peoples abandoned us. But the others were never with us in the first place. Our statesmen merely imagined they would be there once the Americans were. It is even more important to note that the weight of our own causes is inherently less burdensome than that of causes not our own.

The key question is: For what purpose should American influence reach any part of the world? Our Founders were sure that our government's actions abroad should be ancillary to its domestic purpose, namely, to enable the American people to live peaceable lives while strengthening their commitment to the principles and virtues that make America different from other nations. When Washington spoke of "our interest," of course he meant that statesmen should be asking of any situation "what's in it for us?" But his copious references to the "justice" that should guide that interest, as well as to what he called the "indissoluble connection"— at least for Americans—between moral virtue and success, leaves no doubt that the "greatness" he and his generation expected America soon to achieve had to do with its character. What Americans would do with or to any other peoples would be important only insofar as it affected the quality of what America itself would become. This, the Whig approach to expansion and greatness in the 1840s, the Lincoln/Seward midcentury Republican doctrine, contrasted with Stephen Douglas's Democratic approach: Greatness equals size and power, period.

America's twentieth-century interests radiated farther into foreign lands, and its power put into its statesmen's hands tools that seemed apt to shape them. But the size of interests abroad cannot erase their foreign quality. Where foreign situations impinge directly on our interests, reasonable judgments are possible about actions to deal with them. As we consider whether it is in our interest, say, to disarm North Korea or Iran of nuclear weapons, just as we considered whether or not to make war on Saddam Hussein's Iraq in 2003, we can weigh in the scales of interest the cost to ourselves of doing it against that of not doing it, and in the scales of justice the harm and good of our actions. But when foreign situations concern primarily foreigners (e.g., when we try to uplift Iraqis, Afghans, or any other peoples—inevitably pleasing some and displeasing others among them—or when we try to settle quarrels between them) we can find no basis for judging the justice of what we do. Nor, since we cannot control how foreigners leverage our influence for their purposes, can we gauge the impact of what we do on our interest, or anybody else's.

Among the countless illustrations of this is a 2008 battle in the city of Basra between two Shia militias, one of which was urged by our statesmen and supported by our air strikes. The Americans who planned the 2003 US invasion of Iraq, which freed its Shia majority from Saddam's oppression and who thought in terms of democracy, never dreamed that they would be stoking a war among the Shia. Yet there was the war, and there they were stoking it: "We were expecting one thing but we saw something else," said Ali Hussam, forty-eight, a teacher. "But unfortunately with the presence of this new government and this democracy that was brought to us by the invader . . . made us kill each other. And the war is now between us."[9]

America's power reaches to the ends of the earth. But power is not to be confused with the capacity to serve your or anybody else's interests. That takes calculation undimmed by illusion.

ASPIRATIONS AND OPINIONS

One illusion, shared by Republicans (Secretary of State Condoleezza Rice) and Democrats (Senator Hillary Clinton) alike, is that *all mankind lives in one global village and shares the same aspirations.* "We just have to believe," Secretary Rice told the State Department staff on taking office in 2005, that all other peoples want democracy and decency as much as we do. Unlike Elihu Root in 1912, she did not explain why it was reasonable to believe this, much less why believing it had become obligatory. This axiom defies explanation if only because it is the reverse of reality, and not least because the few Americans who profess it are the only people on the planet who believe it.

The same is true of the corollary axiom: *All the world's diverse cultures are compatible and commensurable.* Consequent to that axiom, we must regard the differences among cultures as proof positive of their equal value and must refrain from judging them by any standard of value other than their own. The problem is that only one culture, that of American Multiculturalists, claims to do that. In fact, all of mankind's cultures exclude each other, and the American Multiculturalists' embrace of others' cultures is merely theoretical—*vide* their insistence that all real cultures are or must be "moderate," and their harsh judgments on non-Multiculturalists, especially American ones.

In fact the first datum that strikes the sentient traveler is mankind's diversity—in the ordinary sense of the word. Our Multiculturalists, like Stanford's David Starr Jordan a century ago, conclude from their relations in the faculty club and five-star hotel that intercultural relations are no problem. But if you listen sympathetically to folks from a different culture, preferably in their own language, or even if you read their cultural icons in translation, you find yourself amid hopes and fears, goals, paths, and signposts different from yours. And if you do it again with another, and then another culture, you realize that they all differ from each other as much as each differs from yours. Sometimes, you just don't get the point of what they are saying, don't see what they find so funny or sad, good or bad. Or you don't appreciate what takes Shia clergy so many years to learn to reach the rank of Ayatollah, or the fine points of the old Mandarin imperial exams. Usually you find yourself repelled by mundane things like habitual lying, gratuitous cruelty, oppression, and self-abasement. And you realize that these folks' habits of mind and heart are more like skin than like clothes: They are grown rather than chosen. If the globe is a village, the neighborhoods sure feel different.

Our Founding Generation had no trouble with that and gloried in America's differences. They knew that God creates all men equal and endows them with the inalienable right to live as they please—and that mankind's many components please to live very differently from one another. They had no doubt that they and their fellow Americans understood better than others how man should live, and they declared independence precisely so that Americans might live as we choose. Just as surely, they knew that all other peoples thought and lived according to different lights that, dim or distorted, were *their* lights, their business. Our business was to make *our* lights shine. Our right to our ways was as good as others' right to theirs.

But this was not relativism, because our Founders knew that America's ways ranked ahead of others' in the continuum between barbarism and civilization. They never questioned that Americans could and would live amicably and profitably alongside all manner of despots, primitives, and barbarians. They believed that the key to relations with any of them, the way to get what could be got in peace, was to be clear about, to keep in mind, just how different each was. And, of course, dealing with foreigners would remind Americans of how blessed was our uniqueness, how high our calling. This would teach us to be patriotic and to think of foreign relations in terms of limits—on them and on us. As W. H. Seward admonished France: "Nations are not authorized to correct each other's errors except so far as is necessary to prevent or redress injuries affecting themselves."[10]

By contrast, the axiom of cultural equality—the converse of which is that neither our ways nor theirs have any intrinsic worth—produces American statesmen wary of American patriotism but convinced that they can do anything that strikes their fancy with foreigners. In practice, the axiom means that all cultures and religions should be taken moderately—that is, not seriously. Multiculturalists believe it is wrong to take seriously in its own terms any culture—especially American ways and Christianity. Following the axiom's logic, our statesmen believe that any and all cultures, when taken moderately, amount to multiculturalism, and hence that theirs is mankind's universal culture. Thus it follows paradoxically that the more they detach themselves from and look skeptically upon America's peculiarities and interests, the more they serve what they imagine to be the transcendent goals and universal culture of the global village, the more they imagine themselves entitled to do great things in all that village's neighborhoods. Beginning with Woodrow Wilson, our statesmen have touted the formula: Because America wants nothing for itself but seeks only to further mankind's universal aspirations, it is entitled to ask for (and why not to *impose*) much on mankind's recalcitrants. Of the many things that may be said of all this, the least debatable is that it is very, very peculiarly latter-day American and quite foreign and incomprehensible to anyone else. Hence, our global-village neighbors may be forgiven for regarding American statesmen alternatively as imperialists, busybodies, or rubes.

It is dangerous to barge about a global village that exists only in one's imagination. Our Progressive statesmen believe in their own beneficence, strive to please foreigners, indict their fellow Americans for insufficient commitment to please, are convinced that good folk everywhere will applaud them, and are distraught when this does not happen. But you should know that any number of foreign governments and peoples hate passionately, for example, that opinions about Jews and Americans in today's Arab world make those that circulated in Nazi Germany seem mild. Note, for example, the cartoons about Jews in Saudi newspapers.

Nor are such penchants peculiar to the Arab world—indeed scapegoating and slaughtering innocents seems to be more widespread in our global village than multiculturalism.

So in *this* village, on *this* planet, few things are more pregnant with trouble than taking responsibility for others' travails. Our statesmen would have done well to ponder that politicians from Benin to Bangladesh might take seriously their lighthearted indictment of the United States for causing "global warming" and for imputing to it, and to America, violent weather's ravages. Typhoons have ever decimated the peoples of the Bay of Bengal, the death tolls rising along with the population. But in 2008, a Bangladeshi politician gathered a following to force America to pay for resettling Bangladeshis affected by flooding, preferably in the United States, on the ground that "everyone knows" America is responsible for global warming and hence for the typhoons. This sentiment is contagiously imitable. Whereas floods, droughts, and wind once led the victims to theodicy, now thanks to our statesmen they build constituencies for wreaking punitive damages on the American people.

You would think that people who handle such dangerous things would be more careful with their axioms. One reason why our statesmen are not is that they imagine what they call "world opinion" to be all-powerful and good. When you read the statesmen of America's first century, including even the ebullient Theodore Roosevelt (of whom it was said that he moved as if to John Philip Sousa's march "Stars and Stripes Forever"), you get the sense they realized they were treading among countless deadly foci of greed, that they were handling fearsome things. But because a new generation of statesmen, beginning in the 1890s, imagined a permissive environment, they dispensed with reticence and calculations as lightheartedly as men of the north might doff woolen underwear and drop weapons were they to step out of snowy, wolf-infested forests onto a tropical beach among dancing girls.

Elihu Root explained the new environment: The intentions of foreign governments had almost ceased to matter, because in more and more places, power was passing to peoples. And whereas governments might have self-serving opinions about justice, the people would demand impartial justice. "First, there has come to be a public opinion of the world; second, that opinion has set up a new standard of international conduct which condemns unjustified aggression; and third the public opinion of the world punishes the violation of its standard. . . . When any people feels that its government has done a shameful thing and has brought them into disgrace in the opinion of the world, theirs will be the vengeance and they will inflict the punishment."[11] Woodrow Wilson spoke of "world opinion" as the just jury of mankind, and of course the UN was supposed to be the place whence world opinion would exercise its beneficent, omnipotent rule. The 2008 Beijing Olympic slogan put the axiom succinctly: *"One world, one dream."* Never mind that Tibetans dream of being rid of the Chinese, that Bulgarians dream that Serbs are really Bulgarians while Serbs dream that Bulgarians are really Serbs, that the word "Arab" is an insult for Persians while the word "Persian" serves the same function for Arabs, and so on *ad nauseam*. Though our statesmen no longer confess faith in omniscient, omnipotent, beneficent world opinion so boldly, alas, much of what they do makes sense only in terms of it.

America's Founders cited "a decent respect to the opinions of mankind" as the reason for declaring publicly "the reasons" for independence. But it did not cross their minds that this "opinion" should have the authority to approve or disapprove of what Americans were doing. "Decent respect" does not mean "subordination." Nor did they imagine that Chinese or Africans would know or care how Americans live, or that it would be any of their business. The Declaration's immediate foreign audience was the court of Louis XVI, which conditioned making war on Britain on being sure that its American colonies really intended to detach themselves. Beyond that, the Declaration aimed at that "opinion," that civilized sector of humanity, to which "the laws of Nature and Nature's God" were "self-evident truths." The authors were under no illusions about how many such folks existed. Nevertheless, early American diplomatic documents are obviously written to persuade civilized readers. Long, detailed, closely reasoned arguments, they really are the kind of stuff good lawyers would prepare for expert, impartial juries. But again, these documents reflect the Americans' understanding of what justice required of them rather than any confidence that many others shared that understanding.

Early Americans also dealt with "opinion" in the sense of prejudices that may work for you or against you. Lincoln and Seward's Civil War diplomacy rested substantially on the fact that the British and French masses were antislavery. On that basis they warned the British government in 1861 that were it to get on the wrong side of the American war, it would suffer even "more general" "domestic convulsions" than it suffered from fighting in America in the previous century.[12] Their successors cultivated favorable opinions of America by taking delegations of Chinese, Japanese, and Latin American delegates around the country for months, showering them with good will and cheer. And Theodore Roosevelt's dispatch of America's new white battleships around the world showed that nothing so builds a favorable opinion as mighty armaments that come in peace. All this goes under the heading of dealing competently with one of international reality's components.

Making axioms from your imagination is something else. There was more reason in the twentieth century than previously to believe that Europe's statesmen represented what V. E. Orlando called "sacred egoism," that is, demands impervious to justice. Moreover, twentieth-century statesmen have been thus, less because of personal perversity than because they have been more answerable to their peoples than their forebears had been. Woodrow Wilson's generation of Americans had more contact with foreigners than had J. Q. Adams's. Nevertheless, Wilson's indulged its own imagination that European peoples were going to force their governments to be good world citizens. Sadly, the world's peoples had it in for one another and still do. So in a world of varied opinions, most at odds with one another, which ones will you choose as constituting "world opinion"?

Beginning in the 1950s our statesmen, who should not have anointed any foreigners as arbiters, chose precisely the wrong folks. Anyone who remembers those years has vivid images of American statesmen treating the dictators of what came to be known as the "Third World," men like India's Nehru, Egypt's Nasser, and Ghana's Nkrumah, as moral icons. The image of "the noble savage" has seduced generations of Westerners. The US government put great emphasis on what President Dwight Eisenhower called "people-to-people diplomacy," meaning precisely dubbing such people "world opinion" and courting them. The peak of this came in the Kennedy Administration's most memorable act, reducing the scope of its 1961 attempt to rid Cuba of Fidel Castro and the Soviets because, in UN ambassador Arthur Schlesinger Jr.'s view, the invasion's defeat would be preferable to a victory opposed by "world public opinion." But the Third World's peoples proved themselves more savage than noble, and their squalid, predatory, hypocritical leaders became objects of disgust. Americans did not have to learn about how Secretary-General Kofi Annan had turned the UN's economic sanctions on Iraq into the Oil For Food scandal to view him as just another fauna of the Third World.

LEADERSHIP AND IDENTITY

For five decades, the Soviet Union's division of the planet embarrassed our statesmen's axiomatic claim, embodied in the UN, that Progress had transcended statesmanship's rules as well as America's peculiar character and interest. During that plurality of our century, they developed a fallback axiom: *We Americans are the natural leaders of* [fill in the blank: *"the free world," "our allies," "the stakeholders in the international system"*]. *As such, we have a unique responsibility to reflect and abide by their consensus.*[13] This differs only superficially from the original notion that America has a duty to submit to "world opinion" because it is merely the most progressive part of the "global village." The difference lies in taking a step back to something closer to what Woodrow Wilson had in mind: Though America's interests are global, its influence and responsibilities are limited to the world's democracies, or at most to its progressive states. These are the states of which it is the leader. But this leadership must, according to one contemporary formula, "respect the collective will of our democratic allies."[14] And in fact Presidents from Harry Truman to Bill Clinton explained countless times that they might have decided otherwise in foreign affairs but for the need to please or not displease too badly "the allies."

This axiom is problematic in theory and bedevils practice. The fact that several countries are allies does not make them a collectivity. Nor does democracy or lack thereof fuse multiple wills into one. Always, will is individual. The more countries are allied, the more diverse their joint will is bound to be, the more likely it is that some will favor course of action A while others will be partisans of action B. With whose consensus should the consensus-seeker join? Which allies should you please more, and which less? Seeking consensus for its own sake guarantees that you will get the opposite.

Collective will was no more a real thing in the 1950s than in 1919 or 2008. While in the 1950s Europe's democracies surely faced a common if not collective threat from the Soviet Union and had a common interest in warding it off, the interest they took in doing so was just as surely unequal. In 2008, as the US government considered whether to support Ukraine's and Georgia's applications for membership in the North Atlantic Alliance, its Western members, led by Germany, opposed the applications in deference to Russia while its Eastern members, led by Poland, supported it precisely to keep Russia at bay. No a priori judgment is possible about which of these sets of wills, if either, coincides with America's interest. Appeals to democracy and collegiality only obfuscate the substantive political nature of the decision.

Alliances are about peace and war. Because differences about such things stem from attitudes deeply rooted in peoples, they are not naturally amenable to consensus. Modern Europeans' axiomatic attitude toward violent conflict—stop the violence and call meetings—flows from what they presume to be the twentieth century's lessons, to wit, that the outcome of battles is irrelevant because violence settles nothing. Peoples who have such attitudes will not change them for the sake of consensus. Nor is it possible to convince those who believe that foreign cultures can be reformed that they cannot be, or vice versa. Such opposing views cannot be reconciled by splitting the differences between them, least of all by crafting what former National Security Adviser Condoleezza Rice called "bridging documents." In short, it is all too easy to base an alliance on willful neglect of irreconcilable, contrasting wills.

Unwillingness to confront and be responsible for political choices may be the fundamental reason for our statesmen's eagerness to confuse America's interest with that of mankind, the UN, or, that failing, the part thereof we call "our allies" or "the free world" or "the democracies." That is why talk of America as the collectivity's "leader" invariably ends up subordinating the will of the leader to that of the led. How else can our statesmen pretend to unload onto others responsibility for what they do? Such cynicism is preferable to truly believing that other peoples care about our safety and well-being enough to hazard their own. Whether any ever did is less important than the fact that, in our time, the notion that the American people deserved the attacks of 9/11 is almost as widespread among Europeans as it is in the Muslim world.[15] The media images of America on which modern Europeans have been raised range from unsophisticated and uncool to enemies of all good things. Hence you are forced to conclude that trying to confuse America's interest with that of even our most traditional allies is a bad idea.[16]

Combining the notion of international leadership with that of collective security doubles the misunderstanding. America's Founders believed in their bones that they were leading mankind, precisely because they knew their civilization was so different from others'. That is why they insisted on acting independently and unilaterally. This is the difference between leading by exhortation/cajoling and leading by example—between "do as I say" and "follow me." In international even more than in personal affairs, nothing so convinces others that they ought to follow you than your confidence in your own actions. Confidence bolstered by successful example needs no words. Nor can words make up for reticence—much less for failure. While early Americans were not shy about their pride in their special ways, they did not proselytize. Rather, they concentrated on maintaining independence, confident that their success would compel due respect. After World War II, peoples from around the globe needed no exhortation to besiege an America brimming with success and confidence with offers to follow and imitate it.

Conversely, approaching foreigners with projects that you may undertake on condition that they agree to take part tells them that your interest in the project is not great—else you would do it regardless. It also invites them to set the price for their participation as high as your market will bear, as advantageous to themselves and as disadvantageous for you as they can get away with. And since the subject matter is war and peace, you will lead them reasonably to conclude that you are not terribly serious about what you are doing.

CHAPTER 3
/////////////////

IDEAS HAVE CONSEQUENCES

Ideas have consequences.
— RICHARD WEAVER

In 1989, Francis Fukuyama's article "The End of History?" convinced many influential Americans that the parts of mankind that matter had settled once and for all on liberal democracy as the optimal way of life. It followed, as Chalmers Johnson wrote in 1995,[1] that the big qualitative question having been decided, force having become passé at least in major international affairs, henceforth hearts and minds would be attracted to nations that peacefully offer the greatest material good for the greatest number. This dogma, that international affairs are contests for "hearts and minds" and that America must attract mankind to imitate and support us, is perennial catnip for American Progressives. Liberal democracy's peaceful millennium was supposed to have arrived before World War I, then after it, then after World War II, then again after the end of the Cold War. But because questions about how human beings should live are not subject to closure, whoever dallies with this dogma misunderstands America as well as the rest of the world.

THE DOGMA

The Nobel Peace Prize for 1912 went to former Secretary of State Elihu Root, father of the turn-of-the-century Hague and Geneva conventions as well as of the World Court—the man who popularized the concept that peoples would force their own governments to act lawfully toward one another. President Woodrow Wilson's scheme for eliminating war, the League of Nations, was based on confidence in that concept: The world's publics would constrain aggressors from within and without. Instead, in Root's and Wilson's day, public opinion made World War I even bloodier, poisoned its aftermath, and later pushed the German and Japanese publics to war while softening resistance to them in the rest of the world. Republican and Democratic leaders, from Charles Evans Hughes and Herbert Hoover to Cordell Hull and Franklin Roosevelt (the latter until after the fall of France in 1940), also embodied that soft thinking: Hughes by inventing naval arms control treaties that ended up enabling Japan's conquests, Hoover by trusting America's security to a treaty that outlawed war. Public opinion was supposed to enforce them all. On Roosevelt's behalf, Hull lectured world public opinion to imitate America's self-denying ordinances. Later, because John Kennedy and his successors contraposed winning "hearts and minds" in Vietnam to winning military victory, they disabled America and enabled North Vietnam to win politically as well as militarily. Nor did 9/11 shake this dogma's hold on our statesmen any more than Pearl Harbor had. George W. Bush responded to an attack on America by declaring war on "terrorism" and "extremism" rather than on anyone in particular, in part because, like his immediate predecessors and as is taught at Harvard's Kennedy School, he believed that the world's peoples will abandon their antagonisms and identities to join an "international community" of democratic prosperity.[2] Perennially attractive, this simpleminded, dangerous nonsense now goes under the label "soft power."

This is not to deny that ideas, attraction and repulsion, love, hate, and contempt play arguably the greatest role in world affairs. But the contemporary notion of "soft power" trivializes that massive reality by passing it through the narrow, parochial optic of American Progressive thought.

Let's look first at how Progressives have defined "soft power" in their own image. Having done that, we will examine the realities of the habits—

and passions—of hearts and minds, the complexities of what moves men and nations. We will then turn to understanding how attraction and repulsion affect today's conflicts. Our point is to trace guidelines for sailing safely through the storms of human sentiment.

HOW THEY SEE IT

While America's Founders were sure that their City on a Hill would light the world and John Quincy Adams exhorted foreigners to admire America and "do likewise," they also realized that passions and habits would lead most of the world's peoples along paths radically different from ours. Since the Progressive era, however, presidents and their advisers have supposed that successful, peaceful, universal imitation of America (by which they mean themselves) is ineluctable, while giving lip service to the diversity of human motivation.

Each component of our foreign policy establishment projected its own narrow intellectual, social, and political preferences onto foreigners. The Kennedy School's Joseph Nye, author of the best-known book on the subject, only invented the term "soft power."[3] Other Liberal Internationalists, as well as Realists and Neoconservatives, add to, minimize, or emphasize parts of Nye's definition. But few dispute its main points.

Soft Power

Nye writes that soft power "is the ability to get what you want through attraction rather than coercion or payments. It arises from the attractiveness of a country's culture, political ideals, and policies. When our policies are seen as legitimate in the eyes of others, our soft power is enhanced."[4] It is about getting others to "buy into your values."[5] Explicitly, Nye presents soft power as a reproach, a better alternative, to the Bush Administration's 2003 invasion of Iraq, which he takes as the prototype of power politics. Any military success and any prestige that might come from going to war without "a second [UN] Security Council Resolution," he argues, must be offset by a loss of "legitimacy."[6]

Note the assumption necessary for this to make sense: The world's peoples and governments hold America (and presumably themselves as well) to a notion of legitimacy defined substantially by the procedures of the United Nations. Americans (and presumably other peoples as well) make themselves attractive or unattractive by getting or failing to get sufficient UN blessing. Attraction thus defined is a surer means to success in world politics than "coercion or payments," "carrots" and "sticks." That is because avoiding such tools of "hard" power makes others look favorably upon your values—that is, it shows others that your values are the same as theirs—namely, nonviolence and UN procedures.

To believe this, one would have to accept that force, threats, and bribes, honor, fear, and interest, play second fiddle in matters of life and death and none at all in the most important of things, how governments vote in the UN. One is tempted to ask: "On what planet?" Who lives by this supposed standard of legitimacy? What does it avail its supposed adherents? How does it punish violators? Nye does not address such questions.

Nye cites other sources of attraction: We Americans are "the world's number one exporter of films and television programs." We publish "four times as many scientific and journal articles as the next runner up, Japan." We rank first in Nobel Prizes in chemistry and economics, and in the proportion of students who study abroad. Four-fifths of mankind admire our scientific and technical advances. Three-fifths like American music, movies, and TV. Half like American ideas about democracy. But, alas, we fail to realize this potential by doing things like fighting in Vietnam and Iraq, using military power, and pursuing policies that displease others—refusing to transfer American wealth to foreigners to stop global warming, supporting Israel, and so on. Thus we give America a bad image. But you must ask: "Bad to whom?" and "So what?"

Nye suggests we take lessons from Europe, "the superpower of soft power." France is first in Nobel Prizes for literature. The rest of Europe gets the silver and bronze for Nobels in physics and chemistry. France is the world's leading tourist destination. Europe leads in life expectancy. It gave the world soccer! European youth culture is more uninhibited than America's. Europeans have not fought wars recently. And so on. More important, Europe translates all this potential into solid (dare we say hard?) soft power by following policies that frighten no one and attempt to please all (especially those who threaten it, except of course Israel). Polls show that Europe is even more popular with non-Europeans than with Europeans themselves. But we—not Nye—ask, so what? How does any of that keep Muslim governments from blackmailing Europe and their peoples from invading it? How does it help Europe resist Russia's stranglehold on its natural gas supply?

Nye also tells us that the Soviet Union's stock rose in the polls when Mikhail Gorbachev projected a nonthreatening image in the late 1980s, but that, previously, the USSR's cultivation of high culture, massive efforts to organize support, even Communist ideology, prevented it from being "a serious competitor with the United States in soft power during the Cold War."[7] This, alas, is ignorant.[8] In fact, although billions of ordinary people shunned or fled any and all things Communist from Communism's 1917 inception to its demise, the USSR during its heyday attracted hundreds of thousands of Western intellectualoids—including some advisers to US presidents—who controlled (and mostly continue to control) the commanding heights of education, the media, finance, and government bureaucracies. This asset rivaled in size the Soviet Union's military power itself. Indeed, as Gorbachev's incompetence was destroying the Soviet Union, the rising poll numbers that Nye cites did not indicate that more ordinary people were moving to Communist-controlled places. On the contrary, peoples in socialist countries were flowing westward faster than ever, voting with their feet. Yet Western elites—precisely those who subscribe to Nye's notion—were sending billions of dollars in unsecured, taxpayer-backed loans to Moscow. These people were responding not to polls but to the congruence between their own and the Soviets' values. Soviet socialism's substantial soft power was at work here. But Nye does not explain that power, perhaps because it gripped him to some extent.

The point is that Nye's book is neither a study of mankind's hopes, fears, reasoning, and passions, nor is it about how to make foreigners do what Americans want. Rather, it defines the hopes, fears, and passions of Nye's class, which includes contemporary American statesmen—maxims peculiar and strange to mankind. Nye reproaches fellow Americans for not adhering more closely to those maxims. Hence "Soft Power" is not about empowering America but about making Americans do what people like Joseph Nye want—people such as meet at the Davos World Economic Forum, teach at places like Harvard's Kennedy School, and rule the prestigious media—and the many more who look up to them.

A Power Vacuum

By focusing on the supposed sins of the lesser beings who are America's majority, this notion of soft power sucks positive intellectual and moral power out of America while eliciting, empowering, and helping to define the animus of America's enemies.

Note the similarities between the reproaches to America that are the core of the concept of soft power and the accusations that the Soviet Union leveled at America for three generations, that European anti-Americans have thrown at us for two, and that contemporary Islamists have taken up. Shorn of their perfunctory Muslim verbiage, the texts of the September 2007 videotapes supposedly by Osama bin Laden are terribly familiar. America is too violent. Its economic system fosters insecurity and rapacity. It is culturally backward and insensitive. Unwilling to subject itself to the common rules of mankind, it exploits other peoples and ruins the environment. Its insensitivity to global warming is destroying the planet.[9] It should escape no one that such indictments of America have less in common with Islam, or even with Marxism, than with the prejudices of Joseph Nye's class.

In sum, although soft power is power indeed, our statesmen misunderstand it.

The Three Schools

Along with Nye, Liberal Internationalists, Neoconservatives, and Realists look abroad and see what is important to themselves, not to others. Neoconservatives see struggles between democrats and totalitarians. They expect majorities in foreign countries to defer to America because its sponsorship of democracy tends to empower them. But Neoconservatives typically abstract from the fact that each and every *demos,* and parts thereof, wants to be free to do things that other *deme,* or other parts of their own *demos,* do not want—things that may be incomprehensible to Neoconservatives—and that some *deme* dream of destroying America.

The Realists see the world divided between moderates and extremists. They expect foreigners to match their own willingness to limit their country's claims and their worship of "stability." Just as Lyndon Johnson could not understand why Ho Chi Minh, North Vietnam's dictator, could refuse his offer of billions of US dollars plus an increased role in South Vietnam in exchange for agreeing not to take it all by war, James Baker could not understand why US offers of money and increased influence would not attract Syria's al-Assad to curtail his military pressure on Lebanon and American troops in Iraq.

For Liberal Internationalists, mankind struggles to free itself from traditional society's ills—underdevelopment and prejudice—and to access the blessings of modernity. Technocrats at heart, Liberals believe the world must surely cooperate with their benevolent, modernizing, multilateral expertise. Hence Arthur Schlesinger Jr. could not imagine that were America to entrust its foreign policy to multilateral institutions, especially the UN, the rest of the world would not defer to Americans like himself as mankind's natural leaders.[10]

Note the similarities: What is important to each "school" is essentially void of moral, political, or intellectual content and consists rather of self-admiration. But look at reality without the schools' blinders: Democracy enables whatever any *demos* might fancy at any given time, and preaching moderation abstracts from the *quality* of the things that anyone should favor or oppose. Which of the many ends that modernity, technology, and organization should anyone serve? In short, the three schools do not explain why anyone should value their particular value-free sets of values as each of the schools value them.

The schools are similar as well in their low regard for the American people. The Realist complaint, best articulated by Henry Kissinger, is that Americans demand simple solutions to complex problems, oscillate between isolationism and total war—they are immoderate.[11] Neoconservatives blame the American people for insufficient willingness to promote their ways.[12] Liberal Internationalists share the other schools' complaints and also blame Americans for insistence on narrow national interests and narrow national prerogatives.[13] In short, the American people do not lend themselves sufficiently to their betters' foreign policies. Nevertheless, each school discounts the American people's distrust and is confident that foreigners will trust it to reshape their lives.

Much as many might like to affect the world through policies (e.g., the Realist dream of buying Arab goodwill by promoting Arab interests against Israel, the Neoconservative one about supporting democratic revolutions in places like Saudi Arabia or even China, or the Liberal Internationalist one of subordinating American troops to the UN or imposing carbon taxes on US industries), policies are costly and require the American people's agreement. So the easiest way for the foreign policy schools to express themselves is through the US government's cultural policy. This they can do without national debate, through Beltway culture wars. But because they take seriously only the culture of their own narrow transnational community, they imagine that their own likes and dislikes must trump others' customs, religions, and prejudices. Not taking other cultures seriously results in a halfhearted mixture of pandering and contempt.

The Common Denominator

For example, the Bush team's soft power approach to the Muslim world combined MTV broadcasts in Arabic with the promotion of female suffrage, and lectures about the need to "unfreeze" the region's regimes. In July 2006, the US Department of State granted one Toni Blackman, a rap lyricist, vocalist, actress, and writer, the title of US Hip Hop Ambassador. It is easy enough to point out that this represents a very partial view of America, one that many Americans as well as foreigners find corrosive. In France, for example, the most popular rap group calls itself *"nique ta mere"* (f—— your mother). French rap, which imitates the music of US black ghettos, has become the marching music of Arab-French youths who, like their American counterparts, burn, deal drugs, brutalize women, and predict the death of the state.

At the same time, Bush sent his former press secretary, Karen Hughes, to the Arab world to preach women's rights. Her female audiences told her they were quite happy, while males mostly thought her subversive. As for images of happy Muslims in America, they confirmed America's enemies in their belief that America is at once subversive and weak. As Undersecretary of State for Public Diplomacy, Hughes told the Organization of Islamic Conference in Washington:

> The vast majority of people in our world, Muslim, Christian, Jewish, Hindu, Buddhist or those of no faith at all—want to live secure lives of opportunity—this is not a goal owned by any country, but a shared human goal—despite differences of language or culture or skin color, so much more unites us as human beings than divides us. Yet we live in a world where misunderstanding and mistrust are spreading, often being fanned by extremists. . . . One of our great shared challenges is to isolate and marginalize these extremists, and nurture our common interests and values by finding ways to bridge differences and doing a better job of truly listening and seeking to understand each other.[14]

This was less a statement of fact—if the audience already agreed there would have been no need to state it—than the invocation of a creed. Pitifully, she added: "And tragically, the vast majority of those being killed are Muslims." The Bush Administration surely did not intend this. But by her statement's logic Muslims could alleviate this tragedy by killing a greater percentage of infidels. In short, US public diplomacy represents America as dissolute, dumb, and dying to please.

By their nature such images of America can appeal only to those foreigners whose tastes coincide with those of the American elites who market them: aging yuppies who wish they were young ghetto types or celebrities, and above all trendy leftists. Hence the US government's Arabic-language TV station, Al-Hurra, combined these images with coverage of the world from the perspective of . . . America's enemies in the Middle East. On December 12, 2006, it treated with respect speakers in a Teheran conference who were denying that the Holocaust had taken place. Thereby it stroked many of the region's anti-Semitic conspiracy theories, including that the US government or the Zionists plotted the attacks of September 11.

Note also that the Bush team coupled its revolutionary cultural assertions with refusal to ensure that any revolutions succeed. Perhaps the primary examples are in Lebanon and Egypt, where Syria and the Mubarak regime, respectively, kill or imprison those foolish enough to identify with America. In his 2005 State of the Union address, President G. W. Bush urged Egypt to lead the Islamic world to democracy. Pursuant to that, Secretary of State Condoleezza Rice encouraged Ayman Nur to run in the elections that President Mubarak allowed. But at the moment that popular support began to flow to the opposition, Mubarak jailed its chiefs and spurned Rice's entreaties on their behalf; Nur got five years of hard labor. The hard fate of these pro-Americans moves hearts and minds more than Joseph Nye's soft power.

WHAT IT REALLY IS

Seriousness must begin with the realization that most of mankind is moved by hate and fear no less than by sleepy soft power. Solipsism blinkers from our statesmen's minds that men in every civilization have found joy, humor, and moral and spiritual uplift in slaughtering and torturing their innocent fellows as well as in charity or contemplation. The ideas and passions by which Arab masses shout "God Is Great" as they watch replays of burning Americans jumping to their deaths from the World Trade Center or videos of Americans' beheadings differ only in proper names from the soft power that animated the Austrian, Lithuanian, and Russian civilians who joyfully helped the Nazi *Einsatzgruppen* force innocent Jewish women onto piles of corpses to be shot in turn; or from the soft power that filled the French crowds that bayed for the blood of thousands dragged to the guillotine, and who sang as they passed the bloody heads around. Similarly potent soft power animated the Aztecs who propitiated their gods by ripping beating hearts from their captives, and the Iroquois who slow-roasted theirs. In *The Education of a True Believer,* Lev Kopelev reports that the Communists who collected the last bits of grain from Ukraine and southern Russia in 1934 to make absolutely sure that some 10 million farmers would starve rejoiced they were "realizing historical necessity" against "enemies of the people." What fulfillment might self-appointed "saviors of the planet" find in erasing the "carbon foot-prints" of "enemies of the planet"?[15] The point is that psychological em-powerment comes from sources more diverse, more powerful, and less benign than our statesmen's notion of soft power comprehends.

Reducing ever varied, ever changing human soft power to "attraction," and supposing that there exists any universally accepted code of legiti-macy, is self-deception. Repulsion energizes human beings at least as much as attraction.[16] Nor is attraction identical with affection, since that usually requires respect, which is compatible with fear, which is a natural reaction to power. In fact, soft power or attraction most often emanates from ca-pacity to do or prevent harm. A nation's (or an individual's) incapacity to hurt you is not nearly as attractive as its capacity to protect you—or as the fact that it is refraining from hurting you. Charles de Gaulle observed that power draws men to wrap themselves around it—out of a combination of love, fear, and interest. The Romans used to call the complex of qualities that leads nations to defer to one another *gravitas*—the capacity to weigh upon events.

Gravitas and Ephemera

All great power combines love, fear, and interest. The most ironic of Ma-chiavelli's statements, that unarmed prophets always fail, was part of his powerful, unarmed campaign against Jesus who, unarmed and crucified, is the origin of Europe's civilization. Machiavelli's campaign depended far more on stoking his readers' resentments, fears, and interests than on logical argument.[17] Yet though he counted on superiority in "unarmed power" being decisive in the long run, he pointed to Moses, whose sword augmented the force of the Commandments he had brought his people. Nevertheless, Machiavelli bet that the kind of civilization inherent in his message would do to Christianity what Christianity had done to the Ro-man Empire and to the Barbarians. He knew as we all do that the greatest changes in the way peoples live happen when those who lack powerful ideas, or who have abandoned them—people we call Barbarians—succumb to the "soft power" of those who have them. But barbarism and civilization are relative terms.

This leads us to ask, who, in the confrontation between Islamism and contemporary Western civilization, is the most bereft of ideas? Willingness to kill and die signifies seriousness. Which side proves that it represents something worth killing and dying for? That side will attract others. One can imagine third-century AD Romans rejoicing in their civilization's attractiveness to the Barbarians in terms similar to Nye's definition of soft power. But while the Barbarians admired the Romans' technology, they had long since lost any awe of the Romans. Which side today represents nothing but the lives and comforts it fears losing? Which side has the most potent combination of ideas and swords? A hint of who today's Barbarians may be comes from the fact that while few Muslims convert to Christianity, Western governments, celebrities, and trendy folk have converted to Islam, professed affection for it, or censored criticism of it.[18]

Every nation that has exercised influence in the world has done so on behalf of a way of life, of aspirations that held its people together and attracted foreigners. The persons each such nation sent abroad personified a way of life—"a particular vision of politics, economics, culture, and ultimately . . . of human nature and the meaning of life itself." Thus James Kurth famously identified the Spanish Hapsburg Empire with the soldier-priest Ignatius Loyola, the French empire with egalitarian teachers of high culture, the British with disciplined, liberal administrators.[19] Like other successful peoples, of which the Romans were the prototype, they lived lives that others wanted to imitate. These serious men were open to adherence and imitation but neither imitated others nor imagined themselves part of any universal community. The Catholic Hapsburgs, the Protestant British, even the representatives of secular France (most of whom were Catholic) lived disciplined lives whose very successes accredited their causes, and they gloried in setting standards.

Kurth describes the post–World War II generation of American leaders—the Eisenhowers and Marshalls—in similar terms: They personified a country victorious, rich, and benevolent, whose movies showed a way of life that the world could barely imagine. Their America had always been attractive. Millions had migrated to it, Americans had always thought their ways worthy of imitation. But the American people had resolved not to imitate conquering Rome or equipped themselves physically or morally to impose their ways—much less to follow others' leads. That is why the world followed them.

But after 1945, as a substantial part of mankind besought America for help and protection, another generation of statesmen grew imagining that the world was just as eager for America's guidance. This new generation, unlike the Eisenhowers and Marshalls, neither won wars nor elevated the human spirit. Rather, since the 1950s it only lost wars, after sacrificing lives, treasure, and allies. Many who sought their protection—Iranians, Kurds, Angolans, Vietnamese, Lebanese—found betrayal, justified by the logic of Realists such as Henry Kissinger and James Baker, even as John F. Kennedy and Jimmy Carter spoke in Neoconservative terms about paying any price, bearing any burden, to support freedom and "human rights." But losing wars, abandoning allies, is inherently repulsive. Liberal Internationalists' deepest wish seems to be integrating America with the world. But the America they project—a mixture of self-absorbed celebrities, academic bureaucrats, and seminaked figures gyrating to loud music—gives the impression that the Americans' god is in their bellies and loins: a fat, cowardly god, repulsive in his pretentiousness, shallowness, and impotence.

And yet these Americans seem to think that, under thin appearances to the contrary, the whole world is just like them. Well, it isn't—and neither is America.

Religion

Ignorance of religion is perhaps the defining cultural characteristic of America's foreign policy establishment. The University of Chicago conducted a massive study of "fundamentalism"—by which term the study means the phenomenon that some people seriously believe the tenets of their religions. Peter Berger, my Boston University colleague, observed that the study's premise—namely, that such seriousness is unusual and hence problematic—is wrong.[20] In fact most humans, no less bright than the study's authors, take their own religions seriously. Because they do, it is possible for them to understand others' seriousness. Only small and peculiar groups, such as the study's authors and our statesmen, take no religion seriously and hence are baffled by all. That's a problem.

The several strains of American Progressivism make it difficult to imagine why some people would blow themselves up to kill those they regard as enemies of God. In *The Lexus and the Olive Tree*, Thomas Friedman expresses the view of Liberals and Realists that the modern global economy will entice Muslims to be less passionate about what they think God demands of them. The Neoconservatives believe the prospect of freedom will do the same. These sophisticated Americans may not realize that they are as insulting as any Western trader who ever tried to buy any primitive's patrimony by dangling beads. They may not realize it for the same reason that Robert Kagan, as Neoconservative as they come, described early America as a "theocracy" (a modern pejorative unknown at the time) that was followed by a "reactionary revivalism" that barely veiled the fact that Americans really worshiped "at altars [of] mobility, growth, and the enjoyment of life."[21] He neither realized nor cared that he was insulting most of his fellow Americans because he could not take seriously anybody's concern with God.

But willingness to die in God's service is less peculiar than the contrary. Few churchgoing Americans have not sung the old hymn "Faith of Our Fathers," the second stanza of which reads, "Our fathers chained in prisons dark, / were still in heart and conscience free. / How sweet would be their children's fate, / if they like them should die for thee." Every Boy Scout has pledged "on my honor to do my duty to God and my country." Even at tender ages, those who recite this know that they are promising forfeiting life itself. And, of course, moral disdain for one's own life is the *sine qua non* of military life—which our demilitarized statesmen cannot imagine any more than they can imagine churchgoing. No wonder that the suicide attackers' world is beyond their moral and intellectual horizon.

Religious illiteracy also limits your ability to distinguish between religious orthodoxy and heresy. The difference between them is not a matter of opinion or of which sect wins. It is just as objective as that between poisonous and wholesome mushrooms. For example, the division of the Muslim world in elite discourse, from the White House to *The New York Times*, between "moderates" and "extremists" or "fundamentalists," refers to American secularists' subjective preferences, but to no reality. The divisions that matter to Muslims, and hence matter objectively, are not just those between Sunni and Shia, but also, among the former, between Wahabis and advocates of other modes of practice, and among the latter between people who hold different views of how the Hidden Imam will return. These divisions are social and political—even racial—as much as they are religious. But intellectually to untangle the elements, one must take them seriously.

The problem *du jour*, Islamism, the mixture of Islam and politics in the context of anti-Westernism, must be understood piece by piece: The Sunni and Shia aspects are different, often antagonistic, and differ according to the regimes under which they live. Moreover, and this is the key point, some variants, especially Wahabism, are especially foreign and threatening to mainstream Islam. Note for example that Wahabism preaches, and has practiced, mass slaughter of supposed polytheists, and that it puts Shia first in that category. It is significant as well that the religious antagonisms overlap and strengthen racial ones. Hence Sunni Islamists sometimes insult other Sunni by calling them "Persians," meaning both Shia and tools of Iran. Ordinary politics mixes orthodoxy and heresy as it uses them.

But while the sources of heresy are many, heretics have in common that they depart from their faith's strictures—from the fundamentals—to appease their passions in their faith's name. Heretics are not fundamentalists. That is why usually, but not always, heresy forges closer links with politics than does orthodoxy. The distinction between moderation and extremism brushes over such vital details and lumps into the same categories even people who may be at odds with one another. So when you hear someone talk about moderates and extremists, realize you are listening to an abstraction from reality. Moderate about what? Extreme about what? And so what?

For those who run American foreign policy to regard religion as a negative factor in the world, to be overcome by "moderation," that is, by watering belief down to a point pleasing to unbelievers, is to place America in the role of enemy to all the world's sincere believers in God. That is not power.

Secular Concerns

The secular parts of human motivation spring from people's inexhaustible will to be above others. Peoples are good at finding reasons to take from others, to dominate others, to eliminate others. Words cannot undo this human reality. Much as anyone might imagine that neighbors would set aside the blood feuds of dime-size origin jointly to pursue million-dollar jackpots, that they might forget their olive trees for the chance to drive Lexus cars, the reality is that most are likelier to dream that getting the neighbor out of the way is the key to getting the Lexus under their tree. We must realize that secular interests, like religious identities, exist in their individuality, place by place, piece by juxtaposed piece, and must not imagine that you can exercise impartial influence among them.

It was impossible for President Wilson to champion the Italians' and the Slavs' incompatible demands in 1919. His attempt to ride horses going in opposite directions had to end up as it did, making things worse for both, and for America.

Alas, just about anything that distinguishes one group from another may set off the innate human tendency to affirm the group's identity by destroying the other.[22] We know it from Thucydides' account of how a small controversy between fifth-century BC Corcyra's two parties spiraled into a conflagration that consumed them both, from accounts of how the 1947 independence of India sparked the ancient opposition between Hindus and Muslims into the murder of nearly a million, from the memory of how easy it was for Hitler to turn a most civilized people into destroyers of civilization by feeding their resentments, from how Serbia's Slobodan Milosevic rose to power in the 1990s by an impassioned recall of the ancient antagonism between Serbs and Albanians, from America's own history in the 1790s, the 1860s, and since the 1960s. That fuel is inexhaustible, ever dry.

Contempt

But much as fuels need oxygen to burn, hate blazes mostly when accompanied by contempt. Much as we may hate persons, ideas, and institutions, yet we may recognize that they are beyond our capacity to affect. Or fearing the objects of our hate, we respect them. Like hunger, unsatisfied hate gnaws at much of mankind. But once the object of hate no longer inspires fear, when you imagine it in range of your reach, contempt replaces respect. Then people savor pent-up hungers, rejoice in reversing roles, rush to realize dreams of vengeance. That is why Machiavelli, following Aesop, reminds us of what we already know: that the smallest amount of contempt will blow even tiny resentments into flaming hate—even create hate where debts of gratitude might have existed. That is why weakness and impotence are secular mortal sins—unpardonable and unpardoned. *On the bright side, while others alone can decide whether they hate us, we alone, exclusively, control whether others hold us in contempt.*

As a general rule, managing foreigners' resentments is a more promising approach to dealing with their passions than trying to please. Practically, the power of opinion depends on time, place, and circumstance. For example, superficially and ex post facto, one might judge that the Polish people's ecstatic adherence to Pope John Paul II in 1979 was sure to sweep Poland to freedom and prove that religion's power is overwhelming. But had a Stalin been ruling the Soviet Union, he would have drowned in blood the Poles' jubilant cries of solidarity. On the other hand, the Pope did not delude himself that all who responded to him with shouts of "we want God" were drawn to his message of personal holiness more than they were moved by their secular hate of Communism.

In short, there is more to soft power than our priests of "Soft Power" and their august congregation understand.

Let us now see how it really works in our time.

HOW ATTRACTION AND REPULSION MOVE PEOPLES

Two ideas define the opposite limits of error: On one side, Stalin's well-known quip, implying that the Pope's lack of army divisions signified he had no power; on the other, the US Central Intelligence Agency's confidence, in the 1950s, that its apparatus for influencing the world's media could play public opinion like "a mighty Wurlitzer [organ]." In fact, opinion is very powerful, and manageable for good or ill—sometimes, to some extent. Stalin knew this. He expended energy and shed blood to organize the Comintern, the world's most capillary system for the controlled diffusion of a (per)version of reality. Stalin also knew well enough to bow before the fact that the Russian people would not fight Germany for the sake of godless, internationalist Communism. Hence he banished Marxist rhetoric for the duration of the "Great Patriotic War" for "Holy Mother Russia" and provided the Red Army with plenty of priests. The CIA, however, diffused propaganda that pleased its monochrome writers rather than their diverse audiences. It never learned that the message must be relevant to the audience. It learned nothing from serial failure. During the Iraq War, the CIA paid hundreds of millions of dollars to contractors, including Washington's Lincoln Group and London's Bell Pottinger, to fill the Iraqi media with material to the effect that the war pitted all of them together against extremism.[23] This fit US policy but meant little to people being bled by religious and ethnic divisions, whose objects of fear and hate were close at hand.

From Opinion to Power

When an image is applied inappropriately, you know it must be very powerful. Thus, in the winter of 2006–2007, as the two main Palestinian factions in the Gaza Strip were fighting each other for power and booty, one side, Fatah, took to insulting the other side, Hamas, by calling them "Shia" and even "Persians." Of course the distinction between Sunni and Shia is important to Muslims. But no one doubted that all sides in the Gaza Strip were of pure Sunni Arab extraction. Why then the insult? Because while Fatah's financing was coming from Sunni Arab states (and not a little from the US government, more on that below), financing for Hamas was coming through Damascus but ultimately from Iran—the citadel of Shia power. Still, the two Palestinian sides had been clients of powers on opposite sides of the Sunni—Shia divide for a long time without coming to blows. In Gaza, the Muslim war against Israel had overshadowed the divide. But the divide became relevant and bloody when all sides came to see it as a part of a larger war between Sunni and Shia raging in Iraq, and in Lebanon as well, and sensed that Israel had left the field to them.

In short, specific events made this centuries-old divide especially relevant in our time. Iraq's 2003 liberation changed that country from the major threat to Iran to one whose Shia majority augments Shia Iran against the Muslim world's Sunni majority. And as Iran sponsored Lebanon's Shia majority and Shia demographic growth surpassed that of Sunni, the balance of power between the main parts of the Islamic world changed further. The rise of a historically oppressed minority struck terror into Sunni regimes that rule none too tenderly over Shia minorities. Hard as it may be for Westerners to believe, Iran's development of nuclear weapons is directed at the Sunni world at least as much as at Israel. Hence the budding nuclear cooperation between Egypt and Saudi Arabia aims at the Shia threat. The hate had been there. Circumstances produced the opportunity on one side and fear on the other that fanned it into flame.

This storm's winds may propel or hinder many causes. The mutual hatreds and fears of regimes inherently weak and sitting atop half the world's oil reserves are inherently manipulable by far greater powers from the rest of the world. The US government, as mentioned, financed Fatah in Gaza and helped rally Egypt, Saudi Arabia, Jordan, and the Gulf States against Iran. It did so on the ignorant premise that it was strengthening "moderates" against "extremists." But these American categories are artificial, unserious. Taking seriously what actually moves people is a prerequisite for successful manipulation. That is what Saudi Arabia did in 2007 when it began to finance Hamas as well as Fatah to focus them on what unites them—fighting Israel—rather than on differences between Saudis and Iranians. The Americans refused to understand how irrelevant their distinction between moderates and extremists really is. The Saudis merely underestimated both sides' lust for power.

Politicizing Opinion

Now consider Islamism—how some people revived fervor for a religion by deemphasizing God, seeking to realize Islam "in concrete form" within their societies by emphasizing disdain of Euro-American civilization.[24] How did it grow so? Certainly not by *force majeure*—Islamic societies are weak by all standards—but rather by juxtaposing a little cunning, a little moral strength, against the Western world's prevailing intellectual nihilism and moral weakness.

Since their inception in the 1920s, the various Muslim brotherhoods have fed on the widespread realization that the Muslims who run their societies are generally impious and self-serving and that they ape Westerners shamelessly. Logically, if false Muslims empowered by dealings with the West are the problem, the solution must be true Islam. The millions of people who think this way are not "fundamentalist," "radical," or "extreme," as Westerners are wont to call them, much less "Islamofascists." By the same token, the nominally Muslim Middle Eastern rulers who did not hinder the world's access to oil at market prices until the 1970s were not thereby "moderates." The misleading categories flow from the fact that Western elites equated religion with bad, and movement away from it as good. Hence they believed that they would earn the Muslim world's thanks by helping to secularize it. Reality proved more complex. In fact, urging Iran's Shah to carry out a "white revolution" against Islam in the 1960s and 1970s—which alienated him from his people and set him up for overthrow—was a pillar of American policy.

Few remember that Islamism's first big success, to which it owes much of its further development, came when the Ayatollah Khomeini's weak Islamist resistance to Iran's secular Shah was first strengthened by massive Soviet patronage, and then helped into power by the Carter Administration's deep misunderstanding. The Soviets, despite their atheism, understood that political resistance to Middle Eastern regimes allied with the West was likeliest to come from Islamists. Hence they supported the exiled Shia Ayatollah Khomeini in Baghdad through their ally Saddam Hussein—a Sunni atheist who had killed more Shia than anyone since the Wahabi wars of the early nineteenth century. They also took Ayatollahs to Moscow's Patrice Lumumba University and then continued to support them once back in Iran. In 1978, a Soviet radio station in Baku, Azerbaijan, tied the Shah's deviations from the Koran to the people's daily troubles, and to his association with America. Meanwhile the Palestine Liberation Organization (PLO)—Sunni, atheist, and largely Soviet-controlled—acted as Khomeini's military arm. Thus Sunni gunmen paid by an atheist power midwifed a Shia regime. Revolutionary slogans switched the focus of Islam from Allah to the Mullahs, and from the supernatural Satan to the earthly one, America. The Islamists' pretense of piety did not affect the reality that they were secularizing Islam. They acted as reincarnated prophets and pointed to earthly devils. Shifting the focus from eternity to politics eventually diminished their own authority. But after 1979 they had power.

Because the US Establishment's ideological lenses skewed perceptions of reality, America itself unlocked the Islamists' door to power by persuading the Shah not to let his elite corps, the "immortals," drown them in blood. "The Ayatollah Khomeini," wrote Princeton professor Richard Falk in *The New York Times,* "has been depicted in a manner calculated to frighten. . . . His close advisers are uniformly composed of moderate, progressive individuals . . . who share a notable record of concern with human rights . . . resisting oppression and promoting social justice. Iran may yet provide us with a desperately needed model of humane governance for a Third World country."[25] *Time* magazine was of the same opinion: "Khomeini believes that Iran should become a parliamentary democracy. Those who know the Ayatollah expect that he will settle in the holy city of Quom and resume a life of teaching and prayer."[26] US Ambassador William Sullivan compared Khomeini to Mahatma Gandhi. Blinded by their commitment to their own very particular view of the good, disturbed by knowing that the Shah did not quite live up to that view, not realizing how having tried to live up to it at all had been ruinous, and perhaps seduced just a bit by Soviet propaganda that placed Khomeini in the "progressive camp," America's best and brightest were involved in a battle of ideas with only their own blinkered ones in mind.

The simpleminded distinction between moderates and extremists, the confusion between moderation and secularism, ignorance of the ways in which sects within both the Sunni and Shia traditions influence behavior, and the facile equation of fervor with fascism lead logically to the conclusion that Americans are at war with Islam itself. But the US government's attempts to soften this by indulgence of Arab regimes is precisely wrong. American patronage of false Muslims, such as Saudi princes, inflamed the faithful, while projections of American popular culture poured the gasoline of contempt on hate's fire.

Contempt is what turned Islamism's hate to mass murder of Westerners. Europe's and America's passivity in the face of ever growing terrorism richly earned it. Even though the region's early anti-Western terrorists were aggressively secular, Western acquiescence to any and all who killed or humiliated Westerners made them de facto paladins of the Islamic world. Terrorism had long been arguably the main currency among the Middle East's internally weak potentates. Egypt's Gamal Nasser, head of the first of the region's independent, secular regimes, bet successfully that if he used irregulars rather than uniformed soldiers for small-scale attacks on Western and Israeli interests, he could avoid retaliation. That was the origin of the *Fedayeen,* whose *Fatah* faction, led by one Yasser Arafat, morphed into the PLO. Arafat, paid partially by Egypt, then by Jordan, then Syria, Egypt, and Saudi Arabia, but mostly by the Soviet Union and in the end by Iraq, the European Union, and the United States, became a small hero to the Arab world by bombing school buses, shooting up airports, and hijacking planes. But his soft power really grew when his group killed Israel's athletes at the 1972 Olympics and was not hunted down and destroyed for it. Not only did Germany release his men but, in November 1974, shortly after his PLO had murdered twenty-six Israeli schoolchildren, Arafat addressed the UN General Assembly in New York wearing a pistol and was applauded. The Arabs' anti-Westernism became fashionable in fashionable Western circles, and Israel became unfashionable.

Many Westerners convinced themselves that there *just had to be* ways of deflecting the terrorists' wrath. One way was to convince themselves that terrorist leaders like Arafat are relative "moderates," proper objects of state honors, parties to treaties, recipients of funds, in the hope that they would become what one might wish them to be. Most Europeans, and the Left part of the US political spectrum, including the US State Department, came to believe that Arabs who kill Israeli civilians are not really terrorists but "resistance fighters." Fear, it seems, bends minds as well as knees. These Western reactions to terrorism are further evidence that soft power flows from the hard kind. But as the Muslim world sensed this change in soft power, it did not doubt that bravery on their side had shown up the Westerners' contemptible cowardice. Because career atheists such as Arafat and Saddam Hussein had made the Europeans, and even the great Americans, eat their own words about not rewarding terror, and made them smile at humiliations, thankful for the bloody spittle, Muslim hearts accepted them as defenders of the Faith. Pride in one's own and contempt for others made heroes even of the vermin who pushed an elderly Jew in a wheelchair over the side of a hijacked cruise ship in 1985.

In 1979, the Ayatollah Khomeini became a hero even to Sunni who despise Shia when he imprisoned the entire staff of the US embassy for over a year—a textbook *casus belli*—and got away with it. He showed how easy, safe, and fun it is to hurt Americans. Contempt for the West also brought about a truce in the fundamental conflict between Islamists and their proximate, indeed ultimate, enemies, namely, the secular regimes where they live, the false Muslims they say are their main enemies. But because these enemies are hard targets that bite back hard, they inspire only hate—not contempt. By contrast, the Americans bite ineffectively, and the Europeans are toothless. This is not the place to itemize the causes of the Islamic world's contempt for Euro-Americans. The point is to note how essential an element of Islamist soft power that contempt is, and that attempts to propitiate the Islamic world can only confirm and deepen it.

The power of Islamism is indeed "soft": existing largely in the realm of words, ideas, with just enough force to affirm seriousness. The Americans have prescribed soft-power antidotes: Neoconservatives, democracy; Realists, rule by secular strongmen; and Liberal Internationalists, economic development assistance. But none of these touches either Islamism's religious substance or the vital fact of contempt. Moreover, since all would increase the Muslim world's Westernization, they amount to prescriptions of booze for a hangover. For their part, the Middle East's secular regimes have dealt with Islamism's symptoms by co-opting its rhetoric, directing its violence toward the West, and repressing it internally. This only puts off the religious-cultural reckoning. This reckoning, however, is necessarily and exclusively the Muslim world's business. Contempt, alas, is a global currency.

Capturing Hearts and Minds

The soft power of the Soviet Union, by contrast, was substantially a work of art—awesomely created nearly from scratch and sustained by hard work. The Soviets invested much and expected everything from their apparatus forcefully to spread and inculcate ideas. Of course, the idea that human organization could scientifically change the human condition had captured many "commanding heights" long before Lenin's 1917 *coup d'état* in Russia. By that time, the world's existing socialist parties had already organized themselves internationally, and the factions thereof that split from them hoping to follow Lenin's example formed the skeleton of a worldwide organization to spread the idea.[27] But the Soviets, as the saying goes, thought globally and acted locally. The local Communist parties themselves were one conveyor belt for Moscow's message, from which another subordinate layer radiated out into the various components of local societies: women, youth, each category of workers, each profession; students, musicians, journalists, lawyers, librarians, professors. Even the military was targeted with a message tailored to it, in its particular circumstance, raising hopes to which Communism offered fulfillment, and resentments to which it offered revenge. Overlaid upon this network was another set of groups run directly from Moscow, ostensibly apolitical, and targeting persons with specific concerns: Were you for peace? Did you care about public health or some other cause? Some Soviet-sponsored organization would adopt you and your cause, redefining it in its own way. Implicit in the ensuing messages was the assertion that Moscow was the ultimate scientific authority.

Influence on specific items of world politics was the Soviets' immediate aim, of course. But the ultimate aim was nothing less than what the great Communist theorist Antonio Gramsci called "hegemony" over cultures: In contemporary terms, that meant soft power waxing very hard. Following Machiavelli more than Marx, Gramsci thought that exercising hegemonic power over language can make opposition impossible.[28] Soviet soft power worked methodically, massively, to achieve cultural hegemony for keeps.

The Soviets went about it in military fashion. The idea was for the Party to control the "commanding heights" of cultural life, and those of economic life, thus denying "the class enemy" the intellectual as well as the material wherewithal of survival. Control would be achieved by placing persons under Party discipline in the posts that control subordinate posts. Optimally, as in the Soviet Union and Eastern Europe, the Party people on top would have the power to choose who could practice any given profession, and even who would eat and who would not. In countries where Communists could not wield violence, they would wield as much bureaucratic force as they could to exclude, and as much prestige as possible to delegitimize, those they could not control. Since Communist organizers could count on material as well as organizational support, they conquered more and more positions of influence and grew in numbers.[29]

Soviet soft power's limitations and strengths are most evident from what it did and didn't accomplish in the free world. Farmers proved impenetrable. It barely reached into what Communists considered their natural constituency, "the working masses." Even in Communist-controlled labor unions, for example, many members disaffiliated as they could and joined rival organizations. One reason for failure with "the workers" is that, despite the Communists' soft-pedaling of atheism in "mass propaganda," it proved impossible to proceed as if there were no clash between Communism's belief in itself as the final authority and most people's belief in God. In a few social sectors, however, primarily among intellectuals, government workers, and journalists (here, too, religion was a limiting factor), Communists reached deeply, coming close to making anti-Communism a disqualification for advancement and even employment. By the mid-1980s, even as the penultimate pages in the USSR's history were being written, Strobe Talbott (eventually President Clinton's Deputy Secretary of State) expressed on behalf of *Time* the US foreign policy establishment's consensus condemnation of President Ronald Reagan for having suggested that the Soviet Union was not eternal.[30] It seems that "elite" audiences that imagined themselves as shapers of human clay more easily identified with the Communist potters than with audiences composed of the clay.

But the Soviet Union moved the masses' hearts and minds less by its apparatus for words than by its looming military power. Joseph Nye's point—conventional wisdom in academic circles—that the Soviets' 1956 crushing of the Hungarian Revolt, the 1961 building of the Berlin Wall, the 1968 invasion of Czechoslovakia, and its military buildup cost it soft power—is reality upside-down.[31] In fact, after those events, more and more Europeans began to see danger not in the Soviets but in resisting them. Soviet "mass propaganda" had always depicted the Americans as warmongers. But as Soviet military power was rising and America's was in relative decline, Europeans began looking at Americans as warmongers. Europeans bent to Soviet "peace" propaganda in the 1980s as they had bent to Nazi "peace" propaganda in the 1930s, and as they would bend to the Arabs' in our time.

Within the Soviet empire itself, however, hearts and minds were captive, not convinced. There the hegemonic apparatus of cultural control, overlaying and substituting for spontaneous civil society, made its version of reality "the effective truth." Ordinary people sustained this pretense of reality by speaking the lies demanded of them. But the culture choked. It did not satisfy, did not make room for human emotion, much less for the highest human aspirations. Even Nazi culture had engaged more human elements than that, through its Dionysian spectacles. To say that Communist official culture left people hungry for spiritual life is an understatement. Fear of small consequences, of liberty and life, and anxiety for careers and livelihoods—these were the official culture's glue from bottom to top. Naturally, a culture so dependent on fear had to keep the fear quotient high. Once the Soviet regime let fear drop below a certain point, any opening for truth in public, for public expression of naturally attractive ideas, would free hearts and minds to leave captivity.

In sum, the Soviet organization of soft power was as powerful as can be imagined. But the substance of its message was not. In 1979, the Communist regimes held all the commanding heights of culture. With an official monopoly on truth, and on politically acceptable language, they had just about fulfilled Gramsci's definition of cultural "hegemony." But the culture was empty.

Just Words?

Tiny were the openings through which Pope John Paul II pushed his big agenda. True, Communist regimes had never eliminated or subjugated the Catholic Church entirely. Especially in Poland, the government had spared remnants of a capillary network of bishops and priests. But the Communist regime ridiculed and reviled religion, pushing its ideas out of the public square, its language out of public discourse, and its adherents to society's margins. The attractive power of the regime's material rewards and the unattractiveness of life on society's margins bolstered its message. Because the Catholic Church had nothing left but its message, its attack on Soviet culture under John Paul II had to consist of nothing but words, and nonpolitical ones at that.

Whereas Islamists were attacking reigning regimes by politicizing themselves, John Paul II attacked them by preaching spiritual Christianity. Studiously without political words, he evoked each individual's God-given freedom and responsibility, solidarity with fellow humans, love of family and country—that is, how Christians should live in private and in public, and why. The contrast with the regime's official prescriptions could not have been sharper. His audiences delighted in his speaking publicly truths that the regime had made politically incorrect and banished from public discourse. They delighted in hearing in public a language so unlike that of bureaucrats. And as they cheered him together, they discovered one another. His most subversive words were Jesus' "be not afraid."[32] Wielding that soft power, unmixed with any of the hard kind, John Paul II triumphed over a mixture of proven efficacy. And not just in Poland. In the 1980s, ordinary people throughout the Soviet empire, and in Moscow itself, began to wear crosses though knowing little of Christ. They knew enough, however, thus to tell one another that they identified with the one idea according to which souls exist, independent of tyrants big and small, because they are immortal.

Few of the Soviet empire's elites doubted that their moral weakness had undermined their physical power. Hence, sincerity notwithstanding, the 1990s saw officials from Boris Yeltsin to Mikhail Gorbachev and even Vladimir Putin cozy up to Christian symbolism and tradition, if not substance. Putin himself began wearing a cross and forged an alliance with the Russian Orthodox Church. While much of the former Soviet empire's physical landscape remained bleak, the churches were refurbished, their repainted golden domes glowed, and Moscow's enormous Christ the Savior cathedral, which Stalin had razed, was rebuilt to its original glory. The power that made these things happen seemed to speak for itself—but not to all. The stewards of American soft power knew better. One Norman Pattiz, member of the US Broadcasting Board of Governors (BBG), told

The New Yorker in 2002 that "it was MTV that brought down the Berlin Wall." Those millions who chanted "we want God" to John Paul II must have had Britney Spears in mind. Did you not know that American soft power had destroyed Communism?

CONCLUSION

While the power of ideas, of attraction, repulsion, respect, and contempt is a classic subject, "soft power," conceptualized in Joseph Nye's book, is merely part of the mentality of the Kennedy School's alumni—and of the significant many who wish they were. This mentality is defined as much by what it ignores as by what it deems important. We begin to grasp its most distinctive feature when we realize that Nye's book does not even mention what John Paul II did in Poland, or for that matter Christianity's role in the fall of the Soviet empire. The Soviets themselves always deemed religion the deadliest of enemies and were publishing editorials in *Pravda* to this effect through the mid-1980s. But Nye's readers would never guess that there had been a deadly clash of ideas. Our soft potentates exercise a cultural hegemony scarcely less pervasive than the Soviet Establishment's. But that hegemony has weakened them because their culture is emptier, less attractive, and more vulnerable than that of the Soviets—because it is softer. Unlike Machiavelli and the Soviets, our cultural hegemons do not take their cultural opponents seriously.

Why indeed are Westerners who think in terms of soft power unable to take seriously the world's "softest" and most potent force? Some suppose that gods are mere pretexts, tools, or cloaks for secular enterprises, or that they are advanced cases of a common mental disorder, or simply the opiates of the downtrodden. Mere ignorance. Not much knowledge or reflection is needed to differentiate the hard uses that rulers have made of Christianity from its naturally compelling core. Reflecting on that bare core points to the essence not just of any religion's power, but to what gives power to any and all ideas—namely, that ideas can transcend earthly power, that they can mediate between man and God.

That mediation is power. Isaiah (53) described God's Anointed as one who "hath no form or comeliness . . . no beauty that we should desire him . . . despised and rejected of men . . . smitten of God . . . cut off out of the land of the living . . . his grave with the wicked." Isaiah's argument is that God's instrument is unremarkable except in that he is God's instrument. By the same token, the Gospels never describe Jesus as an imposing figure, but rather as riding on an ass, mocked, abandoned, and crucified. He left only a short dozen of scared nobodies with the world's most unlikely tale—a resurrection that none of them had seen happen—and the fantastic promise that faith in it means eternal life with God. And yet Jesus is the defining source of the world's defining civilization. This can be so only because, within each human being, a soul feels kinship with its own and the universe's maker, regardless of human power or prestige. As we have suggested, only America's and Europe's twentieth-century elites have been able to convince themselves that they have no souls—only soft power.

Incapacity to understand spirit cripples understanding of flesh. Speaking of freedom without explaining for what purpose and by what right we are free neither inspires nor explains. Aimless freedom repels. Moreover, most cannot tell the difference between the desire for freedom and the desire for power over others. The US Declaration of Independence made clear that we are free *vis-à-vis* temporal power as well as one another because all are equally under "the laws of Nature and Nature's God." That understanding, once a pillar of the American mind and not the least source of America's attractiveness to foreigners, is now foreign—indeed alien—to those who use the term "soft power." Thus insensitive to higher power, the mentality of soft power is opaque as well to lower but nevertheless potent human sentiments: fear, honor, interest, love, hate, and contempt. Today's soft nihilism disables you from grasping and dealing with hearts and minds that struggle over any visions of good and evil important enough to kill and die for.

The worst thing you can do is to define America as open to any and all cultures and ideas. By so doing you tell us to risk our lives for the privilege of believing in nothing, and convince mankind that Americans are empty shells.

CHAPTER 4

DIPLOMACY
Medium, Not Message

How we act will affect the main issue more than what we say.
Once we have set our plans in order, it will be easy to find words
to fit our deeds.
> —LUCIUS ANNIUS, LIVY, BK. 8

In the fourth century BC the League of Latin Cities was deciding what
its envoys should say to the Romans, who were about to attack. Lucius
Annius's comments focused the discussion on reality: First decide what
really matters to us, what we want, and what we are going to do about it.
That will speak loudly for itself. Words can emphasize or deemphasize,
or color our actions. But they are worse than silence if they diverge too
far from reality. Worst of all is to speak without having decided on actions, as well as to act as if speech were a substitute for action.

DIPLOMACY AND REALITY

Diplomacy is the verbal representation of a persuasive reality. The words'
sounds, soothing or snarling, do not persuade. Nor do the speaker's per-
sonality or résumé, except as they reflect on his reputation for telling it

like it is. Reality itself convinces—sometimes even without verbal expression, or through nonverbal expression. In 2006, Syria did not use words to convey to the Lebanese people that they had better knuckle under, or to the United States that it had better lean on Israel on Syria's behalf and leave Lebanon to its mercies. The Syrians simply murdered every prominent Lebanese they could who dared oppose them, used their Lebanese Shia proxies to win a war against Israel, and acted as headquarters and quartermasters for Sunni guerrillas killing US troops in Iraq. No words that Syria might have spoken to Beirut or Washington would have so bent American and Lebanese leaders to take account of Syria's interests. And Washington's carefully crafted words of opposition to what Syria was doing did not speak as loudly as Washington's acquiescence to it.

Diplomacy worthy of the name refers to indubitable realities. When it evokes consequences that affect a foreign government's actions, the consequences must follow naturally from the natural relationship between those actions and the realities of which that government is aware. For others to believe that things will happen as you say, they must know that you do not have to go out of your way to make these things happen, that you would not wish to prevent them, or perhaps that you cannot prevent them. Such diplomatic representations are *warnings*. Like yellow road signs that indicate curves, they command respect irrespective of any arbitrary speed limits or threats that might accompany them. Russia's message to Ukraine and Georgia in 2005 that their failure to pay world prices for natural gas would be followed by interruption of deliveries was such a warning. For Russia, cutting off the gas served political as well as economic interests and was a natural response to failure to meet its price. The cutoff took no effort.

By contrast, *threats* are more akin to white speed-limit signs. Since there are no natural consequences of going sixty-five instead of fifty-five, and the highway patrol imposes fines sporadically, drivers naturally take the signs' threats with grains of salt. Perhaps the quintessential example of a threat was the United States' "declaratory policy" during the Cold War to destroy the Soviet Union, but in a manner that would not have mitigated damage to the United States. Few took this threat seriously, because carrying it out would have done America no good and caused America's own destruction. Almost by definition, threats are at least partially empty.

That is why the very notion of "declaratory policy" (perforce different from the real thing) advertises unseriousness. That is why *competent diplomats do not threaten. They warn.*

Because bluffs, tricks, and lies have short legs, effective diplomacy is about frankness and truth. It is about honesty as well, because speaking dishonestly to others leads a government to be dishonest with itself—a deadly addiction. After 2002, the George W. Bush Administration declined to choose forthrightly among competing objectives and grievances concerning Iraq. It did this largely to finesse intramural disputes as well as to persuade prospective allies and mollify opposition to whatever it might do. But obfuscation gained it no allies, compounded internal disagreements, and ensured that the resulting conflated, confused objectives would not fit the means it was willing to use.[1]

Precise language, whether in formulating negotiating positions or in drafting agreements, is indispensable for minds to grip reality. Precise language is also a precondition of meaningful negotiations because it helps make you conscious of what is really important to your side, and enables you to press the other side for similar clarity. Because few experiences are as disconcerting as realizing "I didn't really mean what I said" or "they didn't mean what they said," you must choose your words not for the effect you think they might have but for how accurately they represent reality. If you prefer effect to substance, or to the extent you forget that effect comes from substance, you are in danger of seducing yourself with your own words or of confusing your press releases with reality. You may end up being the only one who believes you. So be accurate, and don't be afraid of letting reality take care of the effect.

The flowerier and more abstract your words, the less likely they are to be meaningful. As we observed in Chapter 1, words are your mind's link to reality. Concrete nouns and active verbs keep that link strong. Moreover, since the longer the talk the likelier it is to contain words that you will be forced to define in unexpected circumstances or that you may have to re-ingest, you had better "keep it simple, stupid!" Minimize self-befuddlement by being brief.

The modern notion that imprecision of language preserves your options by conveying multiple possibilities is too clever by half. In fact, making policy means choosing among options—narrowing, not multiplying them. *A fortiori,* among the worst things diplomacy can do in executing policy is to confuse imprecision with subtlety, because pursuit of subtlety may lead you to bite your own tail. *Directness is the greatest subtlety.* If you wish to avoid specifying what you will do, silence is a straightforward way. There is another as well: John Quincy Adams used the passive voice to convey the Monroe Doctrine's strong expression of US interest in the Western Hemisphere while avoiding commitments. Theodore Roosevelt urged diplomats to have the courage to "say what you mean and mean what you say." Simple lesson, but hard.

Lack of courage is one reason for the modern maxim that imprecision, "creative ambiguity," in language preserves diplomatic options. This maxim culminates in the modern fashion for creative ambiguity in agreements as well, of which Henry Kissinger became the chief advocate and exemplar.[2] Thus envoys from both sides present objectives susceptible to substantially different interpretations and end with agreements that each interprets as it pleases. "Diplomacy" is the wrong word for this sort of thing. "Charade" is more accurate. But for whose benefit (or to whose detriment) is the charade? Why pretend that minds have met when they have not?

These questions are especially relevant to democratic governments that conduct diplomacy on behalf of pluralist societies. Such governments, often unwilling to decide between competing prescriptions of what to do, may formulate ambiguous negotiating positions and let the course of international negotiations resolve intramural differences. In fact the US approached many of the Cold War's most important, long-running negotiations—especially over Vietnam and arms control—in this unprofessional manner. Leave aside that this gave the other side a major say in what US policy turned out to be. Note simply that the real negotiations were among the several sides within US government and politics—that is, that the Americans were really negotiating with one another—and that the so-called agreements that came from these diplomatic encounters were not international agreements at all.

Kissinger touted the Paris Peace Accords of 1973 as the end of the Vietnam War and accepted a share in that year's Nobel Peace Prize for having negotiated it. But the other recipient, North Vietnam's Le Duc

Tho, honorably refused the prize, knowing as well as Kissinger did that peace had not been the negotiation's result, but rather that the United States had agreed not to interfere in the North's military consummation of victory. The negotiations had really been the translation to the Vietnamese of an argument among Americans about how fast or slow, how thinly or thickly disguised, the US surrender would be. The North Vietnamese had been interested spectators to arguments among Americans.

Similarly, any doubt about the purpose and effect of the ambiguities and pseudotechnical complexities of the many US positions in the series of arms control negotiations that began with the Strategic Arms Limitation Treaty and the Ballistic Missile Treaty of 1972 was ended by Russian candor after the Soviet Union's collapse: Whereas the Americans had officially aimed to forestall, then minimize, the Soviet strategic forces' capacity to kill US missiles on the ground as well as to prevent a serious Soviet antimissile defense, the real argument had been among Americans about whether the actual capacity to fight nuclear wars mattered at all. For most of the Cold War, the intramural winners were those Americans who believed that actual capacities do not matter because the mere possession of nuclear weapons made all sides equal. That is why the Soviets invariably and successfully pursued strategic superiority, sometimes within the agreements' studiously ambiguous provisions, sometimes by outright violations, with the Americans' full knowledge and without the Americans' serious objection. The most candid expression of the intra-American debate's results, National Security Decision Directive 192 of 1987, remains classified Top Secret. Acknowledging the scope of Soviet circumventions and violations, it stated that nevertheless the United States would practice "exemplary compliance" with the treaties. In short, the balance of power *vis-à-vis* the Soviet Union mattered less to the US government than the balance of power within itself. It was, and remains, an officious secret that our statesmen's diplomatic process covered intragovernmental politics.

To whom then was the diplomatic charade useful? It was useful to US officials averse to risking the public's ire by staking out their preferences too clearly and debating them too publicly. But the fog of words in which they confused their fears and hopes benefited foreigners who held fast to reality.

The foremost feature of diplomatic reality, and the one most often set aside, is that diplomacy and words can neither create nor change basic intentions, interests, or convictions. Diplomacy is a medium, not a message, regardless of the message's contents. Hence to say "We've got a problem. Let's try diplomacy, let's sit down and talk" abstracts from the important questions: What will you say? And why should anything you say lead anyone to accommodate you?

Your Own Reality?

The diplomat's worst and most frequent mistake is supposing that foreigners must think, value, hope, and fear more or less as he does—that is, that foreigners are made in his image. But in fact such attempts to live in a reality of your own creation are foredoomed because foreigners' minds, counsels, and decisions are theirs alone, not yours. Imagining otherwise goes by the name "mirror imaging." It has led incautious statesmen to assure their domestic publics that certain foreign interlocutors mean well and to bolster confidence that a particular negotiation will yield good results.

The problem is that whenever human beings identify themselves with any proposition, their interest in accrediting themselves pushes them to continue accrediting that proposition regardless of its worth. That is, departures from reality are addictive. That is why Pinocchio's nose stretched exponentially as his lies stretched reality. The farther from reality, the greater and ever less credible must be the further pretenses to uphold it. Hence whenever a diplomat or statesman representing a democratic country states publicly that his foreign counterpart is a man of good will and that the negotiations are likely to be fruitful, he becomes a hostage to his own statements, removes some of the other side's incentives for friendly or even for honest behavior, and places himself in the position of having to pretend that the negotiations have been fruitful even if the fruit is bitter, and to pay with substantive concessions for his counterpart's mere willingness to continue meeting him. After all, if the negotiations had never been a good idea, the statesman is to blame, and if the counterpart is as good as the statesman says, any failure must be due not to the counterpart but to himself.

DIPLOMACY AND IDEOLOGY

The tools of effective diplomacy are the ones that convey the aspects of reality likeliest to move foreign governments to do as you wish. What those aspects are and how they are to be orchestrated is always in dispute. Thucydides' account of the diplomacy by which the Spartan Brasidas conquered Thrace is one example of how diplomacy may be adjusted successfully to balance means, ends, and circumstances. Brasidas's diplomacy is the polar opposite of ideology.

With only 1,200 hoplite infantry, many of whom were unreliable Helots, Brasidas could not force his way into a vast, faraway country, much less overrun it. The combination of his army and diplomacy brought success because he crafted each partial objective so that success would enable him to pursue the next, and he scaled his tactics, demands, and tone in the circumstances at hand to achieve that partial objective. History has no better example of making offers that are hard to refuse.

Brasidas crossed Thessaly without the locals' permission by bringing a few friendly local notables to the border, assuring the Thessalian cities' representatives that he meant no harm and giving them the impression (not the promise) that he would wait for the cities' permission before crossing. When the envoys went home for consultations, he hurried through. Brasidas had got all he needed. Then, having reached the barbarian chieftain Perdiccas, Sparta's ally who had paid for his coming because he wanted help against his enemy Ahrrabeus, Brasidas told him he really had come to fight only his own enemy, Athens. After forcing Perdiccas to make a deal with Ahrrabeus he moved on, again without losses.

His conquest of the first Thracian city, Acanthus, set the pattern for the rest. It was harvest time. The Spartan army did not harm the Acanthians' fields. Brasidas presented himself as a liberating friend, shocked at the possibility that the Acanthians might not receive him as such and declare for Sparta. He did not ask for much, not to station a Spartan garrison (he could not have spared the troops anyhow), nor for Acanthian troops (he could not count on them). He only asked the city to reciprocate his friendship and to benefit from selling him food. But should the Acanthians spurn his good deal, he said with crocodile tears, Spartan troops would ravage the harvest. So, since accepting Brasidas's offer cost little and yielded benefits while refusing it would have been *dispropor-tionately* costly, the Acanthians accepted. Brasidas's real objective being the Athenian stronghold of Amphipolis, he needed only to make sure that the lesser cities would not aid the Athenians and would move a little in his direction. So the little that he asked of Acanthus was all he needed. There would be time enough later for tightening Sparta's grip.

He moved on Amphipolis fast, on a snowy night, surprising the guards at the key bridge. The city awoke to find him occupying its land-ward approaches. Because Brasidas knew that a strong Athenian naval force was within a few days' sail, he crafted proposals easy for most of the city's diverse population to accept, likely to isolate the few inclined to refuse, and therefore likely to put the city in his hands before the Athenian squadron could arrive:[3] He promised that if Spartan troops were allowed in they would take nobody's life or property, nor change any political arrangements. Anyone who wanted to stay, including Athe-nians, could do so in safety. Anyone who wished to leave could do so with all his belongings. This proposal made sure that whoever might want to die fighting the Spartans would be seen as a mere agent of Athenian imperialism. As a result, the city gave itself up just before the Athenian ships arrived. Brasidas's proposition had been just attractive enough, and just scary enough, to get enough of what he needed in a particular circumstance at a particular time. It included verbal argu-ments against Athenian imperialism and a few positive incentives to encourage Thracians to defect from Athens. But Brasidas made his argu-ments sound better and his benefits seem sweeter mostly by shifting the balance of fear in his favor. And the little he asked for in the short run would enable him to get more, more easily, in the long run. This diplo-macy's assets outweighed its objectives. It was solvent. In each situation Brasidas's deeds and words leveraged each protagonist's complex wants and fears into the desired result.

Thucydides' Brasidas teaches us that for diplomacy to deal concretely with complex human motivations, it must tailor arguments, attitudes, demands, incentives, and disincentives to fit particular audiences in par-ticular circumstances. Hence there can be no such thing as an ideology of diplomacy.

AMERICAN DIPLOMATIC IDEOLOGIES

For the past hundred years, however, American diplomacy has been largely ideological, dealing more with constructs of its own creation than with reality. Ideology reduces complex nature to simple categories. Because twentieth-century American elites imagined humanity in their own images, they have sought to move men primarily through economic carrots and technocratic sermons. Force and fear have been there too, but as adjuncts or last resorts. Above all, latter-day American diplomacy has been allergic to connecting ends and means.

The standard preamble of latter-day American diplomacy has been something like: "Different from others, we Americans do not want anyone else's territory or goods. Nor do we want special privileges. This thing we ask of you today is good for both of us, even more for you since we have so much already. By agreeing, you will gain materially, right away, at our direct expense. Over the long run, our experts will teach you to be like us and keep you out of bad international company. You must want this. Thank us, please." Hence American money, food, and experts flowed into Europe after the twentieth century's world wars. In the 1960s and 1970s they flowed to the Third World and, in the 1990s, to the former Soviet empire. But whatever else American involvement produced, it surely did not produce lasting gratitude. More to the point, its simplemindedness makes it a poor prototype of diplomacy.

We may properly speak of American diplomacy generically because its main schools are variants and consequences of a single ideology. Here is its intellectual genealogy: Beginning in the 1880s, even as Republicans like James G. Blaine and Democrats like Grover Cleveland held fast to the Founders' tradition that viewed America as unique, a few of the few Americans who thought about relations with the rest of the world began to think of our country as simply a more advanced part of the international community. They thought that with America leading the way, mankind was fast progressing to a way of life qualitatively superior morally as well as materially to what mankind had ever known. Calling themselves "internationalists," these Progressives wanted to increase America's role in the world for the good of mankind, which they identified with America's good.

They were a heterogeneous lot, including advocates of military power such as Alfred Thayer Mahan, Henry Cabot Lodge, and Theodore Roosevelt on one side, and pacifists such as David Starr Jordan, Nicholas Murray Butler, and Andrew Carnegie on the other. In the middle were men such as Secretary of State Elihu Root. But in the early twentieth century they split; the Liberals focused on reforming the international system and called the Rooseveltians "isolationists" and "warmongers" for defending US national interests through traditional means.

Though Woodrow Wilson came to personify Liberal Internationalism, that position conquered both political parties and remained *de rigueur* in America's highest social circles until the Cold War. By the 1940s, however, Liberal Internationalism had run afoul of reality enough to lead some Liberals—Professor Hans Morgenthau and Henry Kissinger are the best known—to formulate the subideology of "Realism." But while Realism disagrees with Liberalism about the details of human motivation, and despite semiserious qualifications, it agrees on the essential point that all men in all times and places are motivated alike.[4] By the 1970s, "mugged" by the failure of Realism as well as of Liberal Internationalism to stem the Soviet Union's growing threat to America, some Liberals and Realists gathered around the two old ideas: Ideas matter, and we should rally around American ideals. But though these "Neoconservatives" believed that mankind hungers for freedom and democracy above all, they were indistinguishable from Realists and Liberals in viewing mankind through blinders of their own making.

Liberal Internationalist Diplomacy

In January 2007, when China successfully tested an antisatellite weapon, *The New York Times* argued that China did not intend the weapon to serve its obvious military purpose—namely, in case of war to destroy the satellites on which the United States is asymmetrically dependent—but rather that by it China was challenging America to join in a treaty to demilitarize orbital space. Hence *The Times's* editorial called for a conference.[5] According to the *Times*, which represented the views of the US State Department, armaments exist to be dealt with by arms control treaties. It assumed that China thought likewise. Moreover, the question of what to do if the treaty were violated, other than sign another one, was beyond the sociointellectual pale of the paper's influential sources and readers—the ideologues of Liberal Internationalism.[6]

Prominent among them is Harvard's Thomas Schelling, recipient of the 2005 Nobel Prize in economics for teaching two generations that international negotiations are to be understood in terms of game theory.[7] Schelling explained that the proper US response to North Korea's acquisition of nuclear weapons "should have been to encourage the three countries most threatened, Taiwan, South Korea, and Japan . . . to reaffirm their commitment to [the nuclear antiproliferation treaty] and [their] non-nuclear status." This would have reaffirmed "the importance of the nonproliferation regime." Schelling's assumption of course is that this "regime" is equally important to all in the same way—an assumption built into the matrices of the "games" that he posits as the underlying reality of diplomacy.

Schelling writes that he derives this assumption from the fact that "there was, for much of the Cold War, a surprising, effective, direct, and entirely unofficial conversation involving policy makers and 'military intellectuals' from all nuclear powers, including enemies, whose purpose was to learn and disseminate knowledge [regarding nuclear weapons, war and peace.]"[8] The possibility that agendas different from his own might have driven that conversation's other participants does not enter his mind.

The ideology that diplomacy is self-enforcing is deeply rooted. Elihu Root, Theodore Roosevelt's Secretary of State, taught twentieth-century Americans that conferences, by themselves, could solve the world's disputes. In formal settings, recalcitrant statesmen would be bent to law and justice by their peers, who embody reason. By 1915, this had become conventional wisdom. Former President William Howard Taft, future President Herbert Hoover, and near-President Charles Evans Hughes, along with some Democrats, formed the League to Enforce Peace, to promote an organization of countries that would agree to submit all their disputes to arbitration. In 1916, President Woodrow Wilson addressed the League and effectively joined it. His 1919 proposal for a League of Nations was a variant of this idea. All such schemes involved notions of joint pressures on those who would not accept the dictates of the international community. But because all trusted in the intrinsic power of words alone, and hence in the value of meetings and agreements, all shied away from concrete enforcement.

For European governments and the US State Department, calling a conference is the "school solution" to any problem. The alternative is to call a bigger conference. The more governments and parties represented, the bigger the alliance or coalition, the more authoritative, the more forceful is the consensus supposed to be. Hence in 2004–2007 when Britain, France, and Germany, joined by the United States, sought to persuade Iran to cease production of weapons-grade uranium, they warned that noncompliance would lead to discussing the matter in the UN Security Council. The Europeans did not promise to do certain intolerable things if Iran did not comply. Rather, they invoked the UN precisely because they did not have it in them to do such things and knowing full well, as did Iran, that the UN would not do them. Whatever seriousness their position possessed came from the assumption that their petition would weigh more heavily if more signatures were on it.

This view of diplomacy, however, abstracts from the essential question: Why should a foreign power bend its will to any other at all? What can one government, or several allies, or many, bring to the table to bend it? Whence comes the power of diplomacy? In fact, bigger coalitions are not necessarily more compelling and are less likely to focus on your own objectives. When governments seek out alliances because they are afraid to stand on their own, the alliances become the sum of fears, and their objectives become lowest common denominators. In the 1920s and 1930s, Britain and France each found in the other's irresolution toward Germany excuses for their own.

Asking for agreement to any course of action to which you have not committed, and making the other's adherence a condition of your own commitment, telegraphs your fecklessness. Thus in 2002, when George W. Bush asked European governments to endorse an invasion of Iraq while insisting that he had not yet decided whether it was necessary, he *earned* the rejection he got. Moreover, as governments adjust their own objectives to accommodate those of coalition partners, accommodation it-self becomes a rival focus. In 1990–1991, as the US government sought the broadest possible coalition for the Gulf War, it neglected to explain to itself what precisely it wanted from that war and embraced the objective "Iraq out of Kuwait" because it was the Coalition's common denominator. The point here is that focusing on meetings, coalitions, and agreements—the so-called *"mechanisms"* of diplomacy—confuses externalities with re-sults and puts the proverbial cart before the horse.

That confusion is the essence of Liberal Internationalist diplomacy. Since 1925, the Carnegie Endowment for International Peace, first led by Root's pupil, Nicholas Murray Butler, and later by Alger Hiss, has been gathering the kinds of people to devise and staff the international "mecha-nisms" of Liberal Internationalist diplomacy. The most historically impor-tant of these mechanisms include the Washington naval agreements of 1921, the Kellogg-Briand Treaty that outlawed war in 1928, the UN char-ter of 1946, and the US-Soviet arms control treaties between 1972 and 1987. US diplomacy in the interwar period consisted largely of urging na-tions to abide by treaties, chastising them for not doing so, and seeking better "mechanisms" to make better treaties. Republicans William Borah and Herbert Hoover were no less sanguine about "mechanisms" than Franklin Roosevelt's Secretary of State Cordell Hull. Among the most pa-thetic figures in the history of diplomacy, Hull threw words such as "inter-national law and morality" and "respect for treaties" at Japanese tanks in China and German ones in Poland.

But for this ideology, the actual behavior of nations was always less important than the process, and it remains so. Thus one Robert Gallucci, who negotiated the US–North Korean "Agreed Framework" of 1994 for President Clinton—which was supposed to keep North Korea from ac-quiring nuclear weapons and which the Koreans violated repeatedly from the very first—commented on the George W. Bush Administration's signing of a similar agreement in 2007 that a bad agreement is no reason to stop making agreements. George Perkovich, the Carnegie Endow-ment's director of nonproliferation programs, added that although North Korea's promises had not been worth much in the past, and there was no reason to believe that it would fulfill the new ones, it was worth buying them anyway because of the hope that the talks might lead to "a broader exploration of steps to prevent instability in North East Asia."[9] Thomas Schelling might have said that, or Nicholas Murray Butler.

Today's Liberal Internationalist ideology, however, differs from that of the early twentieth century in that whereas earlier generations trusted that the emerging international community included the world's peoples, the "international community" in which today's Liberals place their faith consists strictly of the officials who inhabit the world of well-heeled meetings. In this the Liberals resemble the Realists but differ from the Neoconservatives. But whereas Realist ideology sees foreign officials seeking to maximize their power, sometimes even at the cost of comity, Liberal ideology sees them as instinctively drawn to cooperative schemes for development—precisely what drives the Liberal Internationalists themselves.

Realist Ideology

After the interwar generation of American statesmen had failed to impede disaster by their words, after the Japanese and German peoples had proved that popular enthusiasm can sustain aggressive war, and since not words but rather massive bloodshed had stopped them, some hazarded the notion that dealing with nations' clashing interests must involve concrete incentives and disincentives. They called themselves "Realists."

To be sure, working-level diplomats had dealt with reality even under Cordell Hull. You need only read the memoirs of Ambassador Joseph C. Grew regarding Japan and those of Robert Murphy regarding Germany to realize that. Once engaged in war, some of Elihu Root's Liberal Internationalist pupils reawakened their "harder" side—for example, Henry Stimson, a pacifist as Hoover's Secretary of State, served with distinction as Secretary of War during World War II. Stimson combined belief that military sanctions are essential to international affairs with faith that war could be done away with.[10] Walter Lippmann's influential 1943 *U.S. Foreign Policy: Shield of the Republic* made clear that words had to be proportionate to deeds. The men in charge of US diplomacy in the postwar period, such as Dean Acheson and George F. Kennan, never doubted the difference between words and deeds. Ohio Senator Robert Taft, "Mr. Republican" of the 1940s and early 1950s, had never ceased looking at reality as George Washington had.

Realism, however, is something else. It differs from Liberal Internationalism (in theory) because it recognizes divergent interests among nations and proposes using incentives and disincentives to harmonize them.

The ideology of Realism accepts the basic Liberal principles: Realists are value-free, meaning that they profess no preference for any notion of goodness or evil over any other. Nevertheless, by and large, Realists share the Liberal tribe's political prejudices. Hans Morgenthau, who codified the term, was proud of his anti-anti-Communism. Realists recognize expressions of belief, but they posit that talk of values, of good and evil, better and worse, just gets in the way of dealing with interests. Because Realists believe that all governments seek the same thing, power defined in terms of interest, they assume that there are no fundamental differences between governments. Consequently, because governments are essentially interchangeable, diplomacy becomes like a board game. Realists believe they know the rules because they also assume that all governments approach the game as they do. Like Liberals, Realists don't bother much about the proportion between the things they do and the ends they seek.

Practitioners have defined Realism's meaning for diplomacy. Some of them—preeminently Henry Kissinger—worked it out theoretically as well. In the books that brought him to prominence, Kissinger argued that the Eisenhower Administration was wrong to think in terms of political and military victory over the Soviet Union.[11] "Maximal objectives" would lead to the unpalatable choice between general nuclear war and surrender. The proper way to manage the conflict was to realize that it was rational for both sides to eschew victory and avoid defeat, and hence that competition should consist of bargaining over limited gains and losses through limited efforts. This was Thomas Schelling minus the game-theory jargon. In other books, Kissinger emphasized his belief *(a priori)* that all members of the international system have at least as much interest in maintaining the integrity of the system itself as they have in their narrow national priorities, and that sooner or later they must recognize that interest.[12] Like

Liberal Internationalists, then, Realists identified the US national interest with the cohesion of the "international community" and advocated soft-pedaling America's claims. That became the practical essence of Realism.

Realism ruled American diplomacy through most of the 1960s and 1970s. In that period's two main international events, the Vietnam war and the US-Soviet détente, American officials, led by Schelling disciple Robert McNamara in the 1960s and by Kissinger in the 1970s, strove to reassure the nation's adversaries that America did not aim at victory, only at adjusting differences.

This ideology set the tone in the Cuban Missile Crisis of 1962. The Soviets had placed intermediate-range missiles in Cuba. At that time the US advantage in strategic forces was overwhelming, and the Soviet Union might not have been able to get a single bomber through the US air defense system. Nor could it get a rowboat into Cuba, much less a fleet, past the US Navy. But though the real factors were disproportionately on the American side, the Kennedy Administration framed the crisis in Kissinger-Schelling terms, as a confrontation of interchangeable "scorpions in a bottle," whose equal, primordial interest was not to sting one another. Realists could not imagine that the Soviets might have calculated, quite correctly, that the American team's peculiar view of itself as a poor scorpion was blinding it to the balance of power it enjoyed. And, in fact, the Kennedy-McNamara team "managed" the crisis to a result more favorable to the Soviets and unfavorable to America than the *status quo ante*: Nothing that the Soviets could say or do could have forced the United States to remove its missiles from Europe, nor to guarantee that Cuba's regime would survive as a Soviet ally. By contrast, once the United States had blockaded Cuba it hardly had to say or do anything to force the Soviet Union's removal of its missiles from the island.

Thus, Realist diplomacy began its reign by replacing strategic calculation with "crisis management." Instead of conveying reality, it conveyed our statesmen's desire to get out of trouble regardless of the price. The Realists replaced facts with their own subjective reality.

Kissinger's involvement in Vietnam began with his 1967–1968 advice to the Johnson Administration that it "pause" bombing North Vietnam. Giving up whatever military advantage the bombing was providing America, whatever pain it was inflicting on the North, would convince Ho Chi Minh that the United States would not seek victory and would "make sacrifices for peace." Kissinger argued that North Vietnam would bargain for a mutually acceptable solution once the "pause" reassured it about the boundaries of "the matrix" and enticed it by prospects for modest gains. Only a generation later did Kissinger admit that while he had urged giving up America's means of pressure, North Vietnam never considered giving up its own, and that because of the North's "implacable determination,"[13] "America would have to pay the same price for compromise [he might have said defeat] as it would for victory." "In retrospect," wrote Kissinger, "America did not need to pay any price for the opening of negotiations."[14] For the price America paid, North Vietnam sold nothing, not even promises. Kissinger's *supposition* about what North Vietnam would do in the future was enough for him to trade America's concrete advantages for promising words. But North Vietnam's officials never spoke those words. Kissinger imagined they were in their minds. But they existed only in his own. This made sense only in Realism's pseudoreality.

Détente made sense in the same way. Why, in 1972, should not the Soviet Union have accepted Kissinger's generous offer to give up the massive US advantage in antimissile defense in exchange for maintaining but not increasing the Soviet advantage in offensive missiles—especially since Kissinger coupled that offer with access to US grain and technology on credit? How could it be that, as Secretary of Defense Harold Brown put it seven years later, "when we build they build [intercontinental missiles], when we stop they build"? Why would the Soviet Union have pocketed the US concessions and used US economic resources to do the opposite of what it had pledged? Because seeking after superiority made no sense in his Realist mind, Kissinger himself said of strategic superiority, "What in heaven's name do you do with it?" But strategic superiority made sense to Soviet minds. They sought it because they had uses for it. Kissinger could not imagine that they could think differently than he. So, sensing that Kissinger and his President were in thrall to their own ideology, Soviet diplomacy consisted of letting them believe in their own words while the USSR seized strategic advantages. By the mid-1970s, the Soviet Union was ascendant militarily as well as diplomatically, and America was dispirited.

Our time's best-known Realists, James Baker and Lee Hamilton, the authors of the Iraq Study Group Report of December 2006, congressionally chartered to suggest ways of achieving peace in Iraq, gave another example of Realist ideology's practical meaning. To convince Iraq's Sunni population to curtail the war they were waging to reimpose their tyranny on Iraq's Shia majority as well as on its Kurds, the Realists proposed redoubling pressure on the Shia and Kurds to renounce the constitutional provisions under which they were trying to be independent of their former oppressors, and to return large numbers of Sunni officials to their former positions. Our Realists imagined that thus reempowering the Sunnis would lead them to curtail their violent quest for power. The Realists also proposed that the United States arrange for the Arab League, Saudi Arabia, and Syria, which were sponsoring the Sunni war effort, as well as Iran, which was helping the Shia, to come help pacify Iraq. Such proposals invite one to ask, "In whose reality does this Realism make sense?" Only a peculiar ideology could imagine that helping adversaries to achieve their objectives somehow serves the United States.

Thus Realism failed domestically as well because it came to be associated with American defeats and retreats. The Realist establishment's failure to deal with the challenges of the postwar period discredited it, as failures between the world wars discredited Liberal Internationalism. Thus in 1976 Henry Kissinger became the only person in US history against whom both major parties ran Presidential campaigns at the same time: Ronald Reagan won Republican hearts, and Democrat Jimmy Carter won the Presidency by denouncing Kissinger's Realism for having abandoned America's interests and soul.

The Neoconservative Ideology

The realities of Soviet advances and American retreats, passion for America's success, led some Liberals and Realists in the 1970s to start thinking about foreign affairs somewhat as had some Progressive Internationalists of Woodrow Wilson's time: America's way of life is its biggest asset in dealing with other nations, and promoting that way of life is its primary concern. They believed that only bad governments prevent all the world's peoples from getting along. They supported Ronald Reagan's military buildup of the 1980s as well as his assistance to anti-Soviet resistance movements in Nicaragua, Afghanistan, and Angola. Most of all, like Conservatives, they said good things about America and endorsed Reagan's indictment of Communism's evils.

But the label "Neoconservative" by which they became known denotes that their agreement with Reagan's conservatism was coincidental and that they differed from traditional American statecraft. American statesmen from Washington through Theodore Roosevelt had thought about other nations only as these might relate to specific US interests. For them, whether others might imitate America was merely intellectually interesting. But like other Progressives, Neoconservatives loved America arguably less for itself than for what it could do for mankind. So whereas Reagan promoted imitation of the American way of life as part of the struggle against the Soviet Union, for the Neoconservatives promoting that imitation was foreign policy itself. Also, like other Progressives and unlike early Americans, the Neoconservatives did not regard war as a normal instrument of international relations. Moreover, whereas statesmen from Washington to TR had been ever mindful to match their means to their ends, for the Neoconservatives as for Wilson, world democracy was both the indispensable end and the sufficient means.

The triple-blind bet of Neoconservative diplomacy is that the people of any and every country would really like to imitate American democracy, that nothing in any people's habits of mind and heart prevents it from doing so, and that its trying would be good for America. Even were all three premises valid, however, telling people through their governments that they ought to change their governments is as problematic as was the Soviet Union's dealing with every nation through formal diplomatic channels *and* through a parallel party network designed for subversion. Hence Neoconservative diplomacy has always stressed "public diplomacy" consisting of words and images in the mass media aimed at peoples over their governments' heads. Hence also, it has worked through informal organizations intended to strengthen social-political movements that foreign governments can be excused for regarding as subversive. In the Neoconservative scheme of things, formal diplomacy is relegated to conducting routine business with foreign governments while persuading them to take a hand in revolutionizing themselves. This is a tough job for any diplomat.

The Neoconservative pitch to foreign publics is just as tough a sell, because Neocons do not shy from pressing codes of behavior on foreign peoples as well as on their governments, and even from using the words "empire" and "imperialism" to describe what they are doing. Neocon outriders such as the late William Odom write of developing rules of behavior in cooperation with the foreigners he calls "stakeholders" in America's Liberal Empire.[15] But Neoconservatism's pillars are bolder: Robert Kagan's book describes America as a "Dangerous Nation"[16] that interprets its Declaration of Independence as a warrant for making every other people's independence conditional on its meeting America's standards. Norman Podhoretz, the original Neoconservative, writes that America must exercise "benevolent, temporary imperialism." But neither benevolence nor Liberalism has ever much strengthened imperialism's appeal to the subjects of empire. To overbalance any people's natural resentment of submission to foreign masters, the imperialists must at least supply sure protection against physical danger. But the American Liberal Empire does not promise that any more than the Athenian version of the same thing promised it to the Camarineans 2,500 years ago. Hence, like Athens, it should not be surprised when its clients abandon it, voting with their fears.

Encouraging dissidents in foreign societies is easily done. But what end it may serve depends on how well that encouragement fits with words and deeds well calculated to keep them safe physically while transforming their society in ways useful to ourselves. Such means are difficult to imagine. By itself, encouraging dissidents is not a fruitful course of action. Identifying dissidents with a foreign power's machinations makes the target country feel it is under attack and makes the dissidents the object of retaliation—unless and until their sponsor's *force majeure* undoes the regime in which they live. In short, encouraging dissidents is a measure of war, properly treated a such.

Neoconservatives, however, deal with war through euphemism. Joshua Muravchik, one of the movement's leading figures, stresses that the United

States should make no attempt to destabilize the Egyptian and Saudi regimes that have been the source of so much anti-American terrorism, but rather "exert steady continuous pressure for political liberalization." He does not seem to notice that such liberalization strikes at these regimes' vitals. Even when he advocates military measures, as he does against Iran, Muravchik writes: "Let me emphasize that I speak not of an invasion . . . but merely air strikes." In short, destabilization itself is no more a policy than "air strikes" are. Thus Muravchik describes latter-day US policies that have done enough to get pro-American elements in trouble but nothing to rescue them.

The Neoconservatives place themselves in untenable diplomatic situations when they effectively declare war on foreign regimes by denying their legitimacy through public diplomacy, by waging that war through internal opposition to the regime, and then by not even considering doing whatever has to be done to overthrow the regime. Expressing a mixture of peace and war that consists of words alone, their diplomacy amounts to what Theodore Roosevelt called "peace with insult"—neither war nor peace, the worst of all combinations.

Neoconservatives point with pride to how Ronald Reagan's words encouraged dissidence within the Soviet Union. Indeed, the United States and the Soviet Union *were* at war: Mighty armaments stood ready on both sides. Destruction of our way of life was holy writ for Communists. Subversion was their official policy. Returning the favor was the least we could do. Reagan's words were part of a national effort that everyone understood could culminate in the greatest havoc that mankind had ever wrought. By contrast, the essence of Neoconservative diplomacy is to use subversive words naturally fit for war as part of policies that envisage little, if any, unpleasantness.

The first reason why the promotion of democracy cannot carry the weight of US policy is that the world's peoples do not uniformly wish to imitate America. The peoples of the Soviet empire were an exception, and those of Cuba may be as well, because these regimes, whose subjects hated them, described America as the antithesis of themselves. Hence their near universal hate of Communism translated neatly into near blind adoration of America. But in most places, local folk are not eager to reject the local culture, regardless of how it may differ from ours. The second reason is that, as America's Founders knew well, most peoples cannot transcend the habits of heart and mind that bind them. As John Adams noted in his *Defense of the Constitutions of the United States and Discourse on Avila,* which surveyed the revolutions of his day, Europeans and South Americans who cried for freedom really wanted power and were unwilling to recognize in others the rights they claimed for themselves. So it is today. Third, it is as self-evidently true in our time as it was in the 1920s and 1930s that the *deme* in any given place are not necessarily friendly to America. Wishing can neither change nor hide the fact that the peoples of Iraq, Iran, and Palestine freely elected leaders who represent everything that Americans in general and Neoconservatives in particular abhor.

The Sum of Ideologies

We must keep in mind that the three main strands of modern American diplomatic ideology have comingled in all US Administrations since the turn of the twentieth century. While it is useless to speculate to what extent, say, Franklin Roosevelt established the UN as a Liberal Internationalist, or as a Realist, or as a promoter of his vision of America, it is important to note that in instance after historical instance the three strands' interplay made American diplomacy less coherent than it would have been under each alone and fixed it more firmly in the prejudices common to all three. Thus with overconfidence born of solipsism, twentieth-century American diplomacy neglected statecraft's primordial questions: What exactly are we after? What does it take to persuade whom of what? What means are sufficient to what ends?

Consider the diplomatic aspects of the Vietnam war between 1963 and 1975, and of the twenty-first-century confrontation between the United States and Iran over the latter's nuclear weapons program.

The Kennedy-Johnson Administration saw its relationship with South Vietnam through the prism of Liberal Internationalism: US diplomats had to persuade the South Vietnamese government to reform itself democratically, practice Good Government, and submit to a US-managed social revolution (a combination of Liberal Internationalist technocracy and of what today would be called Neoconservatism). Doing these things was the price South Vietnam would have to pay to obtain what the United States advertised as a guarantee of aid sufficient to fight off an insurgency run by the North. When the South's President Ngo Dinh Diem found the price too steep and the guarantee too flimsy, the US government had him overthrown to clear the way for fulfillment of its guarantee—except that its leaders had not been clear in their own minds about what they would and would not do to fulfill it. But they were already sure they would not undo the North's regime to protect the South's. Diem had noticed that and had understood the Americans' limitations better than they themselves understood them.

So had the North's dictator, Ho Chi Minh. The Americans approached him with Realism: They would cause his people some pain for continuing the war and would offer him material rewards for accepting less than complete victory. They spoke with deeds. But the deeds' message was just as much an "uncertain trumpet"[17] as the words. Though the Americans' Liberal Internationalism had led them to overthrow the South's government, their Realism precluded trying to overthrow the North's. This mixture, which made little sense to each of the US government's constituent ideologues, was the common denominator that convinced the world America could be had.

As Iran's Islamic Republic was building nukes circa 2000, Neoconservatives wanted to encourage the regime's many internal opponents to revolt and argued about whether the US government's public diplomacy provided enough incitement. But they did not discuss what such a revolt would need to be successful, never mind whether the United States could or should meet those needs. Meanwhile, the Realist side believed that a variety of small commercial sanctions, the deployment of aircraft carriers to the Persian Gulf, and a *de facto* alliance with Iran's unfriendly Sunni neighbors would eventually persuade the government, in the words of Undersecretary of State Nicholas Burns, to "come to the negotiating table."

What might happen at that table could be imagined by what had been happening in the previously mentioned negotiations between Iran and the European six since 1995—negotiations that the State Department's Liberal Internationalist side deemed essential that the United States join. Quite simply, between 2004 and 2005 Germany had increased its government-guaranteed (read: subsidized) trade with Iran by a factor of 3.5, while Italy and France were subsidizing Iran to the tune of 4.5 and 1 billion Euros per year respectively.[18] But Internationalists, Realists, and Neoconservatives agreed that, while "all options" for dealing with Iran's nuclear program were "on the table," they made clear that they had zero plans for war with Iran and that the thought of comprehensive trade embargoes had not entered their minds. Nevertheless, they insisted that Iran's nukes were "unacceptable." Highly credentialed US policymakers were persuaded that all these approaches worked in synergy. Ordinary folks might be persuaded that threatening words and small hurts amounted to neither peace nor war, but rather to diplomatic malpractice.

DIPLOMATIC PRACTICE

Let us look at diplomacy without ideological lenses. As in all human relations, you must know what you want and what you are willing to give for it; figure out if the other side is at all inclined to give it, and what they may be willing to take in exchange for it. If you and they are in the same ballpark, then you can bargain in good faith. If either or both are not selling, or the prices are unacceptable to either or both, then neither side loses by walking away. Whatever peace existed is not broken. But if either or both sides realize that the two sets of demands and prices are incompatible, that neither can get what it wants without the other accepting losses that it refuses to accept, and if nevertheless both sides continue diplomatic contact, then you had better realize that although the contacts may look like diplomacy, they are really something else: instruments among others (likely including violent ones) of coercion. Fred Iklé calls such diplomacy "negotiating for side effects."[19]

Deal or No Deal?

Diplomacy's indispensable first step, then, is not to confuse diplomacy aimed at agreements that accommodate both sides' interests with the kind that is essentially another weapon of war. Diplomatic contact has always been part of war—and all wars but those of annihilation are in fact efforts to force others to accept a previously unacceptable diplomatic solution. The most typical diplomatic messages during war boil down to "Had enough? Are you ready to accept my terms now?" The losing side might say: "On second thought, we might consider stopping if you were to modify your demands as follows. . . ." During World War I, the combatants exchanged offers of peace that reflected changing fortunes at the front. World War II saw very little indirect diplomatic contact between the main belligerents until the end. All wars since have been conducted at least as much by diplomats as by soldiers. And therein lies the problem: Not all the diplomats involved—especially the Americans—have been duly clear about their role as belligerents. It is a deadly error to enter into or to remain in negotiations with the intent of reaching a mutually acceptable agreement when the other side regards these negotiations as an instrument for forcing its will on you.

Reaching agreement on the basis of both sides' essentially compatible positions requires following certain rules, because breaching any of them tells the other side that you are either uninterested in or unable to reach such an agreement, and that therefore he should either walk away or play by nastier rules. Honest clarity about objectives avoids surprises that lead the other side to conclude that it is being played for a sucker. Reciprocating partial concessions builds confidence in a common purpose, whereas pocketing concessions and using them as bases for new demands is bad faith and augurs worse. Honoring partial agreements builds the larger one and increases confidence in it. Honesty about the relative importance of the points at issue, avoiding bluff, builds credibility and allows all sides to judge whether the deal is worth the price. It cannot be stressed enough that at every stage of the negotiations, and even after the agreement is signed, the two parties will act in an agreeable manner only to the extent that they are really and truly satisfied with the arrangement. Thus, as Iklé teaches, the "threefold choice" between agreement, disengagement, and diplomacy for "side effects" is truly "perpetual."

Side Effects

The success of any side using diplomacy as an instrument of conflict depends substantially on the other side mistaking the situation, and abiding by the rules for accommodating interests with a partner, while the first regards the other as an adversary to be maneuvered into ever weaker positions. In short, a big advantage goes to the side with the fewest illusions about the other and about diplomacy. The stratagems for outmaneuvering an opponent who labors under false beliefs about the nature of the negotiation are as follows.

First, realize that diplomatic contact can be an instrument for military force, for interfering in your opponent's internal affairs, for bribery, for economic coercion, embarrassment, deception, delusion, for manipulating alliances, for gaining time or for wasting his, for stringing him along, for preparing nasty surprises, or for bringing to bear on the other side whatever pressure might bend him to accept the unacceptable. Diplomacy can be an important instrument in bringing any of these factors to bear on your adversary for precisely as long as he foolishly adheres to the rules of accommodation while you don't. And remember: The longer he plays touch football while you play tackle, the farther in your direction the balance of power will have moved, the more *faits accomplis* you will have created, the thinner your pretenses will need to be, because his ever heavier investment in the diplomatic process will press him to pretend that all is well and lead him to throw good concessions after bad.

Second, knowing that diplomatic contact has no intrinsic value, you should convince the other side that contact is so valuable that he must make concessions for the privilege of sitting down with you. Whoever values diplomatic contact itself, and trades concessions to obtain it, makes a basic mistake. Competent diplomats do not pay for social occasions or for the privilege of surrendering their interests. Yet eagerness for talks tempts some to accept cover charges that imply the wholesale abandonment of enterprises. In 2006, Hezbollah set a precondition for negotiations to free Israeli soldiers it had captured in the assault by which it had started the Lebanon war: Israel must cease fire and withdraw. But a cease-fire would reduce incentives to release the prisoners. And, in fact, once Israel ceased fire under American pressure, Hezbollah toyed with the captives' price, kept them, and eventually traded their corpses for hundreds of live prisoners of Israel. Often, the course of the negotiation is set when one side accepts the other's conditions for talks or drops its own. One side's demand that there be "no preconditions" can be a precondition. The real issue is always who will give or take what valuable consideration. *Competent diplomats never regard talks themselves as any part of a real issue.*

It is normal for the party that asks for a meeting, the *demandeur,* to pay some "cover charges" because usually it is asking for some kind of relief or stepping back from an uncomfortable position. Thus in 1957 China asked to resume contact with the United States after having started a military confrontation in the Taiwan Strait and having been bitterly disappointed by the strength of the US reaction and the weakness of Soviet support. The United States was in the position to exact a price. It did not.

Why do American diplomats so often pay cover charges for maintaining contact as well as for initiating it and so seldom exact such prices? Sometimes they believe that lack of contact obstructs international understanding and rapprochement. But governments seldom lack basic information, and they have never had trouble making contact when they want to send messages. As for rapprochement, governments have made basic changes in their orientation toward one another quite without regular diplomatic contact. The "diplomatic revolution" of 1968–1969 in which China ceased to be nominally allied with the Soviet Union and placed itself under the protection of the United States occurred despite the fact that the United States and China had no formal diplomatic relations and that their episodic meetings since 1954 had treated nothing of importance. Reality, namely, the growing power of the Soviet Union that threatened both, pushed the United States and China together in 1968–1969—not diplomacy.

Lots of people who should know better believe that diplomatic contact precludes or lessens the chances of violence. "Jaw jaw is better than war war," said Winston Churchill. But in fact no government with reasons enough to commit or resist violence is likely to set them aside for the sake of mere contact. Such a government may seek or agree to diplomatic contact hoping to deceive its enemy about its intentions. In 1941, Japan protracted negotiations with the United States as its aircraft carriers were steaming for Pearl Harbor, and in 1956 the Soviet Union invited Hungary's Imre Nagy to negotiate as it was preparing to kill him and invade his country. In fact, diplomatic contact is an effective adjunct to war precisely because some people believe it is a substitute for war. But indulging that belief is costly: In Korea and Vietnam, after America had paid for negotiations by limiting its military activities, its enemies killed more Americans than before because they grasped both ends of the diplomatic dialectic.

Diplomatic meetings can produce lots of other things useful in war, like deception and intelligence. An offer to negotiate may tempt a government that was considering making war or imposing sanctions to believe that it might get its way less expensively. North Korea, after 1994, successfully used US willingness to negotiate as a shield. As for intelligence, among the benefits that Iran gained from the American-backed Europeans' diplomatic demarches concerning its nuclear programs in 2005–2006 was to learn how much or little they knew about those programs. More important, it learned how little force was behind those demarches.

Diplomacy can be decisive in war by affecting third parties—and the other side's domestic factions as well. After 1967, Israel's enemies, conscious that Israel had become dependent on the United States, realized that the best way to bend Israel to their will was to persuade the United States to do it for them. Diplomacy became the decisive theater of operations in the Middle East, and the name of the Arabs' game became convincing Americans, by words and by terrorism, that America had to earn its own peace by leaning ever more on Israel to satisfy the Arabs' demands.

Seldom, however, can diplomacy recruit allies to rescue a flawed plan or lead others to exert the decisive force that one is unwilling to exercise on his own behalf. Governments seldom cast their lot with losers. Doubly fanciful are hopes that diplomacy may entice heretofore antagonistic third parties to join a losing cause—for example, the joint insistence of "Liberal Internationalists" and "Realists" that US diplomacy can change the preferences of European states for avoiding the Muslim world's displeasure rather than pleasing America. What words could US diplomats say that would turn such a trick?

Diplomacy's capacity to undermine an adversary government's domestic support for its positions is a potent weapon. Speaking over their counterparts' heads, diplomats may paint the target government's domestic supporters as warmongers and offer domestic opponents the opportunity to present themselves as the peacemakers by endorsing diplomacy. "Diplomatic offensives" can be potent. In the summer of 1940, Adolf Hitler tried mightily to convince the British people that he had made a magnanimous peace offer. He had won the war and now offered to let Britain keep her empire and pay no indemnities simply in exchange for peace. He even sent Rudolf Hess on a nutty mission to convince British aristocracy of his benevolence. Had Hitler's actions matched his words, had he declared a unilateral cease-fire, his diplomacy would have undermined Winston Churchill, the one obstacle to Britain's acceptance of objectively generous terms. But Hitler was impatient and inconsistent. The reality of German bombs dropping on Britain strengthened Churchill and undermined German diplomacy. The point is that to think of diplomacy as an independent factor, as President Bush's spokesman did when he claimed that "diplomacy won" the 2006 Lebanon War, is a childish attempt to escape reality.

At the outset of that war, Arab governments, Liberals of all stripes, and many Realists chided the US government for not using "diplomacy" to force a cease-fire. If we Democrats were in office, Senator Hilary Clinton said, America would have brought peace to the Middle East because we would emphasize diplomacy. But "emphasizing diplomacy" is inherently meaningless. To speak thus is to pretend either that the war's issues are trivial or that words can make them so. Such pretense enables the further pretense that the speaker is not on either side, rather on the side of peace.

There is no such side. Israel and Hezbollah were fighting. Israel's survival and the role of the United States in the Middle East depended on who gained and who lost the military advantage. That would be determined by who won the firefights. The timing of any cease-fire was important chiefly insofar as it affected who would win the battles and how the issues of the war would be resolved on the ground. Whose conditions would be embodied in a cease-fire? What should one's diplomats say to advance whose cause? And why should their words lead any side to accept any peace it does not want? In 2006, the US Administration succumbed to a combination of requests from the Arab world and criticism from

Europe as well as from its political left and agreed to force Israel to accept a cease-fire advantageous to the Arabs. Note well, however, that these pressures were purely negative: The United States asked nothing and gained nothing in exchange for giving in to them. There was no give and take—just demands to give. The United States resisted those demands for some twenty days, arguing that it had no right to tell Israel how it should secure itself. Then it gave in and negotiated window dressing for doing precisely what had been demanded of it and what it had said it would not do. Pressures on the United States to end the war by diplomacy were as much part of the war as Hezbollah's rockets.

WHAT CAN DIPLOMACY DO?
ENDS AND MEANS

Talk and other forms of nonviolent communication can help change the balance of power between nations if they are part of a reasonably well-conceived plan to advance a reasonably well-conceived policy. There is no such thing as good diplomacy in support of a plan whose elements work against one another or whose means are insufficient to the ends. Knowing what nonviolent communication can and cannot do makes the difference between enterprises that can succeed and ones foredoomed to fail.

Iraq, 1991–1998

After the Gulf War of 1991, because both the United States and Iraq, for their own reasons, feared a resumption of the war, each pursued an agenda *vis-à-vis* the other by means short of war. Each faced problems and had fears of its own. Each tried to achieve its ends by leveraging the other's fears.

Saddam's primordial objectives were to consolidate his power, to work around the system of weapons inspectors and economic restrictions imposed on him after he lost the 1991 battle of Kuwait, to diminish the prestige the United States had gained by winning that battle, to break out of the "box" where US policymakers thought they had put him, to make good his boast that he, not America, had won the war, and to rebuild his status as the Middle East's driving force. His problem was that he lacked the force to stop any full-fledged US effort to overthrow him. Hence all his actions had to be such as not to provoke such an effort.

The US government's objectives were to keep Saddam in his box, to eliminate what remained of his missile arsenal and programs for building nuclear, biological, and chemical weapons, and to set in motion changes in the Iraqi regime that would remove the country as a long-term threat. The US problem was that the Bush team had already shown the limits of what it was willing to do when, in the endgame of the battle of Kuwait, it let Saddam crush the Kurdish and Shia revolts that had been about to overthrow him. Namely, it would avoid anything that might result in the breakup of Iraq. Hence there would be no US invasion and no support for popular revolts. Saddam noticed.

Perhaps the biggest factor in the outcome was that Iraq's objective, causing the United States to fear war, was achievable by the means he was willing to employ: recalcitrance, intimidation, and humiliation of inspectors, moving Iraqi troops in ominous ways, and propaganda to explain these events in his way to his Arab audiences. Meanwhile, the United States could not achieve the ends set forth in UN resolutions 687 and 688—force Saddam to compensate Kuwait, to give up weapons programs, or to cease persecuting Kurds and Shia—much less change the regime, without a war it feared just as much as Saddam did. The means the United States was willing to use, limited air strikes, economic sanctions, and UN resolutions, did not excite Saddam's fears. Moreover, Saddam had a higher tolerance for fear than did the Americans. Hence because Iraq's diplomacy was based on a favorable balance of fear, it was able to convey to the United States a more fearful reality than US diplomacy conveyed to Iraq. In sum, Saddam's objectives were achievable by diplomacy. America's were not.

The incident that most clearly illustrated the strength of Iraq's position occurred in October 1994: Saddam moved 80,000 troops to the Kuwaiti border, thereby suggesting he might attack. As they arrived, the US government scrambled to put some 36,000 US troops aboard planes and ships on their way to Kuwait and set another 160,000 in motion. US reserves were called up, and two aircraft carrier battle groups and air wings were diverted from the world's far reaches to the Persian Gulf. But Saddam did not attack. As the US armada neared, he slowly pulled his army back to Baghdad. As American forces were turning around in mid-ocean, Saddam detached an armored division to move toward Kuwait for a day before resuming its northward march. By playing yo-yo with the Americans, by mocking them publicly, Saddam had sent a message: I can make you look ridiculous any time I want.

Through the 1990s Saddam and the United States exchanged two sets of diplomatic messages. In Chapter 5 we will deal with the one having to do with economic sanctions. Here are a few examples from the one concerning the disarmament provisions of the 1991 armistice. In July 1991, the Iraqi forces openly in charge of frustrating UN weapons inspectors held them outside the Ministry of Agriculture while they cleaned out the premises in their sight before letting them in to verify that there were no prohibited materials. The United States answered by obtaining a UN resolution that Iraq had violated the terms of the 1991 armistice. Among the strongest US statements reproaching Iraq was President Clinton's "no options are off the table" in 1998.[20] The United States also stated that "we are not ruling out any options including the use of force." But these words were useless because Iraq knew perfectly well that it was violating, and counterproductively false because Iraq knew as well as did the United States that whatever force the United States might use was not the deadly kind that Saddam feared. By the same token, when Rolf Ekéus, the head of the UN special commission inspectors (UNSCOM), replied "no compromise" to an Iraqi demand that inspection teams exclude Americans, and then compromised by keeping the Americans out of the groups that actually entered certain sites, he violated another of diplomacy's cardinal rules: Don't say it unless you mean it. The Americans did the same by declaring this arrangement "unacceptable" and then accepting it.

Over the next seven years both sides simply followed this diplomatic pattern to its logical conclusion. Just before going out of office, President George H. W. Bush answered Saddam's harassment of US aircraft patrolling Iraqi skies with an attack on an Iraqi air defense site. And just after coming into office in 1993, President Clinton followed a scathing UN report about Saddam's frustration of UN weapons inspection with a cruise missile strike on an Iraqi intelligence building—at night. Presumably, cleaning ladies were the main victims. Thereafter, the United States agreed that the UN inspectors would gather data in cooperation with the Iraqis. Clinton said he had sent Saddam a message. He sure had.

By 1995 the UNSCOM data gathered in cooperation with Iraq showed that Iraq had largely complied with the terms of the 1991 armistice. But then the man in charge of clandestine weapons programs, Saddam's son-in-law Hussein Kamel, defected with documentary proof that the programs were alive and well and that UNSCOM had been had. In response, Clinton publicly asked Congress to approve a CIA program to overthrow Saddam. CIA funds flowed to its friends in Saddam's entourage as well as to dissident Kurds. But because Saddam knew his entourage better than the CIA did, those funds actually ended up in his hands, and because Saddam could do more against the Kurds overtly than the United States was willing to do for them covertly or overtly, the CIA program produced only dead Kurds. Clinton's response, in September 1996, was to fire cruise missiles at Iraqi air defense sites some five hundred miles away from where the Kurds were dying. The messages were unambiguous in both directions.

Iraqi pretenses ended in November 1998, when Saddam announced that he was expelling UN inspectors. In response, the United States launched Operation Desert Fox, a four-day set of air and cruise missile strikes on various buildings, supposedly to "set back" Saddam and "send him a message." Part of the message was Clinton's acceptance of Russia's offer to cosponsor another UN resolution. But UN action consisted of raising the amount of oil that Iraq could sell under the UN's Oil For Food program, about which more later.

In sum, after a decade's diplomatic intercourse, Saddam had reversed the results of the Gulf War of 1991. To the Arab world, he had become the living, mocking symbol of America's and the UN's impotence. By 2000, Arab leaders realized that Saddam was more popular with their subjects than they. He had become their peoples' favorite leader. They worried more about pleasing him than about pleasing the United States. Diplomatically, the United States was more "in a box" than Iraq. This resulted not so much from a disparity in handling diplomacy's subtlest instruments as from the Americans' loose grasp of diplomacy's fundamentals.

Talking to Pharaoh

On June 20, 2005, Secretary of State Condoleezza Rice, speaking in Cairo, said that henceforth the United States would support "the democratic aspirations of all people."[21] Bluntly, she then told the Egyptian government that it "must" let its citizens choose their rulers in free elections. She said that opposition groups "must" be free to assemble and compete in parliamentary elections scheduled for three rounds in November and December. Echoing her president's most recent State of the Union address, she said that the Egyptian government "must put its faith in its own people." But the US and Egyptian governments had different faiths. Hosni Mubarak's ruling party believed it could win fairly, just as it had won unfairly, while US diplomats believed that their favorites in Egyptian politics would gain. But while the government had the power to make things come out as it wished regardless of public opinion, the United States did not.

The Egyptian people found both their own government and the Americans arrayed against them. In the elections' first round, as the Muslim Brotherhood candidates were winning more seats than the government candidates, the government moved with a heavy hand to scatter voters and seize ballot boxes. Then the government turned the second and third rounds into traditional farces. The first round's outcome surprised and displeased the US government as well. Secretary Rice shifted to Realist mode and, far from condemning Mubarak's heavy hand, declared: "We cannot judge Egypt." By May 2006, the Pharaoh's son and anointed successor was received at the White House while the leaders of Egypt's opposition, Liberals as well as Islamists, sat in jail nursing their beatings.

In sum, by combining Neoconservatism and Realism with ignorance and impotence, US diplomacy damaged all it touched—above all what remained of America's reputation for seriousness.

THE WEIGHT OF THE WORLD

In its February 12, 2007, issue, beside a story headlined "The Weight of the World," *Time* magazine pictured a pensive Secretary of State Rice. Its point, that she and her Administration were not up to bringing peace to the Middle East, managing China's rise, Russia's slide, North Korea's armaments, and Africa's tragedies, was based on the supposition that managing the world is the task of American foreign policy. It isn't. Any country's foreign policy, including America's, can only manage that country's interests. Confusing your country's interests with anybody else's, imagining you can bear their burdens, well nigh guarantees you will end up harming all you touch. Your country's burdens are heavy enough. If you manage to bear them well, you will have done your job.

CHAPTER 5

POWER MAKES MONEY

Money . . . will not defend you but will cause you to be plundered all the sooner. Nor could any idea be more false than the popular opinion of wealth as the sinew of war. . . . Good soldiers are the sinew of war and not gold, because gold is insufficient to find soldiers, but good soldiers are more than sufficient to find gold. . . . Money is certainly necessary as a secondary consideration, but it is a need that good soldiers overcome by themselves, because it is impossible for good soldiers to lack money, just as it is impossible for wealth alone to create good soldiers.

—MACHIAVELLI, *DISCOURSES*

Money can't buy the things most crucial to success in war and peace: understanding the peace you need, the enemy that stands in its way, reasonable plans for undoing him, and the moral wherewithal for doing so. Insofar as you have those things, money can help.

Economic development was the US government's chief substitute for strategy in the twentieth century. In Vietnam and Iraq it used military force as a shield behind which economic development was supposed to have caused the wars' issues to vanish. Progressives convinced themselves that increased or decreased commerce would be the ultimate lever in everyday affairs and an undemanding substitute for war. In fact, however, though economic measures can serve strategy, they cannot substitute for it. Nor are they cheap: If they are powerful enough to coerce, they are as difficult and dangerous to wage as military campaigns.

Economic sanctions can be deadlier than atom bombs. Blockades and sieges have destroyed armies and nations. Between 1914 and 1919 the Allied blockade killed more Germans than all the weapons fired on the western and eastern fronts combined. But economic strictures are blunt instruments. Usually, to be effective they must be applied with great stringency to the entire target. In mere foreign policy, the usefulness of economic incentives and disincentives is highly problematic because economic goods are inherently fungible and are enjoyed privately. This means that almost any kind of economic asset can be transformed into another, at a price, and that shortages or bounties will affect a target population unequally. Consequently, unless shortages are dire, they may not disable the target country from doing what its rulers want. Dictators are especially tough targets for economic pressure, since they can shift resources at will, make their internal opponents bear the brunt of sanctions, and increase the relative standing of their own supporters. Of course, positive economic pressure—one form or another of bribery—is always possible. Invariably, however, it is easier to buy people than to make them stay bought.

Nevertheless, the illusion persists that economic power vanquishes. Neither the League of Nations nor the UN was chartered to make war because their framers supposed that economic sanctions were the ultimate weapon. Because American statesmen assume that all peoples are driven by the same fundamental economic motives, the US government applied some kind of economic sanction some 150 times after World War II, and economic incentives are a principal currency in everyday policy. Events, however, have proved that the key to using any of these means effectively is how they relate to everything else the government is doing. Seldom will economics alone accomplish political ends.

WEALTH AND POWER

Confusing wealth with power (or happiness), mistaking means for ends, ranks with the oldest of errors. Pointing this out is a staple of classic literature. Prominent in Herodotus's tales are Greeks who disabused oriental kings of their belief that fabulous wealth and huge retinues ensured happiness and victory. Most memorable is his description of how the poor outnumbered Greeks at Marathon put aside the fear that the Persians' luxurious clothing had inspired in them to attack them at a run, and beat them "in a manner that is not to be forgotten."[1] Thucydides teaches the same lesson by warning that anyone looking at the ruins of wealthy Athens and poor Sparta would overestimate Athens' power and underestimate Sparta's. And yet, he writes, "Sparta ruled the whole Peloponnesus." He did not need to add that it had beaten Athens in the greatest of wars. And as Thucydides describes the Athenians' preoccupation with gilding their expedition to Sicily, the reader senses its doom. Roman writers, understandably, were obsessed with the relationship between wealth and decadence. Livy used examples of incorruptible martial virtue as *images d'epinal* in a history mostly of progressive corruption. Perhaps the least forgettable is the legend of Furius Camillus: He entered Rome with his army just as the city fathers were weighing out gold to pay off Brennus the Barbarian. "Not with gold but with iron is the fatherland ransomed," he is supposed to have shouted.[2]

Between about 1400 and 1800, when most European armies were rented, there was some reason to think that money could buy victory. But Machiavelli pointed out that mercenary armies are unreliable, that the key elements of victory—loyalty and competence—cannot be bought, and that power gives money whatever value it has. When the French Revolution revived the ancient practice of conscription and masses of barefooted, republican Frenchmen bayoneted Europe's parade-ground armies, the last connection between money and numbers of troops went away. It does not take much to recall that poor Barbarians had defeated rich Romans, and poor American colonists had defeated the wealthiest nation of their time. But as industry became more important for warfare during the nineteenth and twentieth centuries, the link between money and power seemed reinforced—at least for those who forget that America lost the Vietnam War.

In our time, Paul Kennedy made the best-known argument linking the two: On the one hand, the ability to pay armies and suppliers is as decisive now as it was when the Spanish Hapsburgs' lack of money lost them the Netherlands—from which loss their empire never recovered. On the other, military power grows out of surpluses in gross productive capacity. Hence Britain became powerful in the eighteenth and nineteenth centuries because mechanization made it possible for its 30 million people to produce as much as 800 million did in other lands.[3] If one takes this economic determinism to its logical conclusion, as many do today, then the United States' economic productivity—which is in a class by itself—destines America to victory after victory so long as its glitz shall last. Still, no one has ever been struck down by an amorphous chunk of GDP.

Human Capital

Some pieces of GDP are more militarily significant than others. We leave to the next chapter the remarkable fact that the United States has not managed to buy victory in any of its wars since 1945. We begin by considering what elements of victory money does buy. Guns, for example. But "buy" is less accurate a word than "produce." Whereas good economics calls for buying the best quality at the lowest price, national security requires control of the resources needed for war. That is the main reason why Alexander Hamilton, in his 1791 "Report on Manufactures," argued for protective tariffs to grow domestic industries that, though economically inefficient in the short run, were essential for military power.[4] For our part, we note that industries consist primarily of people with certain skills. In World War II the United States turned out more military equipment than the rest of the world combined in no small part because it had a population that knew how to make those things, or was willing and able to learn, and had habits conducive to assiduous work. In practical terms, then, the economic factors that translate into the *merely material* elements of military force are not material at all, but rather consist of human capacities and attitudes—"human capital" in economese. Americans, and not just war Presidents, then, must ask how many among us today have it in them to turn out war goods—as well as to use them.

On purely *economic* grounds, complaints about US industries "outsourcing" manufacturing to lower-cost labor abroad have zero merit. But it is just as obvious that the "human capital" of our service-oriented "consumer" society, in which few people know how to make or fix things, bears little resemblance to the one that outproduced the world in World War II. Is mass production still relevant? Could just a few designers and manufacturers supply the physically small needs of high-tech warfare? And would that be sufficient? True, under certain conditions war may not involve large quantities of ships, planes, trucks, and weapons. Certainly, nuclear weapons most efficiently convert small-scale high technology into massive power wielded by just a few people. Recall that President Eisenhower recommended the nukes' "bigger bang for the buck" as the means by which America could wield power without devoting itself too much to it. But then recall that President George H. W. Bush and his successors largely denuclearized the US armed forces, confident that precision weapons would suffice to multiply the power of small American forces. And recall as well that precision warfare requires precise identification of enemies—which has not been latter day America's strong suit. So, it is not clear how contemporary America's wealth translates into military power.

Nor are the shopping malls and college campuses that characterize modern American "consumer society" apt to produce the human capital of soldiers any more than of people to make and fix things. America's producers and soldiers come from the less favored parts of the economy, while the uncalloused hands and undisciplined habits at its apex are as foreign to making and fixing as to fighting. In America, unwillingness and inability to perform military functions have gone along with the spread of the old idea that military force is something that societies can purchase. This will surprise no one familiar with Roman history.[5] And it leads to the realization that wealth often ends up detracting from military power.

Plato had described the merely wealthy as akin to "drone" bees, who live for themselves and neither build, nor lead, nor sting. In our time, Saudi Arabia is as awash in money as was sixteenth-century Spain. Money enabled its ruling class to become even more physically and morally unable to fight than were Spanish Hidalgos, the Yuppies of the Baroque age. There is not enough money in the world to substitute for such people's incapacity to fight for themselves. To describe the Saudis as having power over the oil beneath the Arabian Peninsula's sands is misleading. What power? Any Western country, or Russia or China, or even Iran, could drive them from the enclaves where they live, umbilically sustained by foreign technologies, out to perish in the desert. Nothing the Saudis have or can do enables them to live where and as they do. The Saudis' lavishly equipped forces, staffed by hirelings, do not train seriously and will not suffer for the powerless who pay them. Hence Saudi wealth is not to be confused with power any more than the wealth of seventeenth-century Granada or, for that matter, of twenty-first-century Palo Alto, California.

Power over Money

Interfering with the free flow of goods and services may or may not achieve political ends. It may impoverish some countries, but it cannot enrich any. Because the logic of politics and that of economics differ, because the relationship between economic causes and political effects is complex, and because power is likelier to compel money than money is likely to buy power, whoever thinks of international economic maneuvers must do so as part of a political plan to be pursued mostly by non-economic means. Keep in mind as well that economic stratagems will affect politics at home as well as abroad, and that the value of economic goods in general depends on the balance of power.

First, consider the difference between the logic of economics and of politics. By the economic provisions of the Versailles Treaty, Britain and France intended to recover from Germany some $55 billion of their costs for World War I, as well as to hobble the German economy. Of course, the two purposes contradicted each other. Where would economically crippled Germans get the wherewithal to satisfy the French? The German people, unable and unwilling to draw that much wealth from themselves, ruined themselves by trying to pay with inflated currency. When France attempted to extract real value by appropriating the industries of the Ruhr, the Germans' passive resistance was enough to foil it. Had the Allies' economic geniuses intended to convince Germany that they meant to hurt it but were impotent, they could not have chosen a more apt instrument than the Versailles Treaty's economic arrangements. After World War II, the Soviet Union simply carried many of the German factories in its zone of occupation to Soviet territory, together with their enslaved workers. Thereby it gained some economic benefit. But it gained less than what the United States and Britain got by following the logic of economics: They dispensed with reparations, restored German industry to its owners, and reaped the benefits of free trade with the (West) German economic miracle that followed. The point is simply that the logic of economics, the art of wealth, must not be confused with that of power.

As you look to using America's power over money in international intercourse, make sure that the political effects you intend are direct and obvious. The shorter the term over which you figure those effects should occur, the less likely you are to lead yourself astray. Also, since any large-scale artificial restriction or enlargement of trade will affect domestic constituencies, you may find that the domestic political effects bind America as much as the foreign targets of your maneuvers—that your money may give others power over you.

A Double-Edged Sword

Consider the US government's thirty-year financing of Egypt's regime for some $2 billion per year after President Carter's 1978 deal at Camp David, Maryland, with Egypt's dictator, Anwar Sadat. To many at the time it seemed a masterstroke: For a mere $2 billion, the most populous and civilized of Arab countries was shifting to our side in the Cold War and was making peace with Israel. So long as the Cold War lasted, the mere fact that the Soviet Union was no longer operating ships out of Alexandria (Egypt had expelled the Soviets for its own reasons before turning to the United States) overshadowed the fact that after Egypt had got the main thing it wanted from the deal (Israel's return of its Sinai conquests of 1967) it resumed funding terrorists in Gaza, and that Egyptian foreign policy was as anti-American as it had ever been. Moreover, the fact that Sadat had paid with his life for having gotten as close to the United States as he did made sure that his successor, Hosni Mubarak, would move ever farther from America.

The problem here is not Egypt's treachery. It is the foolishness of expecting that money—especially money given as a kind of entitlement—could possibly move Egypt's ruling class, or any ruling class, more powerfully than the realities in which it lives. The United States never shaped those realities, never created any reason why the Egyptian ruling class should have feared the United States, or imagined that the United States could defend it against its enemies. The United States had the chance to shape them in 1991 after the Soviet Union's disappearance and our victory in the battle of Kuwait. But by 2007, after some $30 billion in economic and $33 billion in military aid, as the Egyptian regime continued to tighten its grip on political life, and as it continued to smuggle arms and money to fuel its factions in the Gaza Strip, the Neoconservative notion that the money might be sufficient inducement for the ruling class to hazard its future in free elections or to support US policy should not have been taken seriously. In short, the money bought America nothing, except the prospect that cutting it off would buy retaliation.

The notion that massive amounts of American money could affect the Soviet Union fundamentally was part of the Realist rationale for détente. Pursuant to Henry Kissinger's notion that shipments of US grain, merchandise, and technology would involve the Soviets in "a network of interests" that would bind them, the US government guaranteed loans that financed $56 billion in sales (in 1979) from some of America's biggest companies. Later, the International Monetary Fund (IMF; funded 17.5 percent by American taxpayers) joined by America's and Europe's biggest banks began to extend unsecured loans to the Soviet government not tied to any specific project—the equivalent of unsecured personal loans.[6] Those who made them justified them in general terms as investments in liberalization, transition, moderating influences, prosperity, and so on. But by the mid-1980s, it was already clear that the Soviets were not paying principal and were using part of the new loans to pay interest—in short that these were not loans but grants, and that the money was fueling the Soviet Union, not redirecting it. By the 1990s, loans were being granted only to pay interest—that is, to maintain the fiction that Russia was not in default, and that the decisions to transfer all those billions had not been irresponsible. The charade ended in 1998 when Russia simply repudiated the debt.

But Leonid Brezhnev had made an even more telling point. In his 1977 Kremlin address to the "US Soviet Business Council," led by David Rockefeller of Chase Manhattan and Pepsico's Donald Kendall, who were profiting from subsidized trade, he congratulated himself and them for having bound the United States to a course of action more profitable to them all than to the United States. He said: "I am looking around this hall and see that our contacts have really become a system."[7] The point here is that some US businessmen saw in the US government's vague desire to influence the Soviet Union a concrete opportunity to make money for themselves by lobbying their government to extend or guarantee credit. For the Soviet regime, what Brezhnev called "a system" paid even more political dividends than material ones.

Money and the Balance of Power

The pro-Soviet lobby's power was limited, however, because Americans did not feel compelled to pay tribute to the Soviet Union. Far different was the political role of Swiss heavy industry within the Swiss body politic on Germany's behalf between 1940 and late 1943 because the balance of power was far different. At the outset of World War II, some 90 percent of Swiss industry's foreign orders consisted of war goods for Britain and France. Germany, through which about half of Swiss trade flowed, was not in a position to object because if it interfered with any Swiss export item, the Swiss would just send it through France or Italy. But after Germany had conquered France, Italy had become its ally, and Switzerland had been surrounded, the Germans showed that they controlled the value of things first by cutting off the coal, and then by delivering less of it for more money. Germany simply ordered Swiss industry to turn over the goods that had been destined for the Allies, to increase production with new specifications, and to do so on credit. Swiss management and labor joined in pressing their government to pay their wages and fund their profits with real Swiss francs on the basis of the Germans' worthless credit. Because the Germans augmented Swiss management and labor's ordinary political power, their government had no choice but to comply.

Having decided what value Swiss money and products would have for them, the Germans left the Swiss with the unpleasant problem of figuring out how much the things that were left them would really be worth domestically, including money. By law, the government was to maintain the Swiss franc's value between 195 and 215 grains of gold. But since local industry and international trade were putting less than half the goods on the market than before the war, workers and owners had little to buy with the nominal payments they were getting. To avoid inflation, the government was forced to issue bonds. Effectively, these were German war bonds. The Germans had used the balance of power to leverage a partially willing part of a wholly unwilling population to buy them. The government gave in, because doing so was necessary to avoid Germany's outright invasion, because Germany alone could decide how much, if any, food or fuel would reach Switzerland, and because big constituencies in business and labor demanded it. The economic pressure worked on the political level because it was part of a compelling military reality.

But what the balance of power giveth, it also taketh away. By 1943, after the battles of Stalingrad and Kursk had decimated the Wehrmacht, after the Allies had landed in Italy, and a year before they had broken Switzerland's siege, Germany could no longer spare the ten divisions needed to take Switzerland, never mind the forces to run yet another set of enslaved industries. So it had to take such goods from the Swiss at such prices as the market would bear. And the Allies' growing prospects made the market bear less and less.

The Allies began by cutting off food to Switzerland. If the Germans intended to receive any goods from Swiss industry, they themselves would have to supply the food to keep the workers working. That would mean taking away food from German troops and laborers—unless the Allies relented, which they offered to do—at a price. The Allies offered a deal, directly to the Swiss but indirectly and mainly to the Germans: They would resume half the shipments of food in exchange for Switzerland cutting deliveries to Germany by 20 percent, and demanding payment in gold. The Swiss were pleased to pass on these demands to the Germans, who calculated that the cost of paying in gold for less stuff than they had gotten for free was less than what they would have to pay for feeding or invading. So they paid. But as the balance of power continued to shift, as the Allies pressed the Swiss to restrict deliveries further, more German gold bought less and less, and the Germans were less and less able to do anything about it.

The changing value of Nazi Germany's gold during the war teaches an essential lesson. Germany needed tungsten ore from Spain and Portugal. The Allies did not want the Iberians to sell it. But since neither Axis nor Allies controlled the Peninsula, both had to pay the going rate for the tungsten (incidentally driving the price up by competitive buying). At the beginning, the balance of power only determined the *mode* of payment. The Allies, who controlled the seas through which food came to hungry Iberians, could not force them to forgo earning the means to pay for it. But they did insist that the Iberians not accept Nazi gold. During 1941–1944, this meant that although the Germans bought as much tungsten as they wanted, they first had to buy enough of the world's only remaining convertible "hard" currency, the Swiss franc, to pay for it. Of course, the first thing that the Iberians did with the francs was to buy gold in the world's only open gold market: Switzerland.

The Allies had no choice but to accept this open money laundering—until the balance of power shifted to the point that the Iberians came to fear the hunger that the Allies might impose on them after they had won the war more than they feared whatever shortages they would suffer from cutting down, and then stopping their deliveries of tungsten to the Germans. So, the more the Germans became prospective losers, the more they found that their money would buy ever less, and then nothing at all, because their suppliers realized that any currency from the losers' hands would buy only trouble.

And indeed defeat deprived of value all things German. In May 1945, the US government "vested" all enemy property into itself. It made no distinction between private and government property. Any and all stock in German companies, as well as currency, became worthless. When Germans lost the war, they lost their property rights—even in their own labor and indeed in their own bodies. Only later did the Western Allies return property rights to German owners.

The Barbarian Brennus is reputed to have said: "To the victor belong the spoils!" But reality is even more poignant: Property is the creature of positive law, and positive law is the expression of power. Hence the value of material things depends on the balance of power. As Montesqieu had pointed out, real commerce can exist only when the powers arrayed on either side cancel each other out because they are equal. But supremacy of power is the proximate objective of war, and economic goods are some of the means. That is why it makes little sense to use economic values as primary instruments for changing the balance of power. Rather, when the balance of power changes, the worth of things must as well. In short, economic stratagems are potent insofar as they are parts of serious plans for victory.

What Does It Take for Money to Represent Power?

Precisely, it takes evidence that the stratagems are indeed part of such a plan. On the eve of World War II the ratio of Japan's economy to America's was about 1:10. Before 1930, America had been a significant outlet for the exports that Japan needed to pay its way. In short, America held Japan over an economic barrel. American tariffs had cut off Japanese exports, and the Japanese knew that the Americans had been debating whether to cut off its imports. They also knew what America wanted: Japan's withdrawal from China and respect for China's independence. No Japanese had illusions of defeating America. Nevertheless, Japan continued raping China, took French Indochina in 1941, discounted US economic sanctions, and prepared to attack America. Why did America's economic power, demonstrated by the sanctions, not convince Japan to give in to American demands lest it be crushed?

The answer is that the sanctions convinced Japan of close to the opposite: America showed it was unwilling, perhaps morally and politically unable, *to do anything other than* cut off trade. Japan knew it could live without the trade by taking enough of China and the Pacific Rim to form its "greater Asia coprosperity sphere." Besides, since US protectionism had already well nigh closed the US market to Japanese products, Japan was already hard-pressed to pay for American oil, steel, timber, and so on. If Japan gave up its Asian empire, how could it live? The United States had made Japan's economic problem but offered no economic solution. Unwittingly, however, the United States had opened Japan's way to what seemed a military-diplomatic solution by sticking to the promise it had made in the 1921 Washington naval treaty not to fortify Guam and the Philippines, even though Japan had violated the nine-power Washington treaty guaranteeing China. That meant the United States remained as unable to defend the Western Pacific as it was averse to doing it. This convinced Japan that if it—quickly—conquered Guam and the Philippines, and reduced the US Pacific Fleet, a weakened and war-averse America might just negotiate a new order in the Pacific within which Japan could live. In sum, Japan miscalculated badly, in part because the US economic leverage misrepresented what America would do *in extremis*. The United States presented *sanctions not as precursors to war*, not as "earnest money," a down payment, on a demand that Japan must choose between life and death, but rather in a way that invited miscalculation.

No one should blame Iran if, in our time, it took the economic sanctions imposed by the United States and the Europeans as evidence not only that it could develop nuclear weapons with impunity—talk aside, no one will stop it—but even that it could wage some wars against America with equal impunity. Why? Size matters. The Iran sanctions were disproportionately smaller than the objective at which they were aimed. Being of what former Secretary of State Colin Powell called the "smart," or highly targeted, kind, they simply prohibited American, British, German, and French citizens from doing business with Iranian companies involved in enriching uranium. Even if the sanctions were to eliminate the companies rather than just make them work through intermediaries, the effect on the Iranian economy would be imperceptible. But enriching uranium is a big and politically popular part of what the Islamic Republic is about. It is also essential in the great standoff between Shia and Sunni, between Persians and Arabs. Hence the sanctions amounted to trying to move a big political mountain with a tiny economic shovel.

The Iranians might have treated the sanctions less scornfully if they believed that they were the "edge" of a big "wedge." Iran imported about half its gasoline and some two-thirds of its food. Its oil industry depends on Western spare parts. Blockades, or even secondary embargos, would cripple its economy and might well lead its electorate to value its standard of living above enriching uranium. Perhaps, perhaps not. But Iran's government surely made clear that it would treat such strictures as war and try to close the mouth of the Persian Gulf with cruise missiles and torpedoes from some four hundred small craft as well as from its own shore. To keep open the world's oil lifeline, the United States would have to wage war. But avoiding war is precisely why the United States and the Europeans imposed the "smart" (read: symbolic) sanctions rather than more painful ones. Pretense of doing something, it seems, is the comfortable middle option between doing nothing and admitting it.

Just as Japan judged the meaning of US sanctions in 1941 in the context of US behavior since 1921, twenty-first-century Iran was sure to judge the meaning of the 2007 "smart" sanctions in the context of the reality that the United States had accepted a series of events it had declared "unacceptable." Thus the United States had pressured Israel to stop counterattacking Iran's Hezbollah pawn in the Lebanon war of 2006 after having supported Israel's right to do so, and had accused Iran of helping to kill US soldiers in Iraqi acts of war—but had not reciprocated war. This reality would have led anyone, including Iran, to ask what other unacceptable things the Americans and the others would end up accepting. If Iran concludes, correctly or not, that it can safely start a war against US and European interests, the economic sanctions that were levied against it will have been part of the reason.

Tailoring economic stratagems to any given political purpose is the main task. Here is an example of how not to do it. On December 19, 1990, Dr. Gary Hufbauer, former Deputy Assistant Secretary of the Treasury for international trade and investment policy, testified before the House joint economic committee in support of the proposition that sanctions alone could force Saddam Hussein to remove troops from Kuwait. The scientific probability they would, said Hufbauer, was well over 99 percent and was based on a model of 105 cases of economic sanctions since 1945. In those cases, the target state did what the state or states that had imposed the sanctions demanded after its economy had declined by an average of 3.5 percent. Since the sanctions that the UN had imposed on Iraq at US request were reducing its economy by over 50 percent, Iraq's compliance was virtually certain. One member asked whether the sanctions were likely to overthrow Saddam. Hufbauer answered that the model did not account for things that the regime held especially dear. No one asked, "How dear is dear?" Nor did anyone ask how the powerless people affected by the sanctions would force the hand of the powerful ones who were not.

In sum, money is a blunt tool. Let us see what makes it so, and why wielding it is difficult.

A BLUNT TOOL

Increases or decreases in economic goods cannot stop, move, or affect whole nations because they affect individuals within them differently. Individuals, not collectivities, consume and enjoy things. Inequality of wealth and power is the invariable rule among all peoples. Moreover, economic goods are fungible: Things can be traded for one another and, often, can be physically transformed into others. The effect of the UN sanctions against Iraq in 1991–1998 illustrates the first difficulty, while that of sanctions against North Korea in 1994–2007 illustrates the second.

The Center of Gravity

The UN sanctions strengthened rather than weakened Saddam Hussein's regime because they gave him more control of a greater proportion of his country's economy than he had ever had. Being partial, their pressure on Iraqi society as a whole never reached its "center of gravity," the regime. Since the UN administered the sanctions in cooperation with the regime, these made the regime a bigger influence over a smaller economy. Most important, the character of the sanctions reflected the contrasting purposes of the governments within the coalition that imposed them. The "smart" sanctions were consistent with the coalition's overall policy. But it was a dumb policy, except for those who administered it and smartly made fortunes for themselves.

Like the 1991 Gulf War itself, the sanctions that followed it aimed neither to overthrow Saddam nor to allow Iraq to break along its constituent ethnic-religious divisions. Had the United States aimed at this, total sanctions would have made sense. Soon, Saddam would have been unable to prevent starving people from flooding away, leaving his center of gravity exposed, shrinking, and collapsing. But the sanctions were never total, never forbade the entry of food or medicine, in part precisely because the United States did not want to collapse that center. Another reason is that although the United States wanted to constrain Saddam, it imagined that it could do so without hurting the Iraqi people too much. The objective was to press lightly enough to leave the center in charge, but heavily enough to change it a bit. Too clever by half. Alas, so long as the regime remained in charge, it would determine its own character. Saddam made the people suffer and used the sanctions to constrain the sanctioners. Saddam knew what he was doing, while the Americans proved incompetent by pursuing incompatible things through economic measures they misunderstood.

The sanctions initially reduced Saddam's shipments of oil from 2.7 million barrels per day to 100,000, sold at discount. Hence his income was reduced from over $50 million to $800 thousand per day—98 percent. The US blockade cut food imports to near zero during hostilities. The people survived on meager rations, hungry, sick, and miserable. Spare parts for everything were cut off.

But $800,000 per day is not nothing. Saddam augmented that by selling some $5 billion in gold and using some $4 billion in cash reserves. That sustained his income at near normal levels until the UN allowed him to sell $2 billion worth of oil per year, ostensibly for food. Moreover, because the United States had no intention of starving out the regime, the sanctions did not cut off food and medicine. Sieges, by their nature, are total and indiscriminate. This was no siege. By March 1991, the UN had delivered 3.3 million tons of food to Iraq, effectively making up for all the food imports missed during hostilities. Moreover, because the US/UN's purpose was to maintain the regime, they agreed to Saddam's demand that any and all food and medicine coming into Iraq be distributed by him. If it were not, some might keep alive the Kurdish and Shia rebels that Saddam was trying to kill. But if the US/UN had preferred preserving their lives rather than the regime's life, they would not have let Saddam use his helicopters and armored divisions against them. Having let him kill his victims, insisting on feeding them would have been inconsistent. So the US/UN gave Saddam more control over what each Iraqi ate than he had ever enjoyed.

The sanctions did not cut off small but significant trade through Jordan, by which Saddam obtained what he needed most to keep his officials happy and his military equipment functioning. The United States paid Jordan to cooperate with the sanctions but imposed no nasty consequences for not doing so. So Jordan took America's money, as well as Saddam's. Since smuggled goods cost more, Jordan's profits increased. But Saddam simply took the extra money out of his people's food budget. As we will see, goods are fungible.

Saddam isolated his regime from the sanctions' impact, making it fall on his enemies, in part by raising the pay of officials and friends to keep up with the inflation that ruined everybody else.

Finally, the UN's Oil For Food program was as perfect an example as one might imagine that managing economic transactions empowers and enriches the managers. The first thing that Benon Sevan did as the UN official in charge of the process by which Iraqi oil should have bought food for Iraq's people was to meet with Saddam Hussein and arrange the program for their own and their friends' benefit. Saddam was given the power, with Sevan's approval, to allocate to certain persons and entities the right to broker the sale of individual lots of oil. The brokerage fees came out of the difference between world prices and the lesser price Saddam charged. Saddam rebated part of the difference first to Sevan, and then to persons around the world in positions to influence their governments to be favorable to him. He concentrated on the ruling parties of Russia and France, which in fact became his most ardent supporters.[8] Iraq might not make as much on the oil as before, but Saddam made more than ever. The other half of the program, the purchase of food, worked the same way. Saddam (and his well-paid UN accomplices) would pay for certain quantities of nominally high-grade food, accept delivery of lesser quantities of lesser quality, and be rebated the difference in price.

While Saddam was profiting from the sanctions and using them to crush his opponents, he gained again by blaming the sanctions, and the United States, for the sufferings of the people being crushed. Triply, he used some of the money he gained from the sanctions to ignite the Arab world with the message that the Americans and Zionists must be punished for the Iraqi people's sufferings. By comparison, our highly credentialed statesmen proved themselves to be little children.

The point here is that the United States employed sanctions to "keep Saddam in a box" and "keep pressure on him" because it was unwilling to simply let Saddam alone or to overthrow him. The sanctions might have made sense as part of an otherwise well-designed plan to overthrow him. Such a plan would have caused the Iraqi people pain for some months but would have eliminated him as a source of trouble for them as well as for the United States. Had the United States decided to just live with him, at least it would not have had to hurt Iraqi innocents and make itself hated in the Arab world. But it compromised between doing something serious and doing nothing at all by doing something unserious. Hence it hurt innocents for a decade, strengthened an old enemy, and made new ones.

The Private Nexus

Keep in mind, then, that economic measures will always enrich some individuals and impoverish others in the target country and in your own. If you can design and execute measures that harness enough private self-interest—positive or negative—to move a foreign government's public policy without giving it even more power to move ours, then those measures may make sense. But for this to happen, you must be sure that the target industries or individuals are close enough to the center of power, the "center of gravity" you want to influence, so that they will force the center to come to their rescue by yielding to you. At the same time, the target industries or individuals must not be so close or dear to the center that it will simply take upon itself the sanctions' burden.

For example, during World War II Allied economic warriors influenced the Swedish and Swiss governments by "blacklisting" influential businessmen—banning them from dealings with anyone in Allied-controlled territory. As the Allies were winning, these people lobbied their governments to do whatever was necessary to get them off the lists.[9] Blacklists worked because the businesses were powerful with government but were not government itself. Had they been that, the government would have made up whatever losses it sustained on one side of its ledger with gains from another.

By that token, sanctions on Iranian companies that purchase nuclear technology abroad make no sense. These are not companies of private individuals, "constituents" of the Iranian body politic who can transfer their private pain to their government. Rather, they are components of that regime, which uses them, or any convenient means, to its ends. The government simply pays nonsanctioned intermediaries. One might speculate on the life expectancy of the manager of a "company" in Iran or, more clearly, Cuba or North Korea, if he were to try pressuring his government to change its policies to benefit him personally. The point is to keep in mind who has power over whom, and what the powerful ones' agenda is.

That is especially so when trying to influence foreign societies by large-scale aid. That American and European aid to Third World countries enriches and empowers despots while impoverishing their societies should have been clear already by the mid-1960s. But by the 1980s even the World Bank was turning out studies that were making the point.[10] Yet in the twenty-first century these governments were recommitting themselves to the same venture under the auspices of the UN/US Millennium Challenge.[11] The salient point is that the money flows through individuals, who use it not just for self-enrichment but also to empower friends. That is as inevitable as water flowing downhill. And this empowerment entails at the very least subsidized businesses that shut out really private, unsubsidized ones. Having acknowledged the problem, the World Bank's officials nevertheless objected in 2007 to Director Paul Wolfowitz's initiative no longer to fund corrupt governments, or even to bypass them when trying to uplift their societies. One can only speculate on the officials' mixture of "idealistic" motives and partnership in corruption.

The public case for such aid does not argue that it renders the recipients pliable, only that it can help lift poor peoples out of poverty through "import substitution" schemes financed by foreign benefactors and maintained by tariffs as well as by "loans" from the IMF and from government-guaranteed private banks, conditioned on the recipient governments implementing policies agreeable to the lenders.[12] In fact, import-substitution schemes enrich the few who benefit from captive markets at the general public's expense, while "loans" to or through governments allow them to unload upon the donors the consequences of their mismanagement and corruption. Such schemes also enrich the people in "donor countries" who manage them. For example, in 1994, the Mexican government secretly warned its favorite people that it would devalue the peso by 35 percent after having drawn foreign capital in with high bond rates. The favored ones took their money out. When the devaluation came, US investors succeeded in getting the US government and the IMF to "lend" the Mexican government money to make good their nominal gains and to condition the "aid to Mexico" on its raising taxes and massively increasing domestic interest rates to service the loans. This ruined millions of Mexicans who had bought houses and cars on credit and further enriched both Mexico's Establishment and certain well-placed Americans. In sum, the privacy of economic goods has a logic that is hard to escape.

Fungible

North Korea is the limit case of a government able to shift its society's resources to its own purposes. In 2006, it tested a nuclear weapon, culminating a largely indigenous effort over twenty years during which its population lived on and often below the edge of starvation. The resources that went into the nuclear program—perhaps 10–15 percent of its estimated per capita GDP of $1,500 did not go into, or was diverted from, food, clothing, heat, medical care—life's wherewithal. In short, the North Korean nuclear program is the ultimate example of the fungibility of resources. During these twenty years, the United States, Japan, and South Korea thought of and dealt with North Korea in terms of its nuclear program and of its "humanitarian crisis." They did so by providing North Korea with economic assistance—in 2005 perhaps 90 percent of North Korea's food came from donations from China, South Korea, and the United States—while the latter two were trying to restrict its access to nuclear technology. Perhaps it occurred to some of them that the North's "humanitarian crisis" resulted at least in part from the nuclear program and that the assistance—the humanitarian part as well as that given as an incentive to North Korea to drop the program—would increase its capacity to neglect the people's welfare, bypass the restrictions, and subsidize the nukes more than ever. But you'd never know it. And so America and its allies ended up feeding the nuclear program they wanted to stop, because they did not understand the meaning of the word "fungible."

North Korea claimed that it built its nuclear reactor at Yongbyon to generate needed electricity. No doubt true. True also that the reactor was generating plutonium, and that pure plutonium is the key ingredient in fission nukes. (North Korea was also gasifying uranium-238 and separating out U-235, the other fissile *sine qua non*.) The Clinton Administration sought to stop the entire nuclear program by giving North Korea means of generating electricity, gratis, that did not produce fissile material: Massive amounts of food (humanitarian aid), a half-million tons of oil for conventional power plants, and two "light water" reactors that would produce much less plutonium. Our statesmen seemed to know that sources of energy are fungible.

But North Korea looked at fungibility from a more consequential angle: First, the energy sources that the Americans were supplying for free freed it from having to pay a large part of its electricity and food bills. The money thus saved could and did go to bolster the nuclear weapons program. Second, it did not forget, as did the Americans, that the nuclear program was the reason that the Americans were providing the free goods in the first place. Hence the program had paid for itself twice over. With any luck, and by the same mechanism, it would pay for itself many more times in later years. And so it did in 2007 when the Bush Administration agreed to turn over the same amount of oil as its predecessor, and in addition to "normalize relations," in exchange for North Korea discussing how it might limit its nuclear program in the indefinite future.[13] By 2008, North Korea had withdrawn the goods and was offering them for sale yet again. Why not?

"Normal relations" also entail fungible economic benefits. Not least is the growing business relationship between North and South Korea. Look closely. It consists substantially of South Korean businesses located on the border or in special zones, which employ North Korean workers at wages far inferior to those they would have to pay to their own citizens. Paying low wages makes their businesses more competitive. These wages, however, are far above the norm in North Korea. Still, no one believes that the North Korean workers get to keep more than a sliver of them. Their government takes the lion's share. That difference between what South Korea pays North Korean workers and what they take home is also fungible into what the North Korean government wants.

Fungibility is an international phenomenon as well. At the same time that the US sanctions meant to discourage Iran's nuclear program might have reduced Iran's economy by perhaps tens of millions of dollars (no one really knows), in 2006 three Chinese energy companies, Conooc, the China National Petroleum Corporation, and Petro China, signed deals worth over $20 billion with the Iranian government for development and exploitation of its North Pars gas field. The economic futility of subtracting moneys inferior by three orders of magnitude to those being added is self-evident. Is there a political logic that overrides such economic nonsense? The only self-evident one is the short-term, private political advantage of the American politicians who can claim to have solved a problem.

Because economic goods are fungible internationally, economic warfare against any country must include all who trade with it. If the United States and Europeans were serious about crippling the Iranian economy, their sanctions would have to impact China and Russia, as well as lesser powers, facing them with the choice of going along or being targets of economic warfare themselves. Secondary sanctions, "we will not deal with those who deal with . . . ," are the sign of seriousness. They are also well nigh acts of war. The point is that while military warfare is local by nature, and political warfare can be local or not, *economic warfare is global by nature*—yet another reason why it is a blunt tool.

THE TOOLS OF ECONOMIC WARFARE

Boycott

Boycott means "we will not buy from you." But it is impossible not to buy gold from Russia or South Africa. They are the world's biggest producers, and gold, like every other commodity, is anonymous: One ounce from point A equals one from point B. The same is true of oil: Regardless of source, it is *almost* as equally useful as its origins are difficult to discern. The initial UN boycott of Iraqi oil in 1990 was enforced less as a boycott than as a blockade at the source. While boycotting French wines and Japanese cars would be easy (they are recognizable and there are plenty of substitutes elsewhere), boycotting American or Argentine wheat would be like boycotting Saudi oil. But the major factor against the effectiveness of boycotts is that really only today's United States and European Union are such big international customers as to cripple their targets by boycotts. Most important is the question: What can you accomplish by boycotting anybody's products? That depends a little on how big a customer you are, and a lot on what larger political plan the boycott may be part of. You must begin by asking what you are after.

Since 1948 the Arab world has used its boycott of everything and anything having to do with Israel—a boycott that extends beyond Israel to all the world's companies that do business with Israel, and even includes persons whose passports bear Israeli stamps—as part of its overall effort to destroy that country. This effort has included a diplomatic full-court press, terrorism, and several wars. But the boycott did not lead the world's economic interests to shun Israel, because the Arab world is simply not a major presence in the world market, except for oil, which is a world commodity. The result would be far different if the United States were to wage on any country the kind of economic warfare that the Arabs wage on Israel: Any US secondary boycott would divide the world and restrict its target to the (much) lesser part.

Economic size matters, as does the relationship between the size of the objective and that of the other means being used. During James Madison's Administration the United States resorted to economic "nonintercourse"—neither buying from nor selling to Britain and France—in the vain hope that the withdrawal of its agricultural produce would cause either or both to stop harassing American ships on the high seas. But both Britain and France cared less about getting American farm products for themselves than about keeping the other from getting them. Hence they did not relent. For Americans, however, selling produce and importing goods was essential. Hence "nonintercourse" lost them money and fueled domestic quarrels. Exasperated and humiliated by 1812, they added their inadequate military force to their inadequate economic one and were lucky to come out of the ensuing war just a bit ahead. At least they knew what they wanted and were willing to fight for it.

The same cannot be said of the late twentieth and twenty-first-century American talk and policies about "energy independence"—read:

the desire to be able to boycott Middle Eastern oil. Leave aside the economic nonsense of dreaming to secede from an important part of the world economy. Discount the prohibitive economic costs and dislocations of truly attempting such a thing. Assume it could be done. Then ask, what would you do with "independence from foreign oil" once you had it? Were you planning to use your independence from the oil states' products to wage some sort of economic campaign against them as part of some larger war? Do you have a purpose in mind for that war? Do you have a diplomatic stratagem up your sleeve that would produce results so great and enduring as to warrant the effort? If you do not have compelling answers to these questions, you might ask why you are even thinking of half-baked preparations for a boycott that you have no intention of imposing, for purposes that you have not thought through, and as part of no war that you intend to wage. Might you be doing it to indulge the domestic political and economic interests that profit from subsidies for "alternative fuels"? Or perhaps because the words "energy independence" sound cool? Such superficiality signals political as well as intellectual weakness that overbalance your economic strength.

In short, boycotts are expensive measures that only a few can afford and that, like other means, make sense only as part of sensible plans.

Embargo

Embargo means "we will not sell to you." Few countries can afford the luxury of cutting off their customers. The famous Arab oil embargos of 1973 and 1979 could not have crippled their targets for the simple economic reason that the sellers of oil were even more dependent on the goods they received from the rest of the world than the rest of the world was on the oil. After all, the Middle East's oil was only about half of Europe's supply and but a tenth of the US supply and a lesser percentage of these societies' total energy sources. And, of course, existing stockpiles would have carried these economies for several months at normal capacity. But the Middle East had become far more dependent on all manner of imports to sustain populations that had grown far, far beyond the capacity of the region's industry—and above all of its farmland—to sustain. Yes, the governments had stockpiles of money. But money is no more edible than oil and can be rendered practically worthless by freezing accounts. Had the United States and Europe answered embargo with secondary embargo and frozen Middle Eastern assets in their banks, the Middle East's physical hunger would have weighed more heavily, much sooner, than the West's mild shortages of fuel.

The balance of economic power was on the West's side. The military balance was even more so. The oil states were open to blockade or whatever devastation the West might have wished to wreak, and their capacity to defend most of the fields was negligible. But material factors were not responsible for these embargoes' power, or for their targets' supine responses. Rather, these resulted from the imbalance of motives: Hurting the Arabs did not cross Western governments' minds, while hurting Westerners rivaled money as a motive for the embargoes. For some three generations, this political imbalance has been key to the relationship between the West and the oil states. In economic affairs, as in others, what you have means less than what you mean to do with it.

The embargo that the United States imposed on Cuba after 1961 is perhaps the most obvious example of disproportion between economic means and political ends. Geography makes Cuba a natural part of the US economy and no other. None of the other countries bordering the Caribbean can supply Cuba's needs or take its products. The rest of the world is far away. If the United States had done to Cuba what the Arab countries did to Israel, namely, refuse to deal with any company or perhaps country worldwide that dealt with Cuba, perhaps not even the Soviet Union could have afforded to sustain it in poverty between 1960 and 1990. Even so, since the US primary embargo-boycott was nearly total, Cuba's free economic intercourse with the rest of the world provided meager life support. But the United States was not trying to overthrow Cuba's regime. In fact it had *guaranteed* it as part of the 1962 Missile Crisis settlement. Yes, the embargo limited the regime's resources. But Cuba's Castro enjoyed a half-century of power and would die in bed. Yes, the embargo warned other countries that following Cuba's path would mean poverty. But Socialists impose poverty on their peoples by the very instruments that secure their power. They can scarcely live without it. And, in fact, Cuba's poverty did not prevent Venezuela's Hugo Chavez, Bolivia's Evo Morales, and Nicaragua's Daniel Ortega from following Castro, imposing food shortages and rationing on their peoples, and making trouble for the United States.

Castro had made Cuba's misery. The embargo worsened it a bit and added to the world's sense that the Castro regime was bad. But the Cubans who continually risked their lives to flee the island were fleeing more than poverty. So the embargo's massive economic force achieved little. Problem was, the embargo ended up carrying the weight of US policy toward Cuba that consisted of impotent exhortation. This had not been President John Kennedy's intent. When he forswore overthrowing the regime, Kennedy promised that the United States would "build a wall of freedom" (whatever that might mean) around the island. He was referring to a set of economic measures and political interference in Latin American politics that he called the "Alliance for Progress," which was supposed to build prosperous, democratic bodies politic in the region resistant to the Castro virus. Castro's cadres would see the virtue of trading their power for their people's prosperity. Sure.

But even the best-designed measures of economic assistance cannot transfer economic fundamentals such as respect for property rights, the rule of law, and small government. And the Alliance's Liberal Internationalist prescriptions of big government, import substitution, and "land reform" (read: expropriation) proved to be the opposite of economic good sense. The Kennedy-Johnson programs of political interference, equally misguided, fostered leftist politicians in Chile, Argentina, Uruguay, Venezuela, Colombia, and the Dominican Republic who ruined their countries. In Chile, Argentina, and Uruguay, they brought civil war. The point is that while the embargo would have been a serviceable part of a well-defined policy to overthrow an island's regime, it was much less likely to complement "building a wall of freedom" in a hemisphere—even if the builders had not been sorcerers' apprentices.

Legal and Financial Measures

A corollary of the Cuban embargo teaches another lesson. Having seized property on the island belonging to US citizens, the Castro regime tried selling or renting some of it to European companies. This led the US Congress, via the Helms Burton Act, to enable those US persons who had title to said properties to sue said European companies to recover the value of the stolen property they had acquired from the thief.[14] The European companies involved, supported by their governments, protested that Helms-Burton made them choose between having assets in the United States or doing business in Cuba as they wished. That indeed was the Act's purpose. The State Department was sympathetic to the Europeans. But if the US government had valued good relations with the Europeans above its own citizens' property rights, the President could have vetoed the Act. Or, if it had valued them equally, it could have recompensed its own citizens directly. Or, if it had valued the principle that Castro must be punished for his theft, it could have brushed aside the Europeans or even overthrown Castro. Instead, the US body politic used economics to try balancing the interests of citizens and Europeans while hurting Castro a little. This was tinkering.

Tinkering as well was the US government's blacklisting of a bank in the former Portuguese colony of Macao, effectively part of China, which provided the North Korean regime's access to the world's financial system. Through it the regime bought military goods as well as the luxuries that glue its elites together—in part with *forged* US hundred-dollar bills. By foreclosing access to the US banking system to banks that deal with that bank, the United States effectively cut this bank off from the world by foreclosing access to the US banking system to banks that deal with it. But since the Chinese regime valued North Korea's cohesion (and since some of its personages also used that bank for their own private purposes), it objected to the US action. Having consulted with China, North Korea refused to attend further negotiating sessions. To mollify both, the State Department pressed Treasury to delist the bank. Treasury then dropped its objection to the bank delivering $25 million to North Korea's account in China that the bank had frozen at US request and removed the bank from its blacklist. In return, North Korea agreed to provide some information on its nuclear program, to reduce it in ways that it would choose, and to continue talking. But of course North Korea reneged and added demands. Why should it not have?

Note that having found a tool for applying pressure to a regime's center of gravity, the US government backed off the pressure precisely because it was hitting the center of gravity. That is because it had invested its prestige in the future of the negotiations and valued that prestige above any substantive effect that the pressure might produce. Hence by easing up on the bank and paying for the privilege of sitting down with North Korea, the US government showed the uselessness of good tools in incompetent hands.

Against Iran, the United States simply deployed a tool too small for the job: Beginning in September 2006, it privately pressured some of the world's largest banks—Switzerland's UBS, Germany's Kommerzbank, and Britain's HSBC—to curtail dealings *with those parts of the Iranian financial system* that relate to the country's nuclear program. This led to lesser banks making difficulties about processing Iranian payments abroad, hence forcing many Iranians to use cash rather than credit. This hurt Iran a little. But to what end? In short, this tool, like any tool, is useful only insofar as one really wants to do the thing that the tool is for, rather than pretend.

Pretend is what the United States did with regard to restricting the finances of terrorists. Since terrorism is anything but the spontaneous, senseless violence of isolated individuals, money is essential to it. Even Iraq's terrorism runs less on ideology or religion than on money.[15] Nor is it any secret where most the money is coming from: principally the "oil states." Those states have governments, none of them permissive. The US government could hold them responsible for terrorist financing that comes from within their borders, but it chooses not to.

Instead, the US Treasury takes a retail approach: It identifies the bank accounts of "charities" and other institutions that are used by persons who have associated with known terrorists or known terrorist organizations. In 2006, the program had designated some 375 persons and entities as involved in money laundering and financial transfers to terrorists. How much money had been transferred by these entities and others undiscovered is anyone's guess, given the diversity and wealth of terrorism's many sympathizers in the Middle East, as well as the multiplicity and flexibility of the channels through which money can be transferred. US monitoring of the international SWIFT network simply led financiers to shift to less obvious channels. By 2006, international bankers had reported to the US Treasury some 14 million suspicious transactions, most of which had nothing to do with terrorism, while an unknowable number that did were unreported. In sum, the US Treasury's achievements, necessary in themselves, would be sufficient to shut off terrorists' finances only if the only terrorists were the ones known, if the program truly targeted the finances of all those who associate with terrorists, and if the US Treasury's international connections could reach the major avenues through which money flows to terrorists. But since none of these conditions apply, no one expects the program to actually cut off the money.[16]

Since most persons who commit terrorist acts had been unknown prior to committing them, trying to identify their immediate support structure makes no sense. In fact, as we shall see in Chapter 6, the "model" of terrorism on which the program is based—that terrorists are outlaws everywhere, supported only by a few "rogue" individuals and groups—is unreal. This brings us back to the fact that terrorists fight for political causes, that those causes are supported by those who count in the oil states, and that the US government chooses not to hold those states responsible. It is difficult not to conclude that while reducing terrorist financing is of some importance to our statesmen, it is less important than many other things.

Indeed, fussing about terrorist finances at the margins hides the fact that, for reasons our statesmen find sufficient but do not advertise, the US government itself as well as its European allies finance terrorists more than Saudi Sheiks. Consider the Palestinian Authority, a quasigovernment that US policy wishes were not quasi. It owes its very existence to the US government's patronage, which it earned by a forty-year campaign of assassinations of innocents ranging from children in Israeli school buses, to Olympic athletes, to airline passengers, to US ambassadors. In 1993, the US government joined the European Union and Arab states in financing it, in the hope that it would moderate its terrorism or just confine it to Israel. The US government accepted at face value its leaders' assurance that they disapprove of their subordinates' and associates' acts of terrorism. In 2007, mindless of the fact that money is fungible, the US government was financing part of the PA, pretending that the money would serve "humanitarian" purposes. US and European "aid to the Palestinian territories," amounting to some $1.35 billion per year, rose by over $300 million over the previous year, as the PA's politics were becoming more violent. Per capita, adjusted for inflation, the United States has given more to the PA than it did to rebuild Europe after World War II. As a result, the PA's massively unemployed population we see on the evening news snaking through its territories with machine guns is rather overfed as well as overarmed. The images suggest that if "aid" did not free these people from the need to earn a living, they might have less energy for militancy. But terrorism earns the PA's living precisely as nuclear weapons earn the North Korean regime's living. Their resource, our statesmen's fecklessness, seems inexhaustible.

The US government also claims that its aid strengthens the PA's "moderate factions." Secretary of State Rice told Congress she would do her best to make sure US money ended up on "the right side" of Palestinian politics. But degrees of moderation among suicide bombers are like degrees of virginity in bordellos. In short, while Treasury documents dossiers to persuade banks to shut down pipelines that feed a few million dollars to terrorists, the State Department supplied "$468 million in 2006, [up] from $400 million"[17] to an entity whose income rises with the level of terror it produces. One might call this supply-side terror financing.

MATCHING MEANS TO ENDS

Though relying on economic measures as the main means for achieving political objectives is generally a bad idea, and despite the fact that even more seldom is it advisable to use weak measures to split the difference between strong ones and none, there are cases in which a mild economic measure may calibrate a message proper to the occasion. Thucydides gives us the classic case that illustrates the subtleties of the matter.

Fifth-century BC Athens and Sparta had agreed to peace for thirty years after a war in which Athens had failed to defeat a Spartan army that had ventured into its home area of Attica. Nevertheless, Athens counted on being able to prevent Spartan incursions if need be by occupying the mountain passes owned by Athens' ally, Megara, leading into Attica. But when Megara switched alliances and butchered its Athenian garrison, Athens lost a strategic position and faced a hard choice: If it destroyed Megara, now a Spartan ally, it would have challenged Sparta to a war that neither wanted; while if it did nothing, it would thereby tell other allies that they could defy Athens with impunity on vital matters. Pericles, something of a paragon of statesmanship, decided to banish Megarians from nearby Athens' markets and to end their access to all ports in Athens' empire. Megara's subsequent impoverishment (Aristophanes caricatured a poor Megarian disguising his daughters as pigs to smuggle them into Athens' market) told Athens' allies that they could not transgress their commitments, while telling Sparta that Athens did not hold it responsible and wished to remain at peace.

Some historians blamed Pericles' "Megarian decree" for the outbreak of the Peloponnesian war because, years later and on the war's eve, Sparta demanded it be revoked. Others have argued that since Sparta proved willing to start the war on behalf of an ally, Pericles' rejection of an expedition to control Megara's mountain passes in favor of economic sanctions against Megara amounted to a half-hearted and foolish bet on peace. But since it was not self-evident whether Sparta would incline to peace or war, it makes sense for us simply to note that Pericles' judgment *might* have born better fruits, and hence that the "Megarian decree" was reasonably proportionate to the ends that Pericles reasonably sought in his situation.

Much less reasonably proportionate were the League of Nations' 1935 sanctions against Italy for invading Ethiopia. We have already noted that Britain and France's joint objectives (the two for practical purposes *were* the League) were mutually exclusive. But both were tall orders: stopping a substantial military move on which Italy had staked much, and cementing an alliance with Italy against Germany. Pursuing either one would reasonably have required major commitments. The League sanctions turned out to be doubly harmful because they sought to stop Italy with disproportionately tiny force. Hence Great Britain and France lost Ethiopia, lost the League, and lost Italy as an ally against Germany. Britain and France also showed Italy that they would have been worthless allies against Germany, and showed Germany that it had nothing to fear from anybody. This incident shows that the League's authors adopted sanctions as their ultimate tool to screen their unseriousness about their commitments.

What is and is not reasonably proportionate to the task depends on how the economic elements relate to the political ones—and here size does not matter necessarily. Consider the disproportionately great effect of Anglo-American economic sanctions against Rhodesia in the 1970s and South Africa in the 1980s. The boycott of Rhodesian farm products, which aimed at no less than forcing the country's white minority to cede power to its fiercest black enemies, forced Rhodesian exports—primarily chrome and produce—to enter world markets through South Africa. Since many were doing so anyway, this added little cost—certainly not enough to convince a whole class of people to do something that they judged, correctly, would force them to give up their livelihoods and start over with next to nothing on new continents. The later sanctions against South Africa, which also aimed at disempowering the white minority, were not even that harsh. US industry in the country, operating under the "Sullivan Principles," simply treated black and white employees alike. And since South Africa exported to the sanctioning countries gold and other commodities, the economic impact was barely perceptible. Nevertheless, in both cases the weak sanctions reinforced a message that the US and British governments were sending to Africa's whites by many means, and that meant a lot to them in their situation.

Africa's whites were acutely conscious of their minority status. Despite their claim—true enough—that they were a "white tribe" that had migrated to their present abodes often before some of the black tribes around them, though their roots in Africa might go back ten generations, they realized that their color and culture were so different from that of their neighbors that they really were foreigners. The fate of whites in other parts of Africa had taught them that these differences would prevent them, in the long run, from living European lives alongside blacks on the basis of equality. The choice was between keeping control of their countries and emigrating. Trying to hold on in opposition to the white world beyond was dispiriting.

In South Africa, where sport is well nigh a religion, the rugby world's exclusion of South Africa's Springboks, as well as the national team's exclusion from the Olympics, told whites that they were being excluded from the only civilization in which they could live in the long run. Much as Africa's White Tribe protested their African-ness, much as they resented the white world, the sanctions forced them to look to joining it. And so they gave in and began leaving. It helped that New Zealand and Australia advertised for Rhodesian and South African migrants. The economic sanctions, albeit economically puny, helped send a cultural message that was decisive in that particular set of circumstances.

In sum, then, the economic tools of statecraft are just like the others: They must be part of a complex of measures that fit a particular objective in particular circumstances.

CHAPTER 6
//////////////

WARS ARE
FOR WINNING

In war there is no substitute for victory.
— DOUGLAS MACARTHUR

Ils ne sont pas sérieux ("They are not serious").
— CHARLES DE GAULLE

Commingling all of statesmanship's tools, the art of war deals life and death to nations as well as to individuals. As men are born and die in pain, so nations are born and die in war. De Gaulle famously wrote of war that it is the *"accoucheuse des nations,"* the midwife of nations, and the *"fossayeuse des decadences,"* gravedigger of the decadent. Losing wars is how most regimes and nations die. Whereas the diplomatic art's fundamental "threefold" choice "perpetually" includes the option of breaking off contact, war's onset narrows the statesman's options to two: victory and defeat.[1] Though not every war seems to place a regime's life at risk, they all do. That is because just as any fistfight can turn deadly, so wars over trifles can grow to consume civilizations, as did the Peloponnesian war and World War I. Because killing and dying engages any regime's legitimacy to the fullest, war is the ultimate election. Peoples may find in foreign war the occasion to betray domestic enemies. Or war may draw them together. Even the strongest nations emerge from even small defeats as if they were convalescent, as America emerged from the Vietnam War—in part because forgiving losers, listening to them, associating with them, is against human nature. Nor does winning necessarily exorcise war's ill effects. Britain and France ceased to be world powers after their costly victory in World War I. Winning merely gives the chance to fulfill dreams—which tests the quality of dreams and dreamers.

Because war has always held life in one hand and doom in the other, classic literature about it ranges from pathos to glory. But classic efforts to *understand* what statesmen had better do in war differ little across millennia, cultures, and continents: Above all you must be clear about the peace that you want to result from the conflict at hand. Only your focus on your peace will make clear the cause for which you fight and hence the meaning of victory. That in turn points out the enemy who stands in the way of your peace and may dissipate somewhat the fog that shrouds the stakes, the powers, and the operational objectives of the various sides, the strategy for overcoming the enemy, and the operations of war needed to make the strategy work. In sum, the classics treat war as statesmanship's perennial *ultima ratio,* demanding full and flexible use of human powers on a case-by-case basis.

While America's Founding Generation debated war and peace in terms of the classics, we saw in Chapters 1 and 2 that our twentieth-century statesmen redefined international affairs in terms of words and concepts that avert the mind's eye from war. They did so wrongly assuming that peace is mankind's natural, default state. *In fact, there is no such thing as peace simply.* Rather there have been, are, and will be as many kinds of peace as willful men establish and keep for themselves—usually over others' dead bodies. Most instances of peace exist as the result of wars, and only so long as they can be defended by war. So, whenever we come across a state of peace, we should ask, *Whose peace is it?* Against whose will was it achieved? By what force? Whose force maintains it against contrary versions of peace?

In short, war's ugliness must not blind us to its primordial function—establishing peace. But whose peace? That's what wars decide. Because human purposes are usually incompatible, some people get bent while others do the bending. Hence war is essentially a clash of purposes. Only derivatively is it a clash of arms. Peace and war are two sides of the same human coin. Failing to grasp that makes it impossible to understand the event that ends war and ushers in peace, namely, *victory: somebody eliminating the obstacles to his peace.* Hence war's essential discipline is figuring out what peace you want, as well as pointing out the mortal obstacles to that peace. Only in light of that does killing make sense.

But though twentieth-century American statesmen largely banished the word "war" from polite vocabulary, they led America in more wars than had their predecessors.[2] They also managed the most remarkable of feats: While America's armed forces won all the big battles, and most of the small ones too, the statesmen—with rare exceptions—did not deliver the peace they had promised. Losing the peace means you lost the war. But losing wars after winning battles is unnatural and begs for explanation. Let us now seek explanation in the truths of war that American statesmen have found too shocking to contemplate: the need for seriousness, for understanding what you are after and what stands in its way, for distinguishing sharply between war and peace, for understanding the enemy's cause as well as your own, for grasping what will make the difference between his victory and yours, for strategy—a reasonable plan to win—and for the steadfast flexibility to meet the war's demands.

SERIOUSNESS

In his memoirs of World War II de Gaulle had written that *un*seriousness about war, not looking it in the eye, was a requirement for "all who wanted to be elected, applauded, or published" in France's polite society of the 1920s and 1930s, and that Franco-British leaders—even after having declared war in September 1939—thought that "war . . . should consist of fighting as little as possible." But denying war had brought it on, and waging it in a phony manner ensured disaster.[3] The mentality of America's rulers, de Gaulle knew, was similar—after all, the 1928 Kellogg-Briand Treaty that presumed to outlaw war had been a Franco-American joint venture. But because de Gaulle had a high opinion of the

American people, he had imagined that American statesmen would take war seriously when the crunch came. They disappointed him.

As the Soviet Union deployed ballistic missiles in Cuba in October 1962, President de Gaulle assured President John F. Kennedy that America could count on France "in peace and in war." He put his country's fate in Kennedy's hands in what came to be known as the Cuban Missile Crisis because he knew that America held the winning cards— but also because he assumed that the Americans had counted all sides' cards as well, that their demands and actions would flow from a net assessment of their own and their enemy's strengths and weaknesses. Strategy grows naturally out of a correct assessment of how one side's strengths match up with the other's weaknesses.[4] In any circumstance, the logic of peace and war demands strict, specific attention to who wants what, what they may be able and willing to do to get it. But the various accounts of the Cuban Missile Crisis are clear on one point: The Americans paid little attention to who was actually prepared to do what to whom for the sake of what and rather focused on avoiding what they imagined would be an undifferentiated "nuclear holocaust." This they did despite the fact that nobody in America had any intention of unleashing such a thing and that the Soviets had even less.

The Soviets' stakes were low and their capacity to sustain their gambit was even lower. Emplacing three regiments of SS-4 and two of SS-5 missiles in Cuba was a gamble that, if successful, would have guaranteed their capacity to get at least some nuclear warheads onto American soil despite their lack of intercontinental missiles. This was of *some* importance, because in those years it was an open question whether *any* Soviet bombers could get through American air defenses. But achieving success in Cuba would have diminished the United States' massive edge in nuclear striking power only a bit. Nor would failure have been serious: If forced to retreat unconditionally, the Soviets would end up no worse off than before. Yet upholding these small stakes in the face of American opposition would require more than they could manage: They could neither force their ships through the US Navy nor project enough power across the globe to defend the Cuban bases and the Castro regime against a vastly more powerful America ninety miles away. The Soviets could have started a strategic nuclear exchange with an America many times as powerful. *But they had emplaced the missiles only to tweak the strategic balance—not to start a war.* Moreover, such a war would not have secured their objective and would have destroyed them in the bargain.

By contrast, for the Americans the stakes were high and the capacity to sustain them was higher. The Soviet missiles in Cuba and Castro's power there were the first undeniable breach in the American people's physical safety and the first enemy base in the Americas in a century. Preventing the missiles from becoming operational, or expelling them and overthrowing Castro, would avoid this and could be secured without breaking a sweat: The Soviet Navy of 1962 could barely get out of port against US opposition, much less survive off Florida. And though a major mutual unleashing of nuclear arsenals might or might not have entailed losses for America, it would have guaranteed destruction for the Soviets. Yet Kennedy et al. managed to convince themselves that the stakes were equally life and death for all and treated the Soviets' nuclear strike forces as equivalent to America's. Our statesmen's subjective reality diverged from objective reality.

For the American side, it was dogma that the possession of nuclear weapons renders irrelevant calculations of relative military power and that "pushing the button" would mean, as Tom Lehrer, a popular songster of that time, had it, "we will all go together when we go."[5] Adhering to that, it was logical for the Americans *preemptively* to do and refrain from doing whatever it might take to avoid hostilities. And indeed, Robert Kennedy, the president's brother, preemptively and secretly offered to Ambassador Anatoly Dobrynin to withdraw comparable US missiles from Europe and to guarantee the survival of the Castro regime in exchange for the Soviets' withdrawal of the missiles from Cuba.

And so de Gaulle watched the Kennedy Administration give the Soviets advantages they had not held before—while under zero diplomatic or military pressure to do so, regardless of massive geographic and military advantages, as well as of its own long-range interests, never mind France's. He wondered, What were the Americans doing? Why, if their fear of war was so overwhelming as to mandate preemptive concessions, had they not just made the concessions? Why had they brandished war in the first place and invited France to expose itself? Perhaps, since the Kennedy Administration at the time denied it had made those concessions, it was using war talk to cover the domestic flank of retreat. Perhaps, on the other hand, it had been as serious about possible military action as about the absolute necessity to avoid it—if that makes any sense. But *surely* it had proved unserious about war and peace. Pronouncing the Americans so, de Gaulle then took France out of the North Atlantic Alliance's military command and led Europe to stop counting on them.[6]

Twentieth-century American statesmen's reticence about the very word "war" coupled with their willingness to engage military forces reminds us of Voltaire's quip that ladies tremble at hearing of certain things, though they do not hesitate to do them. And like those ladies, our statesmen demurely put themselves in positions where "doing it" is inevitable. In June 1941, as Franklin Roosevelt was asking Congress *not to vote* on a motion to declare war on Germany, he ordered the US Navy to "shoot on sight" at German ships in the Atlantic. Is there virtue in "doing it" while saying you're not, or in pretending to do it as a substitute for doing it? In 1950, after Woodrow Wilson's League and Franklin Roosevelt's UN had supposedly abolished war, President Truman sent Americans to fight in Korea but called it a "police action" on behalf of the UN, though some 55,000 Americans died. Why was that not war? Truman explained: The proper objective in Korea was not "victory," as General Douglas MacArthur wanted, but "avoiding a wider war"— meaning that military action could aim principally at *not* doing something. Sophisticated opinion then and later attributed the American people's objections to "no-win war" to lack of sophistication.[7] Is "sophistication" really the right word to describe this sort of thing?

Similarly, John F. Kennedy's 1961 promise to "pay any price, support any friend, oppose any foe in order to assure the survival and the success of liberty" meant in practice that Americans were to shoot and die in Vietnam to "send a message" but not to make war. This was sophisticated because, as Lyndon Johnson explained, "there is no victory in Vietnam, for anyone" but rather "mutually acceptable solutions." Indeed, neither Kennedy nor Johnson called it a war despite (or perhaps because) their critics on the Republican Right and on the Democratic Left called it just that. But the Right wanted an American victory and the Left an American defeat, while the Administration teetered untenably between them.

Contrary to such Democratic pillars as Senators Richard Russell (GA) and even Hubert Humphrey (MN) who agreed with most Republicans that Communists were enemies to be defeated, the Kennedy-Johnson team (e.g., Robert McNamara, McGeorge Bundy, W. W. Rostow, Arthur Schlesinger Jr.) wanted to assure liberty's survival in cooperation with the Communists. But after Kennedy's death a growing part of the Administration, including McNamara, and of the constituency it represented came to see President Johnson and America itself as the enemy in Vietnam. Some wrote that victory for the Communist side was necessary to save the world from American imperialism and nuclear war.[8] The Right then saw them as scarcely distinguishable from the enemy. This domestic conflict's seriousness overshadowed the shooting in Southeast Asia.

Most mythical is the notion that the US government resolved seriously circa 1947 to wage cold war on the Soviet Union, to *contain* and squeeze it to death. In fact *containment* began as a compromise between the Democratic Party's Wallaceite Left's dream of a US-Soviet Progressive codominion of the world, and the desire of many Democrats (e.g., Thomas Dodd of Connecticut) and Republicans (e.g., Roman Hruska of Nebraska) for "rolling back" Communist advances in Eastern Europe and China. Containment's content changed continually over the years. By the mid-1950s the Eisenhower Administration had abandoned the notion of taking advantage of troubles within the Soviet empire. In the mid-1960s the US government began sweeping aside opposition to deals with the Soviets. A decade later it was unanimous in trying to build the Soviet Union economically and to facilitate its "organic" relationship with its Eastern European empire. From then on, to doubt that the Soviet Union was eternal, equivalent to the United States, that technology and history had enabled us to destroy each other but would never let us protect ourselves, was to exclude one's self from the right meetings, dinner parties, and faculty lounges. President Ronald Reagan's suggestions to the contrary ("we win, they lose") were so far out of the consensus of academe, the media, and the US government itself that, as Strobe Talbott wrote, correctly, they were irrelevant to US policy.[9] So while the Soviet Union's collapse was victory de facto, attributing it to our statesmen waging the Cold War seriously since 1947, and even to Ronald Reagan's intentions, is to confuse correlation with causality.

After the Soviet Union collapsed, two Bushes and a Clinton subsequently sent armed Americans around the globe and occasionally even used the W word. But the purposes for which they sent them—New World Order, Democratic Enlargement, and Democratic Transformation—were not such as war may accomplish, nor did their actions fit any dictionary definition of war. Nor did the 1990–1991 Gulf War, because after US forces had won one of history's most lopsided battles, the US government tried to achieve by diplomacy ends that could only have been achieved by war, as we saw in Chapter 4.

In the 1990s American unseriousness shielded Saddam and led Middle Eastern governments to fear and court him more than America. In 1993 Ramzi Yousef and Abdul Yasin traveled from Saddam's Iraq to bomb the World Trade Center in New York. The latter returned and disappeared there, while Saddam's intelligence service smothered America's covert actions in Iraq. In sum, our statesmen were giving substance to Saddam's claim that he had won the war. Then in 2003, as if validating that claim, they overthrew him. But afterward, they occupied Iraq for purposes on which they never agreed. It seems that great power wielded unseriously is not so great.

In sum, twentieth-century American statesmen sometimes wielded the tools of war without intending to make war, and at other times intended war but eschewed the tools. They confused war with actions: with bombing or "boots on the ground," with killing and dying, with campaigns against every physical and social ill, with teaching lessons or punishing, with occupying and building nations. But war is none of these. War is a deadly contest for your peace.

PEACE AND THE CENTER OF GRAVITY

Each regime has needs and vulnerabilities peculiar to itself. Knowing them is key to guarding and meeting them. Competent regimes war in ways that protect their most valuable and vulnerable aspects, the things that sustain them and make them what they are. And they aim at the enemy's most vulnerable vitals, the things the taking, destroying, overturning, or constraining of which make the difference between winning and losing. Clausewitz called such things the "center of gravity." He noted that the Napoleonic wars were contests to defeat the enemy's main force, constrain his capital, while protecting one's own. But, of course, since regimes and circumstances differ, so do the centers of gravity and the foci of wars. Knowing yours and others' centers of gravity is the key to understanding the kind of peace you need, the kinds of wars you must and must not fight, and the way you must fight them. Hence self-preservation's prerequisite is *to shed any sense of entitlement to your peace*, to be ever conscious of how your regime might be undone.

Competent regimes make war in ways that bring them peace, above all internally. Sparta's hoplite army and its location were its center of gravity, because the Spartan oligarchy's primordial need was for ever present military force at home to oppress its Helot underclass. So central was that manpower to the regime that the Spartans seldom strayed far, and never for long. And in 421 BC Sparta offered to give up its objectives in the Peloponnesian war to recover some three hundred hoplite prisoners. By contrast, Athens' primordial need and center of gravity was balance between public-spiritedness and self-seeking in its democratic Assembly. But Athens' natural way of war, naval expeditions of choice, lent itself to aggravating the tendency of its leading men to manipulate war policy for their own interest. By contrast, in the Roman Republic each foreign war relieved pressure on the regime's axis: the precarious unity of its factions. Yet when Rome's wars became ends in themselves, they encouraged those factions to treat one another as foreigners. Perpetual foreign war became civil war.

Some regimes are conscious of their own vulnerabilities, while others are not. Because the fragility of the Communist Party's control of the Soviet Union was foremost in Stalin's mind, "solidity of the home front" was the first of his "five principles of warfare." Soviet political doctrine was to avoid war because no possible gain could counterbalance the danger that war would pose to the regime—even though Soviet military doctrine called for preemptive attack as the opening phase of war. Similarly,

Third World regimes such as Syria, and including China, rarely muster armies to attack across borders. That is because, despite their police apparati and their pretenses of nationalism, such regimes distrust their own armies, never mind their peoples. Hence they carry on war through indirect strategies and essentially private means, including subversion and terrorism, for ends that do not mobilize their own masses or risk invasions. Though otherwise dysfunctional, they war conservatively. Staking little, they can sustain their peculiar peace through all but catastrophic defeats.

Others assume that their centers of gravity are birthrights. At the turn of the twentieth century European regimes stoked popular passions and staked the popular allegiances on which they had rested on a Great War, the worth of whose objectives could not balance the millions of deaths in the trenches. Failing to understand their centers of gravity, they consumed them. Thus having misunderstood their peace, they undermined their capacity to keep any peace. Hence European states in our time do not defend the peace, the civilization and borders established through centuries of war. The causes and justice of the Muslim world's migration to, and pressures on, Europe in our time are beside the point: namely, that because of it twenty-first-century Europe is ceasing to be what it had been, that to retain their peace Europeans would have to control their borders and rule or expel the Muslims forcefully, and that they would not think of it, because that would mean avowing a way of life so worthy as to be worth inflicting and suffering violence. Europeans like their peace, but not *that* much.

America's peace rests on—its center of gravity can be nothing but—a diverse people's common dedication to the founding proposition that unites them. Lincoln explained it best. Few Americans, he said, could trace their lineage to the nation's Founders. But those who "look through that old Declaration of Independence" and believe it will feel "blood of the blood and flesh of the flesh" with the Founders, "and so they are."[10] Protecting and shoring up the American people's common friendship and dedication—our center of gravity—is the statesman's primordial task in peace, and the objective in war. Lincoln's famous 1838 address begins by discounting the possibility that all of Europe's armies combined and led by a Bonaparte disposing of the world's treasure could "take a drink from the Ohio or make a track on the Blue Ridge in a trial of a thousand years."[11] Lincoln then subtly warned that America was vulnerable to its domestic parties' increasing commitment to incompatible visions: slavery as a "positive good," and Negro equality as a political imperative. For the statesman to embrace either horn of that conflict would have meant treating fellow citizens as enemies.

Lincoln's task as a President whose election caused eleven states to start a civil war was the most difficult imaginable: restoring fellowship among all while defeating some. His genius lay in tailoring vigorous military operations to that political priority. Some historians fault him for not having made Negro equality a war aim. But Lincoln knew that no war could accomplish that, and that a war with such an aim could never end, never bring peace. In the 1840s and 1850s the United States' center of gravity had not withstood attack from opposite sides. In peace, Lincoln had sought to safeguard it. In war, he tried to reestablish it. Under lesser statesmen, that took most of a century.

STAKES AND CAUSES

Though always at stake, the regime's survival is usually overshadowed by the stakes *du jour*. Sometimes, small stakes are tokens of very big ones. Thus when Sparta demanded in 432 BC that Athens revoke the "Megarian decree" or suffer a Spartan invasion, Pericles told the Athenians: "I hope that none of you will think that we shall be going to war for a trifle if we refuse to revoke the Megara decree. . . . Why this trifle contains the whole seal and trial of your resolution. If you give way, you will instantly have to meet some greater demand . . . while a firm refusal will make them clearly understand they have to treat you as equals."[12] Pericles resisted the demand and accepted war not because the sanctions were terribly important to Athens' security but because rescinding them under pressure would have meant surrendering Athens' "entire position" of equality vis-à-vis Sparta. Pericles persuaded Athens to offer only what the existing treaty required: to submit complaints to arbitration. He argued that Sparta's humiliating demand for more than it was entitled to meant it had already decided on war (which it had) and had to be treated as war.

Thucydides gives the impression that Pericles' judgment was sound. Perhaps it was not. But surely judging in one's own cause under the shadow of death is hazardous intellectually as well as morally. It is also inevitable.

Prestige is itself a valuable stake, and war engages it as nothing else. Thus in 50 BC Cicero rose in the Senate to argue that in Rome's war against Mithridades, Rome's reputation was at stake more than territory, alliances, and vengeance, and that Pompey must be sent utterly to crush Mithridades: "Therefore consider whether it is right for you to hesitate to continue to support enthusiastically a war in which we are defending Rome's reputation as a great power, the safety and security of our allies, the principal sources of our tax revenues, and the fortunes of a very large number of individual citizens—all matters intimately connected with our national interest."[13] Prestige is worth fighting for because it is a currency in international affairs that often buys peace more cheaply than blood or money.

But for what *substantive* reason does any people actually choose to fight *this* fight? Thucydides answers: "honor, fear, and interest."[14] Yet, another reason underlies them all: Controversies end up being about "them" versus "us." Just as France's turn-of-the-twentieth-century Dreyfus case ceased to be about Dreyfus and simply reinflamed the Left and Right's mutual hatred, cause and identity meld in the minds of men and exist physically in those who embody them—regardless of substance.

Realist and Liberal Internationalist doctrine to the contrary notwithstanding, cold calculations of collective material interest move few decisions about war and peace. If they did, the fact that free trade pays better dividends than rapine to the nation as a whole (as we saw in Chapter 5) would make for a less violent world than our own. Of course, commercial rivalries exist. But they are properly understood as private rather than public quarrels. We should understand "interest" primarily in terms of any regime's constituents' interests in their own primacy and material profit, as well in satisfying their friends and fancies. As Adam Smith argued, the British decisions that inflamed the American Revolution were moved by and for the profit of the British East India Company, not Britain. Nonmaterial private and factional interests are even more prevalent. Thucydides tells us that Sparta's proposals of peace with Athens were thwarted by Cleon, who needed the war to mask his crimes, and by Alcibiades, who was insulted personally that he had not been involved in the negotiations. In *Federalist #6,* Hamilton reminds us that statesmen as famous as Louis XIV and Pericles were said to have made war to satisfy mistresses, while in 1998 speculation, justified or not, was rife that President Clinton had attacked Sudan to divert attention from new evidence of his adultery. So you should ask, "Who *among them* wants what?" And "Who *among us* wants what?"

Of all war's causes, fear may be the most motive and pervasive. Only judgment—inherently disputable—distinguishes preventive wars from acts of aggression. There are as many examples of wars that might have been avoided but were started because men feared that deferring them would mean fighting them later under worse conditions—Sparta started the Peloponnesian war because it "bought" its allies' argument to this effect—as there are of wars deferred that, if fought or threatened in good time, might have avoided later disasters: France did not attack in 1936 to stop Hitler's militarization of the Rhineland, and in the summer of 1914 America did not ally with Britain to dissuade Germany from starting World War I.

Because fear moves war mostly when catalyzed by contempt, as we saw in Chapter 3, arguably contempt is the scariest of war's causes. We need fear it above all because more and more of the world's people hold today's Americans in contempt. As we saw in Chapter 3, contempt has nothing to do with disagreements and is very different from hate. Rather, contempt is the wages of impotence, the expectation of impunity. In our time, foreign crowds shout "death to America" and force American embassies to turn themselves into fortresses lest they be burned to the ground, as was the one in Pakistan in 1979, or nearly so, like the one in Belgrade in 2008. They do so lightheartedly, ever more confident that it is safe. Americans must decide how long to let this confidence grow before increasing the dose of contempt's only antidote: fear.

The word "honor" should be in your vocabulary, if only because more people bet their lives on immaterial considerations than on material ones. Human beings—especially the livelier ones—value primacy, integrity, self-regard, deference, glory, above life itself. Sacrifices for God and country fall into this category. So does revenge. Matters of honor are naturally incommensurable with material interest and can be dealt with only in their own terms. The Muslim world's latter-day eagerness to take offense, its passion for avenging perceived disrespect, should have reminded our statesmen that human beings define themselves by what they honor—and fail to honor.

What indeed is so worthy about *our* way of life, so sacred, that we should kill to make it respected? You had better have answers compelling to Americans and foes alike. You will gain no respect by pretending that nothing is sacred, or that all is sacred and meaningless alike, much less by suffering insult. The signers of our Declaration of Independence dedicated "our lives, our fortunes, and our sacred honor" to America's cause. What is America's honor? What is *America's Peace, America's Cause*? Answering that is indispensable to King Archidamus' proverbial question: What is to be our war?

AMERICA'S CAUSE

Start from the fact that America is made of persons (and their descendants) who crossed oceans to be different from the ones they left behind. From John Winthrop in 1630 to Ronald Reagan in the 1960s–1980s, our leaders have expressed America's primordial cause with the logic of Moses' Deuteronomy: uniquely blessed, Americans must not live as others do. Living by God's laws, we are gratefully to glorify Him and to inspire the nations to do likewise.[15]

The most politically relevant of these laws, the core of America's creed, is "all men are created equal." Until our own time all American politics, domestic and foreign, was based on the proposition that America is different because we are unique in observing "the laws of Nature and Nature's God." It follows that the rest of mankind waste corrupt lives in quarrels that mostly do not concern us. Unlike them, we mean to lead "quiet and peaceable lives," to develop human potential, gratefully to enjoy its bounty. It follows as well that the primary purpose of our foreign relations is to maintain and enhance that difference. Most Americans today would agree with Thomas Paine (1776) that we have no interest in "setting the world at defiance," and with Samuel Cooper (1780) that, unlike Rome, America has no interest in ruling others.[16]

Because living *differently* requires living *independently,* independence is America's primordial cause. Americans fought for it in 1775. For that they will fight eagerly today—not so eagerly for other things. The rhetoric of Woodrow Wilson and his imitators notwithstanding, Americans do not justify killing and dying to disturb the peace of those who leave us alone, or for any cause but our own. President George W. Bush's 2005 inaugural statement that America cannot rest or be free unless and until all the world is free (meaning that we can never be free, never at peace) may well be the most concise antithesis ever of what America is about.

But today, as in 1812, foreign powers and Muslim pirates respect our independence only to the extent we make them fear offending us. Hence our second cause was and must remain to *force respect.* America waged war on Britain in 1812 after bungling diplomacy, neglecting military preparations, against overwhelming odds, and with no strategy. With few exceptions (New Orleans in 1815 and the frigate battles), American warmaking stank. Nevertheless, after two decades in which Europe's powers had not taken America seriously and kidnapped US citizens, the war served notice that Americans would bite and claw as best they could at anyone who insulted and terrorized us. As Alexander Hamilton had argued to George Washington in 1790, while weak America should look the other way were Britain to transgress against us quietly and without bloodshed, were even the great power of the day to do it in a way that engaged America's honor, we should "punish aggression by the sword" regardless of cost.[17] Today as ever, in public life as in private, *leaving no favor unrewarded and no offense unpunished* is the key to respect and a rule of life that you neglect at your risk. Unless statesmen exact multiple eyes or teeth for one, fellow citizens end up paying with arms, legs, and heads.

Doing this requires a military force conceived to dismay and defeat enemies rather than to police peoples.[18] The navy is the clearest example of our perennial choice. Our Founders wanted a navy to ensure that the ocean that surrounds us, the "common possession of mankind,"[19] not be dominated by hostile powers. And Franklin Roosevelt stopped playing Hamlet to the Nazi threat in October 1940 by asking a question that, for

Americans, contained its own answer: "Does anyone seriously believe that we need fear attack while a free Britain remains our most powerful naval neighbor in the Atlantic? Does anyone seriously believe, on the other hand, that we could rest easy if the Axis powers were our neighbor there? If Great Britain goes down, the Axis powers will control the continents of Europe, Asia, Africa, Australasia, and the high seas. . . . It is no exaggeration that all of us in the Americas would be living at the point of a gun."

And, in fact, control of the sea is the natural use for our or any navy. Moreover, navies work best closest to their own shores and worst closest to enemy shores. But today's statesmen want a navy fit primarily to "project power" deep into the Old World's landmass. And so the US Navy struggles to come up with technologies and tactics to survive in shallow "littoral" environments dominated by hostile airpower, where hostile submarines can lurk quietly in the coastal topography. Our statesmen would do well to ponder the historic disaster that overtook Athens' navy—the high-tech wonder of the age—when it was committed to supporting a faraway land campaign.

Problem is, our statesmen's geopolitical priorities seem to be the reverse of what John Quincy Adams explained in President Monroe's famous "doctrine" as the American people's natural ones: What is nearest is dearest. For American statesmen up until Wilson this meant that, beyond our own territory, we would concern ourselves first with our hemisphere, then with the seas surrounding it, and finally with matters overseas only insofar as they threatened the more important ones. When Theodore Roosevelt boasted that had he been President he would have forestalled World War I by weighing in on Britain's side preemptively, he was not saying that Americans should have taken up Britain's causes against Germany, but rather that America's own cause in 1914—keeping danger as far away as possible—required throwing its weight against German aggression. Like Adams, TR would mind America's business, not Europe's. The difference between overseas involvements as American statesmen practiced them from Washington to TR and the way they have been practiced since is the difference between minding our own business and confusing ours with those of foreigners. And, of course, Washington, Adams, Lincoln and Seward, and TR were as clear as Thucydides, Livy (and, indeed, Augustus) had been that your interest, your involvement is related inversely to the distance from home. Serious nations concentrate power whence it radiates: at home. So America must husband honor, blood, and treasure to win the wars that affect us most.

Above all, George Washington taught, America's causes must habituate Americans to an American perspective.[20] In Washington's time, the Napoleonic Wars harmed America most by dividing Americans between partisans of Britain and of France. In the twentieth century, the Cold War's most dangerous aspect was that the Soviet Union's denigrations of America—imperialist, racist, and foredoomed—resonated with influential Americans and still do. The various perpetrators and supporters of terrorism, from Osama bin Laden to Middle Eastern dictatorships to Islamist websites, have picked up those very charges, and the very Europeans and Americans who echoed them during the Cold War kept it up in our time.[21] Whether charges originate abroad or at home is less relevant than the fact that they are always parallel, and sometimes joint, ventures. This happens in part because, as E. E. Schattschneider famously pointed out, conflict expands because weaker parties to quarrels tend to recruit allies far and wide; in part because involvement in others' quarrels naturally leads some among us to take one side or the other. Thus does partisanship over foreign quarrels augment partisanship over domestic ones. Washington and J. Q. Adams were right: We should enlist only in our own cause. And Lincoln pointed in the right direction: America is so endowed that once we get our causes right the rest will take care of itself.

ENEMIES

Enemies are those who trouble our peace by word or deed. Our Founding Generation taught that customs different from ours or downright offensive must not sway us from peace and goodwill toward their practitioners. Hence when Americans circa 1910 began thinking of Japan as an enemy they did so not because of its misogyny and tribal politics, but rather because of Japan's growing resentment of America and the prospect that its naval power might rob our West Coast of peace. But since 1945, regardless of what else Japan may be, it is no threat to our peace.

Neither should we today let China's ever-corrupt Oriental Despotism deter us from the finest relations with it any more than it deterred President John Tyler and Secretary of State Daniel Webster from goodwill toward the China of their day. Reciprocal fascination has always attracted Americans and Chinese to one another. But China is an enemy, much like twentieth-century Japan and Germany, insofar as it tries for hegemony over ocean islands, its possession of which would threaten our peace.

By the same token, though Wahabi Islam is alien and repulsive to us, it becomes our enemy only insofar as it animates Saudi Arabia, has billions of dollars at its disposal, and uses them to foment deadly hatred for Americans through the mosques and organizations it pays for in America as well. And again, while Saudi Arabia's treatment of women repels us, it cannot be our business. Nor is its royal family's kleptocracy. But the Saudis make it our business by being the linchpin of the oil cartel that manipulates prices not just to skin us but to coerce us. Hence the Saudi regime is our enemy. So are the Emirs of Qatar. Their television station that incites hate and murder of us is more our business than their business.

Russia in the eighteenth and nineteenth centuries was both the epitome of despotism and America's closest diplomatic ally—for the finest geopolitical reasons. Because the Russian fleet visited New York in the Civil War's darkest days, as Britain was building Confederate ships and France was trying to take Mexico, Lincoln referred to the Tsar as "my great and good friend." Only Communist rule made Russians think of greatness in anti-American terms. The Soviet Union was the archetypical enemy because its ruling Communist Party saw itself as foreordained to rule mankind, pointed to America as the "main enemy," attracted people from all over the world—not least influential Americans—to its cause, and bolstered that cause with more weapons of all kinds (with the exception of aircraft carriers) than the rest of the world combined. In our time, only the incapacity of Russia's post-Soviet leaders to transcend the Soviet mentality overrides a return to traditional friendship. But it does override it.

Most enmities are not so clear. Take Saddam Hussein. Ever an obscene tyrant, he might or might not have become an enemy. But he became one who led the Muslim world against us in the 1990s, after the US government had opposed his invasion of Kuwait. That invasion was aimed at the Arab world—not us. The US government reasonably might have decided to ignore him and his conquest, or to get along with him. But when, just as reasonably, it decided to oppose him, it hurt him enough to make him an enemy but not enough to finish him. *Unreasonable.* The point here is that some enmities impose themselves on us, while others result from our choices. But these have to be dealt with nevertheless.

Fully to understand who our enemies may be, we must be clear about who, specifically, if eliminated or constrained, will give us our peace. Again, Saddam Hussein is instructive. During the 1990 Gulf War, the official US government view was that Saddam's invasion of Kuwait was "the problem." Undo that, and "the new world order" would march peacefully on. A few US officials argued that Saddam himself was "the problem," the enemy to be undone. And indeed Saddam proved formidable in the 1990s as an inciter, financier, and architect of terrorism. But in the run-up to the 2003 US invasion, the State Department and especially the CIA argued that while Saddam himself had proved to be America's enemy, his Ba'ath party regime was not. Because this particular set of bureaucrats prevailed in Washington, the US government occupied Iraq, trying to preserve as much of the regime as possible. But the regime's remnants were the core of the Sunni "insurgency" that killed over four thousand Americans. They did this with the help of the Sunni states, Saudi Arabia, Egypt, Jordan, and the Gulf States, who deemed the Iraqi Sunni Ba'aths' primacy over the Shia important to their peace. But America's peace did not depend on that. Nothing quite so foredooms a war as misidentifying the enemy or indecision about whether someone or something is to be crushed or propitiated or left alone.

The Palestinians pose a more challenging version of the same problem. Palestinians pioneered modern terrorism and are in the front ranks of its contemporary adepts. But who is the enemy? Whose death or constraint would remove the Palestinians from terrorist ranks? The sad answer begins in 1921, when there was no Palestinian terrorism. Then, under the League of Nations' mandate, the British created the post of "Grand Mufti of Jerusalem," shepherd of Muslims in the Holy Land, and appointed an anti-Semitic monster named Mohammed Amin al-Husseini to it. Through the 1920s, his death or merely his sacking would have ended the murder of those Palestinians who got along with the Jews. By the 1930s and 1940s, al-Husseini's connection with the Nazis and his gang's increasing monopolization of Palestinian society meant that eliminating the problem, "the enemy," would have required killing several hundred. By the 1960s, when his pupil Yasser Arafat secularized his role with the help of the Arab world and the Soviet Union, "the enemy" amounted to several thousand. But not until 1993, when the Israeli and US government handed the Palestinian terrorists governmental power over the West Bank and Gaza and financed them lavishly, were these tens of thousands able to flush the remnants of peace from Palestinian society, fully to control the media, and to indoctrinate a generation into the glories of suicide bombing. Clearly, the Israeli practice of assassinating a few terrorist leaders here and there cannot eliminate an obstacle to peace that includes large segments of a population now bred to war.

Though Christianity disinclines us from paying due attention to it, the fact is that seldom is "the enemy" clearly marked off from the population at large. Trying to split "the enemy" from "the people" is perennial common sense. But while targeting leaders precisely, straining to spare civilians, should help convince the latter to separate their fortunes from the leaders', it also reduces the negative incentives for doing so. Yet crushing all who seem to stand in your way maximizes those negative incentives at the expense of positive ones. But what happens when "the people" are "the enemy"? There is no doubt that big parts of Germany's and Japan's populations in the 1930s and 1940s had "bought into" their leaders' murder cults and that they would not have let go had they not been decimated, humiliated, and starved. Just as surely, majorities of Serbs and Croats considered each other enemies in the 1990s, and only ethnic cleansing set limits to ethnic cleansing in what had been Yugoslavia. Nor is there any doubt that General William Tecumseh Sherman's 1864 ravaging of Georgia helped many Confederates feel that their cause was not worth the suffering. Since this has always been so, you must conclude that the contemporary American notion that war must spare innocent civilians can be counterproductive *to the extent* that "the problem" resides in whole societies. While no population is nearly as mobilized as the Palestinians, nevertheless everywhere "the problem," "the enemy," goes beyond a few leaders and even regimes.

So what does it take to undo widespread impediments to our peace? The only sensible answer *a priori* is: "it takes what it takes"—in short, unless we want to drift in the narcotic hope that movements and regimes that have prospered by whetting appetites for American blood will place themselves at risk to curb them, that those who have fought us will now fight for us, we have no reasonable choice but to do whatever intimidating, killing, starving, and humiliating it takes to dismay them, eliminate them, discredit them, quickly to accommodate whoever may dream of martyrdom, and to be indiscriminate enough so that those around them will turn on them to save themselves. The logic of war demands that you do this to whoever gives you cause: When you designate someone an enemy, you may be mistaken. But failing to acknowledge demonstrated enmity is worse than a mistake.

STRATEGY

Applying the term "strategy" to whatever anyone happens to be doing or wishing at the moment is latter-day American illiteracy. *The National Strategy of the United States,* published periodically by the National Security Council (NSC), and *The National Military Strategy,* published by the Department of Defense, are the official guidelines for the US National Security community. They consist of such wishes as preventing attack on the homeland in addition to a list of activities by various US government agencies. They make *no attempt to show why anyone should reasonably expect what the US government does to achieve the things the US government wishes.* But strategy is precisely the intellectual connection between ends and means: a concrete, reasonable plan for using what you've got to get what you want. The difference between "thoughtless acts" and "empty wishes" on one side and "strategy" on the other is *reason*. A plan qualifies as "strategy" insofar as the success of the operations it prescribes is reasonably likely to put your peace in your grasp and insofar as these operations are in your power to accomplish.

The self-contradictory term "exit strategy" came into use during the Vietnam War precisely because the war's managers had entered into the war without a plan for winning it, hence had failed to bring about an acceptable peace, and were yearning for any peace at all. Of course there should be a plan for ending any war or any other human activity. All human action aims at an end, at a state of rest. But where and how you stop depends logically on why you started. What do you want out of this activity? What's it worth to you? Just as farmers allocate equipment and schedule activities so that they may leave the field with crops, strategists assemble and direct forces so that they may leave the field with their fruit: victory. Game theorists and armchair imperialists may want to commit military forces to kill and die without a plan for peace. But the logic of war demands that the plan for "getting in" be the same as for "getting out"—namely, that it be a strategy for victory.

The logic of strategy requires that you constantly judge the *operations* you are planning by asking how likely it is that, were they to succeed, the enemy would be undone and your peace would happen. Are the tools necessary and proper to that success available, and are you up to using them? If not, it may be worthwhile to suffer in silence or to negotiate such peace as the enemy may give you—before fighting inflames passions. Are your operations aimed at something other than victory? Remember that phony war fools only the phonies who wage it. Are you bringing all of the available tools to bear as best you can? Forbearing any of them, for whatever reason, betrays your people and your troops.

The following cases illustrate the contrast between strategy and pretense thereof.

East Asia

To end America's post-1945 Peace of the Pacific, to establish its own, and above all to strengthen its regime internally, China is mobilizing substantial political and military forces behind a reasonable plan: squeeze Taiwan politically while preparing to isolate and possibly to invade it militarily. Meanwhile to the north, it uses North Korea's nuclear and missile programs (which, like all else in North Korea, exist at China's pleasure) to accustom South Korea to the prospect of a unified, Chinese-backed, anti-Japanese Korea. With Taiwan and Korea in hand, China would control Japan's trade routes, reduce it to subordinate status, and rule East Asia. The United States would have to choose between acquiescing or fighting from an inferior position. In short, China is preparing to win military mastery over the Western Pacific believing, reasonably, that the *growth of mastery itself* may deliver the prize peaceably by creating self-fulfilling expectations.[22]

For its part, the United States built Guam into a mighty base a thousand miles from the problem, helped Japan to build limited defenses against North Korean missiles, and continued to supply Taiwan with military equipment, albeit not top-of-the-line. The US Navy is also retooling its antisubmarine warfare with a view to fighting in the Taiwan Strait. But these tools are neither the best available nor reasonably calculated to succeed because the US government believes that preparing to win the fight would be provocative. Hence US military plans make sense as negative incentives that, added to the positive incentives of peacetime economics, should persuade the Chinese side to limit its noneconomic goals and activities.

In sum, while China aims to constrain American policy through military preparations, the US government hopes to constrain those preparations through economic incentives.

China's medium-range ballistic missiles, some 1,200 of them, most on mobile launchers and hence largely invulnerable to all but area nuclear strikes, line the Taiwan Strait ready either to support an invasion with precursor strikes or more likely just to close down the island's ports with conventional or chemical weapons. The few batteries of American PAC-3 ground-based interceptors and ship-based AEGIS lower-tier interceptors do not stand a chance against them, if only numerically. So China will have the capacity to isolate Taiwan, and everyone will know that. The United States could thwart that by deploying serious antimissile forces in Taiwan, and it could show that, in the crunch, it would attack China's missiles with nuclear weapons. But it will not do either. American aircraft carriers *might* help Taiwan maintain control of the air over the strait—*if* they could operate safely there. But China's submarines—no match for the Americans in the open ocean—are more than a match for US ships when they sit in the hollows of the continental shelf's bottom. And if they fire the 200-knot Russian "Skval" torpedoes at short range, the carriers are sitting ducks for them, as they are for the hypersonic Russian "Sunburn" cruise missiles that can be launched from destroyers, from nearby land, or from aircraft based there.

But isn't there a way to defend Taiwan without getting our carriers sunk? Yes, sure. Like all islands, Taiwan is unsinkable, a much better base for controlling narrow seas than are ships. The United States could prepare to dominate the Taiwan Strait from a fortified Taiwan and thus strike at the notion that its fall is inevitable—the psychological heart of the Chinese strategy. But the US government considers that option too provocative and even threatened to withhold delivery of already pur-chased F-16 fighter planes if Taiwan develops a land-attack cruise missile to shoot back at Chinese missiles on the mainland.

While China's ultimate goal is to push US influence out of East Asia, it cannot afford a US withdrawal so shocking to Japan as to convince this technically superior power to assume full responsibility for itself. Were Japan to do that, it could thwart China's overseas ambitions all by itself. So China wants American forces to remain in Japan, incapable of defend-ing it adequately and inhibiting it from taking charge of itself. But will both Japan and the United States play the roles China wants? The United States' diplomatic pretense since 1994 that it was stopping North Korea's nuclear programs, into which it involved Japan, only aggravated for the Japanese the reality that Korea has nuclear weapons, ballistic missiles, and is so protected by China that the United States actually subsidizes its regime nevertheless. Our statesmen's pressures on Japan to accept North Korea's transparent deceptions about its nuclear program convinced the Japanese that America would avoid confrontation with Korea and China at Japan's expense.

The Japanese realize that the United States is helping to defend Japan much like it is helping to defend the Taiwan Strait: suboptimally. Four batteries of PAC-3 land-based interceptors have substantial capacity to intercept slow warheads and very limited capacity to intercept fast ones. The US-Japanese sea-based AEGIS SM3 antimissile program is designed only to intercept missiles launched eastward from North Korea during the "early midcourse ascent phase."[23] This may protect Japan from some North Korean missiles, but not at all if they were launched from China, nor will the US program defend Japan from Chinese missiles. Most of all, the *scale* of these defenses would not be meaningful against a large-scale attack. The Japanese know that America has the resources to squeeze nuclear weapons out of North Korea and to defend Japan against missiles from anywhere. But they know that the Americans do not even defend themselves against Chinese missiles. So while the United States seems content with a military-political situation that moves inexorably in China's direction, it is an open question whether Japan will be.

In sum, the US approach to the Western Pacific does not amount to "strategy." Our statesmen prefer to imagine that the Chinese would rather not displease the United States than to exploit the "accumulated positional advances" they build to push America out. That hope is not entirely baseless: The American market is so important to China's regime that it may not be willing actually to press its winning military position to actual fighting. But the Chinese are betting that, as the years pass, as they deploy their military assets in the Taiwan Strait and their Korean proxy in the Sea of Japan ever more to maximize the chances of military victory in the crunch, the Americans and their allies' resistance will wane and their accommodations will increase. Regardless of whether fighting occurs, victory would be assured. That's strategy.

Eurasia

Post-Soviet Russia's regime is built on the premise that, in President Vladimir Putin's words, "the dissolution of the Soviet Union was the greatest geopolitical disaster of the century." Hence it aims to reconstruct as much Sovietica as possible. But the Putin regime does not dispose of its predecessor's apparatus for compelling either the Russian people or its own cadres. Because the cadres' loyalty depends largely on privileged access to extravagant lifestyles, which in turn depend on access to the world economy, it is no small vulnerability. Nevertheless, the regime has three assets of which the Soviet Union never disposed: Russia's main exports of oil and gas have brought lots of money with which to build armed forces while providing leverage on neighboring countries, including Europe. The Americans and the Europeans are deeply invested in the pretense that Russia is not an enemy. Above all, whereas the Russian people once blamed Communism for their misery, they now hold the rest of the world responsible for it and cheer their government's truculence.

Russia's approach to economics is strategically significant: Whereas China *earns* money by producing products that the world wants to buy at advantageous prices, Russia *takes it* by exploiting the cartelized oil market, exploiting captive customers, and trying to monopolize Eurasia's energy resources. Hence whereas China sees its pursuit of international ambitions constrained by the need to maintain access to the Western, especially American, markets, Russia's post-Soviet regime seems to have concluded that it can pursue its ambitions by combining the economics of taking with the politics of intimidation.

Russian strategy's operational objective has been to empty, and then to cancel the independence of the peoples whose assertion of it ended the Soviet Union. Ukraine's 46 millions are the most important of these because, were Russia to reincorporate them (Byelorussia, or Belarus with capital in Minsk, never was independent) it would reestablish de facto sovereignty over the Baltic States and Eastern Europe, with Western acquiescence. Thus Russia might again be a world power. But to break down Ukraine's will to resist, to prove to the peoples of Russia's "near abroad" and to the West that accommodating Russian ambitions is better for them than resisting with feckless Western support, Russia initiated a complex of operations in the Caucasus that serve as a strategic point of departure, prototype, and template.

The strategy's first premise, which applies to all of Russia's targets from Azerbaijan to Vilnius, from Abkhazia to Moldova, is the pretense that ethnic Russians and patriotic local peoples are being mistreated by local agents and dupes of the Western powers. Hence Russia must protect them, by armed force if necessary. The second premise is that regardless of how much any of the target peoples in the "near abroad" might identify with "the West" or value their connections with it, "the West" is unable or unwilling to relieve them, and geography makes it possible for Russia to constrain their access to "the West." Third, especially in the Caucasus, each Russian success in any given country makes it easier to impose Russia's political and economic price on every BTU of oil and gas flowing from Eurasia to the West.

The Caucasus—the land between the Caspian and the Black Seas, between Russia, Turkey, and Central Asia—is the home of Azeris, Armenians, Georgians, and countless other nationalities and subnationalities such as Mengrelians and Ajarians. The Caspian Sea basin, from Azerbaijan to Kazakhstan, ranks with the Middle East in reserves of oil and gas. Whether the region's landlocked peoples can sell it to the world without paying Russia's political and economic price depends on the availability of pipelines that bypass Russia and Iran. Geography dictates that these must pass through the Caucasus, especially Georgia. Unsurprisingly, that is where Russia deployed fully the tactics by which it served this strategy.

In 1991, Russia responded to Georgian independence by financing and providing physical backing for non-Georgian nationalities within Georgia as it did in Moldova and Ukraine. By 2001, Russian troops had occupied the Abkhazian and South Ossetian regions, expelling Georgians, effectively severing these places from the rest of the country so thoroughly that, by 2008, Georgia's efforts to reestablish authority there could be labeled "provocations." These triggered an invasion by one Russian motorized infantry army and two tank brigades, preceded by SS-21 ballistic missiles, supported by three hundred fighters and by a naval force that blockaded the Georgian coast. Georgia's four combat brigades had been trained by the Americans for counterinsurgency and for deployment in Iraq, not for resisting invasion. Simply, the Russians had local military superiority and used it. The regime basked in its people's cheers.

The Russians bombed all around the existing oil pipeline that leads from Azerbaijan to Turkey, and their troops occupied and then retreated and again occupied and retreated from the area where Western companies had planned a second and larger pipeline. The point, not lost on Ukrainians, Poles, Balts, and others similarly situated, was that Russia could and would do such things as it pleased and that getting along with Russia on Russia's terms was the best that the peoples of the "near abroad" could expect. In short, the Russian strategy aimed at Russia's greatness against Americans and Europeans at the expense of its neighbors. In operation, that strategy is war itself.

The worth of that strategy, however, depends strictly on the correctness of Russia's evaluation of Western statesmen's character. Against each of its neighboring nationalities, Russia's strategy is solvent, unquestionably. Even were all the neighbors in the long arc from Lithuania to Tajikistan to vow joint resistance, none could succor any other in time of need. Serious opposition could only come from the strategy's ultimate objectives, the Americans and Europeans.

The balance of hard political-military power is against Russia. Although the West cannot defeat each and every Russian foray into neighboring nationalities, it can so strengthen each that every such foray would be more difficult in initial execution and would be followed by enduring, Western-supported armed resistance. Were Russia's new, small professional army to spread, occupying the former Soviet nationalities, it would make itself terribly vulnerable. Nor will the Russian people provide a mass conscript army for such a task. Russia has arguably better and bigger strategic nuclear forces than the United States. But whereas such strategic superiority was meaningful in the 1970s and 1980s when it covered the Soviet Union's massive conventional forces poised to conquer Europe, it is quite useless in our time. At whom would Russia shoot those missiles, and why? There is no way in which using them could further its strategy. So Russia is formidable militarily only so long as the West does not augment its neighbors' hatred of it with weapons.

Russia's strategy is even more vulnerable economically than militarily. Fears that Russia might embargo its oil and gas to the world market are unrealistic. Since Russia does not feed itself and relies on money from oil and gas to buy food, one may ask to what extent the Russian people would endure hunger for the sake of a regime that cannot compel them to endure it. Absent the Soviet apparatus for repression, Russia's regime lives atop a population likely to abandon it if it became the cause of privations. It has to keep the money flowing in, not least because the oligarchs of which it consists derive their pleasures and powers from money, much of which and the enjoyment of most of which is in the West. Moreover, although they settle scores among themselves with gangland murders, disciplining them wholesale in Stalinist style is out of the question.

Hence sanctions on them personally and on their companies, seizure or freezing of their assets abroad, even mere disinvestment in Russian assets would strike at the regime's core. The financial markets' reaction to Russia's truculence—spontaneous and unsupported by Western governments—and the Russian regime's response are an indication of this. After Russia invaded Georgia, its stock market lost roughly half its value, and investors pulled some $35 billion in assets out of the country and cancelled plans for further investment. In world money markets, Russian borrowers were charged risk premiums. This led Vladimir Putin to tell the West that Russia did not want to be isolated economically. Were our statesmen worthy of their jobs, they would demand political-military payment for not isolating it.

Hence Russia's strategy differs from China's. The latter, appreciating what its opponents could do for themselves and wary of provoking them, aims to enmesh them in a compelling situation by steps, none of which lays down a gantlet. While China's progressive constriction of its opponents' options may be warlike, none of its steps is. But each of Russia's steps *is* warlike, lays down gantlets, and exudes contempt for its enemies. In this, contemporary Russia proceeds less like China or the Soviet Union and more like Nazi Germany: In 2008, Vladimir Putin's public belittling of Georgia's President and his undisguised contempt for his American and European supporters were most reminiscent of Hitler's behavior toward Czechoslovakia and Austria in 1938–1939. Adding insult to injury makes sense only against opponents with neither sense nor heart.

Strategy and Terror

Terrorism is a tool that states use in the service of strategy. But it is not itself a strategy, and terrorists *qua terrorists* do not have strategies. Various surveys show that perhaps 10 percent of respondents in the Muslim world, including Muslims in Europe and the Americas, somehow approve of killing innocent Westerners either in the name of Islam or of their race or country, for one cause or another. But those who take any part in terrorist organizations are a tiny slice of those inclined to, while fewer yet are effectively employees of the terrorist protostates, the Palestinian Authority, Hamas, and Hezbollah, none of which has the cogniscence or the capacity to strategize concerning the United States. Nor are the people who call themselves or on whom we pin the name al-Qaeda a "supergroup" that concerts a worldwide movement. Hence whatever thought any terrorist or sympathizer might have on what he and like-minded folk are doing or should do, *it makes little sense to think of "terrorism" or of "the terrorists" as having a strategy.*

Nevertheless, it is imperative to understand *the strategic situation* of the individuals, groups, and regimes involved in terrorism, namely, their insignificance and weakness *in absolute terms.* Once upon a time, the USSR's umbrella extended over the world's Syrias, Iraqs, and Irans, the PLO, and lesser vermin because they served Soviet strategy by demoralizing the West—not least because Progressive propaganda depicted them as expressing the non-Western world's just grievances. As long as the USSR lived, fear of provoking Soviet reaction inhibited US retaliation against them. But since 1989, the Muslim world's various secular, religious, and pretend-religious terrorists have served no state capable of protecting them, of *forcing* anything upon the West, much less of undoing the West.

They are irremediably vulnerable. The freelance terrorists scattered from Londonistan to Detroit stand out among, and are at the mercy of, Western majority populations. They may mount shooting sprees and bomb buses, but only until they elicit the locals' immune responses against their communities. Their survival depends *exclusively* on Western elites restraining Western societies from those responses.

The large, established terrorist groups are not strategically strong either, because the Muslim world's tyrannies where they live, move, and have their being are weak reeds. The tyrants sit atop parties or families that intrigue against them, which in turn sit on populations composed of ethnic or religious groups, many of which regard them as enemies. The politics by which they live consist of paying "security forces" and buying off opposition. The oil states' workers are foreigners. Their overequipped militaries are unreliable politically and stink technically. Their economies consume rent money, produce little of value, and cannot feed themselves. Unable to save themselves from any serious attack, they can be embargoed, blockaded, divided, invaded, and pushed out of livable areas. They can hurt Westerners only to the extent that these are so stupid as to mingle with them. Inured to disloyalty, they are ever ready to sell each other out—never mind their terrorists.

In short, the individuals, groups, and states that have caused havoc in the West have not done so by *force majeure*. Rather, their *force mineure* has sufficed only because the West has indulged them. They have pushed against open doors, found more acquiescence than they or anyone else imagined a generation ago. Were Westerners intent on war, and were the brightest of minds to elaborate a strategy to avoid their destruction, they would have little to work with. In short, *their strength is neither more nor less than our reticence.*

Hence it should be clear that neither the Muslim world's active terrorists nor those who inspire them, enable them, and wish them well pose problems that call for arcane strategizing on our part. Just as clearly, many well-placed Americans prefer we suffer terrorism at the level in which we are suffering it, hoping that it will decrease or not get worse, rather than do the things that would crush the terrorists. Why they prefer this to war is all-important. But it is *beyond our scope.*

Our scope is the art of war. So, for *our analytical purpose, let us imagine* that our society were intent on practicing that art, on establishing our peace over the dead or cringing bodies of terrorists, would-be terrorists, supporters, and sympathizers. Then what? By what plans might America secure the deaths of those who have taken arms against us, make terrorism repugnant to those who now find it attractive, and convince that 10 percent of the Muslim world who now take some pleasure in our discomfort to look on anyone who discomforts us as a mortal danger to themselves? What then might our strategy look like?

Our political objective—to make such people leave us alone—requires that the states that cultivate anti-American terrorists eradicate them. Because only they can do such things, American forces cannot and should not try to purge, to winnow, to police, much less to reform the regimes and societies that produce them. All we can do—and it is enough, and we can do it—is to make war on, to secure the death of, those among them of whom *we*—who are irreducibly responsible for our lives—conclude have *anything* to do with endangering our lives, starting with the regimes, while offering friendship to their opponents. This is akin to organic farming's deadly discipline: turning pests and weeds over to the tender mercies of their natural predators. By the logic of war, lively examples of what happens to those who give us offense motivate others to avoid their fates. The other side of that common sense coin is the lesson of which Secretary of State J. Q. Adams reminded President James Monroe in 1823, the lesson by which American statesmen lived for a century and that Wilson and his successors forgot: If you want others to leave you alone, it really helps to leave them alone too.

George W. Bush's *universally applauded* words of September 20, 2001, that we would *make no distinction* between terrorists and anyone who backs them, pointed the way to putting this commonsense strategy into operation: to *hold regimes liable* for the harm that comes from their jurisdictions, forcing them or their successors to eliminate the people who embody the terrorist causes, disabling and discouraging others from replacing them. Because causes consist physically of *inspiration, money, individuals, institutions, and evidence of success,* the strategy's logical objective is to destroy the above, *whatever it takes* to do that. Bush and his Administration neither followed this logic nor used these words according to their dictionary meaning. Let us see what these words mean and where the logic leads.

How important to terrorism is inspiration? Is it possible to imagine anti-American terrorism ceasing so long as there are TV stations that confect and beam the Sunni world's news and culture in ways that blame America for the Muslim world's troubles and incite those they anoint as victims to take vengeance on us? Their images of funerals stir guts, and their conspiracy theories indict us.[24] Arguably the principal one is al-Jazeera. The Emir of Qatar owns it. Our statesmen have given the Emir no incentive to shut it down, in part because he permits a US airbase next door, partly because prominent Americans have profitable deals with his family. For America this arrangement amounts to renting a base at the cost of protecting the manufacturing of political fertilizer for the troubles that the base's aircraft must deal with. Crushing inspiration could start with closing al-Jazeera. The Emir might well do it, if faced with a compelling alternative: It would not be difficult to turn the Qatar Peninsula over to its oppressed Shia population, who, for their own reasons, would deal harshly with the Emir's family and al-Jazeera's staff. The sight of the Emir caving or crushed would make it much easier for us to persuade other rulers to stop incitement.

Saudi Arabia is at once the biggest source of incitement and the biggest source of money for violent anti-American activities all over the world. Between 2001 and 2009, some $1 *trillion* in oil royalties flowed into Saudi Arabia, nearly all controlled by its royal family's 5,000-odd princelings, not counting cronies. Osama bin Laden was only the most visible of the Kingdom's many spoiled rich kids, whose schooling is Wahabism, who salve such consciences as they have by giving money to anti-Western causes. While the Saudi *government* sponsors only the biggest terrorist groups, such as Hamas, Fatah, and Islamic Jihad, it is difficult to think of any terrorist group that has not received money from the Saudi *regime*— which includes and transcends the government. In short, the Saudis incite and pay for anti-American terrorism because of who they *are*. It is impossible to imagine that they could do otherwise, and hence that the terror can end, so long as they are schooled, moneyed, and unaccountable as they are in our time. What would it take to change this fact?

It is true that our own regime's present proclivities and prejudices make cutting the Saudis off from money well nigh impossible. But it is just as true that actually doing the cutting would be easy. Instantly, US banks (and such other banks as value their access to the US banking system) can freeze the accounts of Saudi citizens. Saudi oil revenues can be placed in escrow accounts. Simultaneously, US forces can seize control of the main Saudi fields and loading centers almost without opposition, pushing the Wahabi Saudis back to their original tribal areas in the Arabian Peninsula's center. This would please mightily the coastal Shia tribes whom the Saudis oppress and who live nearest to the oil. The various foreigners who actually run the oil industry would also get a better deal. On the Red Sea side of the peninsula, US forces could help the tribes who lost to the Saudis in 1921, descendants of the Prophet Muhammed who chafe under Wahabism, to take their historic vengeance. To forestall the interior tribes' resistance, the United States can blockade to deprive them of food and essential maintenance, while letting it be known that the material and financial blockade would be lifted somewhat once the Saudi regime had been replaced, the Wahabis eliminated, and the tribes posed no danger to the world. That would be war.

Failure to meet war with war does not bring peace. America's 1979 failure to avenge Iran's seizure of our embassy in Teheran, US sovereign soil, and imprisoning our diplomats—textbook acts of war—was perhaps the most compelling evidence that anti-American terror is safe and profitable. This impunity also helped bind Iran's many factions to the regime. That is why ending Iran's impunity is essential equally to stopping its terror worldwide and to making Iran's regime vulnerable to its internal enemies. Easily, the US Navy can blockade Iran's essential imports of gasoline, as well as its exports of crude oil—crippling the country—until it turns over to US custody *our* list of malefactors. Any Iranian effort to retaliate by interdicting traffic in the Strait of Hormuz would hardly get out of port and end with the destruction of the bases from which it was launched.

But let us be clear: Persians and Shia *per se* are no more our enemies than Arabs and Sunni. Our strategic purpose is not to weaken Iran against its neighbors. Indeed, Iran is America's natural geopolitical ally. The presence of Shia minorities (and in some cases majorities) in Sunni-ruled countries argues powerfully for our working with them to bring down terrorist regimes. Our strategy just aims to make sure that anyone who harms America ends badly—for that's what it takes to be left in peace.

Deterrence

The surest path to unbloody victory is the prospect that fighting would result in bloody triumph. But if you try elegantly to "deter" the enemy without a military balance unbalanced on your side, and if there is any doubt you are willing, even eager, to reap that imbalance's fruits; if there is the slightest hint that you might not have your whole heart in the fight, above all if the enemy suspects that substituting deterrence for fighting is itself your chief objective, then you will end up having deterred yourself. Strategy is the opposite of bluff.

US "nuclear strategy" is the classic negative illustration. Herman Kahn's epigraph to *On Thermonuclear War* (1959) was, "The [American] planners seem to care less what happens after the buttons are pressed than they do about looking presentable before the event." Even prior to 1963, when Robert McNamara made Mutual Assured Destruction the perennial US nuclear policy, the emphasis on deterrence was so strong that American planners tailored US strikes largely to harm the Soviet Union rather than to spare harm to America. McNamara thought that he could insure America by ensuring that deterrence would "work" by making sure that a US retaliatory strike would kill 25 percent of the Soviet population and 50 percent of industry. Because the whole point was to deter war—not to fight it—it would not matter which Soviets lived or died, what was and was not to be destroyed. And to leave no doubt that the United States had no plans to fight, only to deter, our statesmen chose to build nuclear systems (the submarine-launched Poseidon C-4 and the land-based Minuteman II) that were least fit for killing and destroying the Soviets' own nuclear forces, but best fit only for killing persons and destroying civilian things in Russia.

This ran counter to the logic of war—which applies to nuclear weapons as well as to popguns: The only reason *why* you shoot is what happens *after* you shoot, *because* you shoot; moreover, the only people you want to kill, the only things you want to destroy, are the ones that endanger your life and peace. By contrast, the Soviets planned for nuclear war according to the logic of war.[25] Since civilian damage on America would have done them no good, the Soviets planned to use about a third of their missiles, the SS-17s, -18s, and -19s (designed specifically for this purpose) to destroy US missiles and bunkers. The rest of the Soviet force would have held disarmed America hostage. The Soviets were not eager to fight. They wanted to win by deterring. But *deterring by planning to win* was reasonable because carrying out their plan would have minimized damage to themselves and placed the Americans at their mercy. Their plan was for real, whereas the Americans' plan was bluff advertised as bluff, because carrying it out would only have made matters worse for America.

OPERATIONS

Just as strategy must serve the purpose of peace, operations must serve the purpose of strategy. But the operations of war follow their own logic: Just as screwdrivers are useful only on the screws for which they are fit, so ground, naval, and air forces, diplomacy, bribery, and subversion will serve your strategy only when you use them in the ways for which they are fit. Seldom is good strategy served by operations that do not make sense in and of themselves.[26]

Not least among Thucydides' poignant passages is his description of the Athenian navy's demise through misuse. Fit to roam and dominate the high seas with fifth-century BC high-tech, the navy had been sent to Syracuse's harbor to support a land campaign. The enemy closed the harbor and so hemmed in the Athenians that they could not draw the ships out to dry. Encumbered and their timbers sodden, the Athenians were overwhelmed by crude barges. By the same token in 1943, the Wehrmacht's prized Panzers, fit to rule fast-moving battles, were crushed at Kursk when they frontally assaulted deep fortifications. And the US Air Force's fleet of F-105 Thunderchiefs, fit for delivering nuclear bombs as part of coordinated frontal attacks, ended as wrecks in Southeast Asian jungles, expended piecemeal in a multiyear campaign to attrite North Vietnam's supply lines to the South.

For what operations, then, are US forces fit? What are they good for, and what does "proper use" mean?

Ground Operations

The United States has never been, is not, and never can be a great land power—except in North America. Just as our interests in the Old World's depths are limited, so is our power. By itself, the United States could not have defeated the Wehrmacht in Europe. It is very highly doubtful it could have stood up against the Red Army as part of NATO. Geography is the reason. Land forces from overseas are at big disadvantages. Our Army and especially our Marines are fit for expeditions to the world's rim lands—the shorter, the better. The Gulf War of 1991 was a textbook example of *operational* good sense: B-52 area bombing of Iraqi forces in Kuwait prepared the way for precise strikes by attack aircraft, followed by missile-firing helicopters, followed by tanks. Infantry closed the deal by pointing its muzzles at the survivors emerging from their holes. But in Iraq after April 2003, day after day, year after year, US troops on foot or in armored vehicles patrolled Iraqi streets that were replenished minefields—and some two-thirds of US casualties came from walking and driving around in them. There is no military reason for living in replenished minefields. The US government tried to lower casualties by providing the troops with more body armor and more heavily armored vehicles. But no amount of steel can make sense of using infantry as police, much less in minefields. In short, for the strategy to make sense the operations have to make sense.

Naval Operations

Few nostrums are as misleading as "control of the sea depends on ships." In fact, ships are a good second to the primary method: controlling the land that controls the sea. In fact, the Mediterranean became the Romans' *mare nostrum* after Rome had conquered all its shores, and nineteenth-century Britain dominated the oceans not so much because they were crawling with British ships but rather because it controlled the lands around the passages to and from the oceans: Gibraltar, Suez, Singapore, Cape Town, the Falklands. In World War II, the Allies' Battle of the Atlantic consisted of reaching out from bases in the United States, Canada, Iceland, the British Isles, and ultimately the Azores until the German U-boats had nowhere to hide. In the Pacific, the ships served as bases for conquering the bases that really mattered, the islands. The US Navy pioneered its remarkable method of supplying fighting ships from cargo ships steaming alongside only because its failure in the 1920s and 1930s to fortify Guam and the Philippines had left it without bases in the Western Pacific. The logic of naval operations, then, begins with bases— especially given the range and capability of modern land-based aircraft.

For US naval operations in our time, this means that abandoning our naval air station in Iceland as well as the base complex in the Philippines were mistakes to be rectified, and that building a base in Taiwan and strengthening the ones in Japan will make it possible for our Navy to keep our peace in the Western Pacific, defending these key islands more surely and with fewer ships than would be needed without the bases. Bases and ships, however, make sense only in the perspective of a sensible hierarchy of objectives. The most important of our naval operations is controlling midocean from bases in the United States. The ships being designed and the crews trained for projecting a little conventional power onto distant shores against small-time enemies will be useless for defending the major islands, and ships wasted in halfhearted efforts to defend these islands will not be available for controlling the middle of the ocean.

Aerospace Operations

Because the US Air Force is built on the "airpower" myth, according to which strikes from the air determine the outcome of wars, it is America's biggest obstacle to intelligent air operations. The Air Force became perhaps the chief advocate for Robert McNamara's Single Integrated Operations Plan, reducing US military strategy to mere destruction of the Soviet Union; it lent itself to bombing campaigns against North Vietnam without logical issue; and it led the US government to advertise in advance that it would win its 2003 campaign in Iraq primarily by striking Baghdad "strategically" to produce "Shock and Awe." For the sake of what it calls strategic operations, the Air Force treated support of ground forces as a stepchild, refused any role in naval bombing, built lots of satellites but neglected to defend them, and has been perhaps the most potent intragovernment lobby against missile defense.

The myth of airpower led the Air Force to neglect *controlling* orbital space. The semipermanent, predictable location of satellites makes it possible for any country to defend its own satellites and destroy others'. Moreover, because the places whence ballistic missiles are launched are most easily accessible through orbital space, it is the natural location from which to defend against them. Hence control of orbital space eases, or even makes possible, a variety of military operations. It is achievable by real weapons. This is not the place to discuss such weapons.[27] Our point is simply that protection of satellites and preventing missiles from reaching us through space is a natural focus of American military operations and that it should be confided to people interested in doing it.

WHAT WAR IS NOT

The most contemporary versions of unseriousness about war are rooted in two insights from circa 1990: Convinced by Francis Fukuyama's article "The End of History?," our statesmen became sure that the era of conflict between serious forces about serious things was over. Martin van Creveld's *The Transformation of War* convinced them of that dogma's military counterpart, namely, the destructiveness of conventional as well as of nuclear weapons had made "Clausewitzian war" irrational. No longer would war be waged in pursuit of political objectives according to reasoned strategies.[28] In the future, violence would be by and against irrational primitives. These insights let our statesmen and not a few soldiers imagine that their job would be merely to prevent the subrational quarrels of primitives and terrorists from contaminating our post-Clausewitzian magic kingdom. All they had to do was suppress rogues in the world's backwaters through "Military Operations Other than War." In these "small wars," mere persistence by constabulary forces would ensure success.

And so they rushed to equip and employ US forces for "humanitarian intervention" and "peacekeeping." As well, they sought to prevent or remedy "failed states" and "ethnic cleansing" through "nation-building." The ensuing operations have been what used to be called "imperial wars," including occupations. Since such things are not about defeating enemies, they are not wars. But since they involve killing people and violently getting in the way of what they want, they are not peace. They have brought America more enemies and deepened our statesmen's unseriousness.

In Chapter 1 we saw that the words "humanitarian intervention" and "peacekeeping" only obfuscate war's hard choices. Now let us look at our time's most egregious obfuscation of war: the post-2003 occupation of Iraq, in which our statesmen managed to conflate and confuse multiple figments of their imagination.

SORCERERS' APPRENTICES IN IRAQ

As commonly used, the term "Iraq War" denotes *not* the March-April 2003 campaign that overthrew Iraq's government, but rather the events that followed our statesmen's decision to occupy Iraq indefinitely. That is because the occupying, not the overthrowing, cost over 4,000 American lives versus 138, occasioned the ethnic cleansing of Iraq's previously heterogeneous parts, embroiled America in the Muslim world's sectarian quarrels, weakened it, and discredited its statecraft. The G. W. Bush Administration and its critics equally referred to this as "the war." But what the US government did in Iraq after April 2003 was not a war or an occupation. It was an illogical consequence of the March-April campaign, not a logical one. It neither made peace nor built a nation. Indeed the words most often used to describe it don't fit. Rather its reality was a compendium of often contrasting prescriptions by the Liberal Internationalists, Neoconservatives, and Realists who vied within the Bush Administration. Each recipe self-referential and confused, together they made a mess full of lessons.

Occupations put capstones on wars by killing, imprisoning, and deporting the enemy's troublesome remnants. After World War II, the Soviets crushed resistance to their brutalities. The Western occupiers who weeded Western German and Japanese societies faced no insurrections because all knew they would have dealt with them by resuming the war. But the US troops that stayed in Iraq after April 2003 neither capped a war nor cleansed a society. Rather, because they operated in police mode with shifting, conflicting guidance about whom to police, they *suffered* a war.

The 2003 invasion itself was not a war because President G. W. Bush never resolved the conflicts within his Administration about what America's problems in Iraq might be, who embodied them, and what was to be done about them. Hence the White House's many pronouncements on Iraq's relevance to terrorism, on its role in the Middle East, its regime's brutality, its defiance of UN resolutions, its "Weapons of Mass Destruction"—were about Iraq only incidentally. Essentially, they reflected struggles for primacy among factions, tendencies, in and around the US government. Expressed in generalities, mutually contradictory, and of questionable sincerity, these pronouncements left the troops that invaded Iraq in March 2003 merely with the default mission to destroy Iraq's armed forces and capture a handful of government officials. This they accomplished by circa April 10, 2003. Hence Bush's "mission accomplished" speech on April 30, 2003, was fully justified, strictly speaking.

But what mission? The art of war consists above all of defining the mission, the accomplishment of which brings you peace. The US armed forces' victories in the battles between March 20 and April 9, 2003, could hardly have accomplished missions the government had not defined or that it had not taken seriously.

Prior to the invasion, on March 10, 2003, George W. Bush had signed a secret directive to establish a provisional Iraqi government to which American troops would turn over sovereignty some six weeks after conquering Baghdad. *There was to be no occupation.* As this default plan was unfolding in the latter part of April, American troops were preparing to leave to the applause of some four-fifths of Iraqis, and it was not unreasonable to hope that Saddam Hussein's violent overthrow might inspire similar governments to accommodate our peace to save their own. But as April turned to May, even as General Jay Garner was accomplishing his assigned mission to recruit an Iraqi interim government, President George W. Bush decided to occupy Iraq indefinitely and recruited Paul (Jerry) Bremer to run the country. Whether George W. Bush ever decided what the occupation was to accomplish is hidden in the same welter of conflicting statements and actions by the US government's semiautonomous parts that befogged the purpose of the original invasion.

President Bush did not take responsibility for running Iraq by deciding among alternatives of what he would do to Iraq and how he would do it. Rather, the decision to occupy seems to have been the result of private entreaties by Secretary of State Colin Powell, National Security Adviser Condoleezza Rice, and British Prime Minister Tony Blair on behalf of Saudi and other Arab demands, backed by the State Department and CIA. Each of these parties had their own ideas about what and how. But regardless of what any of the Americans may have thought they were doing, the very fact of US domination served the Arab governments' primordial objective: to prevent Iraq's Shia majority (three out four Iraqi Arabs are Shia) from dominating, and hence to give the Sunni minority the chance to maximize their role. Thus the US occupation was important to the Saudis' peace. But its relevance to America's peace was never clear.

Officially, the US government intended its occupation to produce "a united, democratic Iraq." But the 2005 Iraqi elections confirmed that "democracy" had to mean rule by, of, and for the Shia majority, who insisted that their Constitution allow them effectively to rule the Sunni or to govern themselves apart from them. And since the fundamental fact of Iraqi life had been and would remain precisely the struggle between Sunni and Shia, the moment the US government began to be an obstacle to the Shia pushing their advantage as they pleased, objectively it would put itself at war with the Shia. "Unity," on the other hand, was the banner under which the Sunni fought for control of Iraq's armed forces and intelligence services—the very tools they had used to oppress the Shia under Saddam.

The Sunni mounted an insurrection to bloody the Americans and the Shia, to force them to give them power. This effectively meant war between the Americans and the Sunni. So between 2003 and 2006, even as the Sunni states were decrying the American occupation publicly, and privately financing the killing of US soldiers, even more privately they were lobbying American statesmen to prolong the occupation and to take fuller control of it.

American statesmen floundered, never facing up to the reality of other peoples' contradictory objectives. Officially, the US government described "the war" as between "extremists" of all sects on one hand and against the "moderates" of all sects on the other, with America on the moderates' side. Thus while others were fighting for concrete objectives framed with proper nouns, the Americans were pursuing apolitical phantoms of their own imagination.

Foremost among these phantoms after 2004 was "al-Qaeda in Mesopotamia" (AQIM). In practice, AQIM were persons whom various Iraqis identified as such. There is no doubt that those so identified were enemies of those who identified them. But US intelligence took their word that these were also America's enemies. In practice, US forces did not go after certain people because they were "members" of AQIM, whatever that might mean. Rather, they designated AQIM as whomever they clashed with. And of the few who called themselves that, there was seldom evidence of contact with much less subordination to the organization that had existed in Afghanistan prior to 2001. In short, the designation AQIM was less a matter of epistemology than of convenience.

In our statesmen's collective minds, these apolitical military operations were to screen the political maneuvers that would deliver the prize: a "united, democratic Iraq." The initial US occupation plan was to rid Iraqi public life of the Ba'ath party operatives who had tyrannized it, to hold elections as soon as possible, and to let the winners run the country. By the end of 2003, Colin Powell's State Department, George Tenet's CIA, and

Condoleezza Rice's NSC staff wanted to delay elections. The US government set up an interim—wholly puppet—government under Iyad Allawi, a longtime CIA agent and Ba'athist, dedicated above all to bringing as many Ba'athists into as many positions of power as possible in the hope of satisfying Iraqi Sunnis and their Saudi backers. But this miscarried because the Shia held the Americans to the promise of elections. In January and December 2005, Iraqis voted their separate identities, and the Sunni wound up with less than a fifth of the seats. Thereafter, our statesmen sought to convince the election's winners to pay less attention to those who had voted for them than to those who had voted against them. Thus they proved as illogical about the logic of politics as they had of war's.

Through 2005 the insurgency continued to grow and to take huge tolls of Shia through bombings, shootings, and abductions. This led the Shia to place more of their security in the hands of their own militias, which the Americans called "death squads," and to reject American demands for political concessions to the Sunni. But after Sunni bombed the Shia Samarra golden mosque in February 2006, the United States could no longer prevent war's logic from biting the Sunni: The majority Shia death squads earned their reputation, went on a historic rampage, and essentially won the civil war. By the end of that year, few if any Sunni were left in Shia areas—most of the country outside Kurdistan. As a result, in late 2006 the Sunni clamored for American protection and offered to stop shooting at Americans.

This led our statesmen to invent a fresh phantom: "reconciliation" between "moderate Sunni" and "moderate Shia." That sounded familiar, but the definition had changed significantly. "Moderate Sunni" or "awakened Sunni" or "patriotic Sunni" were now defined as those who agreed to stop shooting at Americans in exchange for protection from the Shia, money, arms, and effective sovereignty over Sunni majority areas. "Moderate Shia" were now defined as the Supreme Council of the Islamic Revolution (SCIR), whose party was in the government and which disposed of its own militia, the Badr Brigade. But while our statesmen and even some soldiers fantasized that these groups had made common cause with us against "terrorism," "extremism," and other abstract nouns, reality was more concrete. Essentially, the Americans were delivering control of

Sunni areas to favored Sunni and of Shia areas to favored Shia, helping them to put down their rivals.

On the Sunni side, Sheiks and Ba'athist generals proposed to the Americans essentially the same deal they had made in Mosul in 2003 and in Fallujah 2004: In exchange for a mutual cease-fire that would reduce US casualties, the Americans would pay, equip, and leave their forces to rule their areas, and to determine election outcomes in them. Even more than before, the Sunni promised to join in fighting the Americans' enemies among themselves—that is, those who *they themselves* point out as common enemies—to be designated AQIM.[29] That such were the Sheiks' enemies there can be no doubt. Believing they were enemies of America's peace was an act of faith in the Sheiks. Delighted, the US government called this an "awakening," baptized the groups "concerned citizens" and "sons of Iraq," and made them the centerpiece of its "surge strategy" of 2007. But to what had they "awakened"? With what were they "concerned"? Whatever their agenda, you can be sure their targets had proper names.

The SCIR politicians around Iraqi Prime Minister Nouri al-Maliki and Abdel-Aziz al-Hakim and their Badr Brigade were in an analogous position. Having defeated (for the moment) the Sunni challenge to the Shia power over most of Iraq, SCRI looked upon the Sadr movement and its Mahdi militia as the most serious challenge to its power and to cementing it in future elections. Displeased that the Americans had effectively given the Sunni-majority areas over to armed Sunni groups, they demanded that the Americans support them in disarming and disempowering their Sadrist competitors in Shia land.

The Americans were delighted to comply, called it a strategy, and claimed victory. By 2008 some 99,000 Iraqis, mostly Sunni, were receiving $300 per month from the United States—their Sheiks and other leaders small fortunes—plus arms and training. One Adel Mashdani, a former Republican Guard officer, boasted to *The New York Times* that he had renamed his outfit, the National Iraqi Resistance council, an insurgent group, the Fadhil Awakening Council. Others were quite open that they welcome working with Americans—but against the Iraqi government, whose leaders they called Iranian agents because they are Shia.[30]

But on October 1, 2008, the Americans began transferring the administration and payments of the "Awakening Councils" and "Sons of Iraq" in Baghdad city to the Iraqi government, dominated by the Shia. The Sunni felt trapped. Talk of resuming the insurgency was rife. But though well-armed, in Baghdad they were surrounded by the enemy.[31] By the same token, however, the "Councils" and "Sons" in majority Sunni areas had almost as much power to keep the Baghdad government at bay as did the Kurds in Kurdistan.

In sum, the Americans' purchase of a truce with one of the war's sides and joining the other against its internal enemies did not, and could not, change anybody's agenda. At best the two US clients would be content with control of their areas, leaving each other alone. Unlikely. But were it even so, this would have nothing to do with the cleverly phrased objectives on behalf of which our statesmen expended so much blood and treasure. And, of course, if any of those to whom the Americans had turned over power were to find it convenient to host anti-American terrorism, they could always attribute it to elements they do not know and cannot control. So while you cannot know who will exercise what option, you should subject any claims of an American victory to the question: *Who precisely won what?*

VICTORY

"Declare victory and withdraw!" Thus Senator George Aiken coated with irony his 1965 proposal to accept defeat in Vietnam. The American statesmen of that era proved to be losers—but not yet such unserious losers as to imagine that pretentious words could substitute for shabby reality. A generation later, American statesmen routinely formulated national objectives in meaningless terms, fudged the designation of enemies, accommodated rather than eliminated them, and called it success. In the case of Iraq, for example, too few in 2008 disputed that the US government had won some kind of victory by reducing US casualties through deals with Iraqis who had been shooting at Americans. When pressed, they argued that the reduction in fighting was good mainly because, as Michael Rubin argued to the House Foreign Relations Committee, it may provide "the space for Iraqi politicians to advance reconciliation efforts."[32] But what, precisely, would any given relationship between groups in another land have to do with our peace? Don't hold your breath for an answer.

In fact our statesmen never decided among themselves what part of the terrorist problem Iraq posed, hence how invading Iraq would solve it, hence who our enemy was, and therefore what victory would mean. Much less did they decide why they were occupying the country. They did not choose among competing analyses of the problem and then settle on a coherent plan for victory against concrete enemies. They compromised with one another, adjusted their definition of enemies and of victory to fit what they happened to be doing at any given time, and claimed that it was all so very complex.

VICTORY AND PEACE

But victory in our time is as self-evident as ever. If you can't celebrate it in peace and safety, with flags flying, bands blaring, and enemies dead or cringing, chances are it's not the real thing. Among other things, victory means being unencumbered to deal with tomorrow's problems. Remember that the natural objective in any fight is to win, to get it over with— not to pass the troubles on to your grandchildren—as the Truman and Eisenhower Administrations passed on their so-called success in Korea. So if your success leaves your wounded sore, if it is not such as to console the dead's beloved, if it exposes their children to the same dangers, and if it ties America down to endless struggles, then think better of George Aiken: Honest defeats are better for America than pretend-victories. At least you can learn from them, above all, that the real peace that real victory brings is worth the price.

CHAPTER 7

////////////////////

USE INTELLIGENCE,
NOT INTELLIGENCE

Intelligence is not to be confused with intelligence.
—DANIEL P. MOYNIHAN

If statesmen grasp their art's essential elements; if they understand their
country's needs and how they may be served by diplomacy, war, and finance; if they know their circumstances, their friends, and their enemies; and if they have a reasonable strategy for securing their peace,
secret information can help. To the extent they lack any of these, information from special sources is likely to deepen indecision and ensnare
them in intellectual traps of their own making.

In the autumn of 1962, fleeing Cubans reported that Soviet troops
were building bases for big missiles on their island. President John F.
Kennedy, under growing public pressure to do something about it, was
hoping that they were merely antiaircraft. But air-reconnaissance photos
left no doubt that they really were the newest nuclear-tipped Soviet
models already in Eastern Europe. In Cuba, they were targeting America
and solidifying Kennedy's image for inept weakness. He had to act. But
before entering into the complex of public relations, diplomacy, and
military alerts known as the Cuban Missile Crisis, Kennedy ordered two

low-altitude photo-reconnaissance flights to get close-ups (at the cost of one pilot). Since these could not have revealed anything actionable, they were not intelligence about the missiles any more than a *Playboy* centerfold is intelligence about females. We begin to grasp the difference between information and intelligence by asking: "What would you do with this tidbit that you would not do without it? What difference does it make?"

The black arts of intelligence and subversion are so attractive—especially to those who know little about them—because of the truisms that knowledge of foreigners' secrets may let us avoid fights or win them cheaply, and that whereas economic force is blunt, diplomacy amounts to asking, and war is hazardous, it can be cheap and effective to put words in the right ears, coins in the right pockets, or bullets in the right heads. But information is useful only insofar as you make intelligent use of it, and even inherently useful knowledge does not craft plans reasonably to succeed, or square your ends with your means. You should think of intelligence as of any other tool of statecraft, from infantry companies to diplomatic demarches: How does this help me to focus America's power on someone or something that, if overcome, will give us what we need? Above all, no lack of intelligence absolves you from the duty to act on whatever information you may have. As for the stratagems of subversion, the US government is the only one that ever mystified them by assigning them exclusively to an intelligence agency, the CIA.

Nevertheless, supposing that intelligence and subversion are extraordinary to the logic of ordinary tools, our statesmen have taken them as further excuses to slip explaining to themselves what they could reasonably expect from them, for skipping the discipline of old-fashioned, intelligent statecraft. But you must remember that when secret information or actions clash with common sense, the safe bet is on the latter. When statesmen treat intelligence officers as soothsayers, when they use them as excuses for not acting on prima facie facts and plead, "How could I act? I didn't have enough intelligence," or "Intelligence made me do it; given the intelligence, I acted the only way I could," they evade their responsibilities, pervert intelligence as well as statecraft. Success in international affairs depends on grasping a situation's fundamentals, on telling friends from enemies, choosing the right objectives, deciding on war and peace, and executing reasonable strategies. For all this, elected officials must rely on intelligence in the ordinary meaning of the word.

The following contrasts how the US government does intelligence with the timeless logic of espionage—a logic that applies to satellites as well as to sleuths. It shows how thorough has been the US intelligence community's rejection of the quality-control function known as counterintelligence (CI), and why that function is the sine qua non of seriousness in this business. It contrasts the US practice of producing "estimates," which hide opinion behind the pretense of knowledge, with the need to act on the basis of what you know for sure and taking responsibility for your judgments. It also explains the age-old, many-faceted ways in which governments interfere in each others' internal affairs.

THE MYTHS OF 1947

The system conceived in the aftermath of World War II brings out the worst in producers and consumers of intelligence alike. Against the advice of the US government's operating departments (State, the military services, Treasury, Justice), the National Security Act of 1947 organized US intelligence largely at the behest of veterans of the wartime Office of Strategic Services (OSS), which President Harry Truman had disbanded at the end of 1945. The argument for a central intelligence agency responsible directly to the President rested on the myth that America had been surprised at Pearl Harbor because no agency existed to "pull together" the information relevant to the Japanese attack, which was diffused within the US government. This was false. In 1941 Army cryptologists had decoded the Japanese message that foretold the attack. They had gotten it through to top officials, who first showed little interest and then warned Pearl Harbor by a routine message that sat in the inbox during the attack. The problem the CIA was created to fix was a myth of its own making.

The system midwifed by that myth cuts against the logic of the craft, which is that armies and other organs of government gather intelligence to serve their operations. Information is intelligence ONLY insofar as it serves them. By nature, intelligence is scouting. Until and through World War II, each of the operating branches of government that dealt with foreign affairs—including the Federal Bureau of Investigation (FBI), which dealt with the foreign ends of domestic problems, chiefly in Latin America—gathered and analyzed the intelligence it needed. As a result, US officials often knew more than they wanted to know: hence Secretary of State Henry Stimson's 1929 statement that gentlemen don't read each others' mail. They lacked good judgment, not information.

World War II's OSS had been an anomaly: Chartered by President Roosevelt, its usefulness to the rest of the government was much disputed. A 1945 report commissioned by Roosevelt argued that OSS had not served America well:

> British intelligence commanders regarded American spies "as putty in their hands." In China the Nationalist leader Chiang Kai-shek had manipulated the OSS to his own ends. Germany's spies had penetrated OSS operations all over Europe and North Africa. The Japanese embassy in Lisbon had discovered the plans of OSS officers to steal its codebooks—and as a consequence the Japanese changed their codes, which "resulted in a complete blackout of vital military information" in the summer of 1943. . . . How many American lives in the pacific represent the cost of this stupidity on the part of OSS is unknown. . . . " The almost hopeless compromise of OSS personnel makes their use as a secret intelligence agency in the postwar world inconceivable.[1]

Nevertheless, the National Security Act of 1947 established a Central Intelligence Agency like OSS, but more so. Concentrating the nation's intelligence resources on national priorities was to eliminate duplication and more efficiently to provide whatever information the Navy, the Treasury, and others might need. Centralized analysis would be free of the several departments' parochial prejudices and self-serving temptations. Reality turned out differently.

Policymakers at State, Army, Navy, Treasury, and so on sent wish lists to CIA, assuming it had a crystal ball. But early on they got into the habit of putting the intelligence cart ahead of the policy horse, as if learning the nature of their task through intelligence were logically and chronologically prior to formulating plans. So, contrary to the logic of intelligence, they levied "intelligence requirements" in generalities—not to support specific plans, but rather to help "maximize options." Questions framed mostly in general terms encouraged US intelligence to answer with opinions. Thus the intelligence community does not ask, "How must we shape ourselves to answer this question?" but rather "What do we have on this?" and, above all, "What do we really think about that?" In short, US intelligence became a classic producer-dominated system, with bias unleavened by responsibility. Intelligence officials have competed to control or "spin" the product for intramural US government purposes. US intelligence knows much less about the world than you think and feels itself entitled to command you to think as it wishes.

Most pernicious has been the intelligence community's claim—which executive officials never rejected forcefully enough—that what they gather defines the boundaries of "what is out there" and that its consensus judgments are official truth, dissent from which is illegitimate. Instead of enlightening American statecraft, US intelligence ended up beclouding it.

Let us see what intelligence is properly about.

COLLECTION

By nature, each military, diplomatic, or economic operation defines the path to be scouted out: the information essential for success. Properly, that path should dictate the human and technical means of intelligence necessary for scouting it. Hence the very notion of all-purpose intelligence collection based on the best technology and the best people—the essence of the US system—is nonsense.

Machines

This is easiest to see with regard to technical systems. Machines see and hear strictly what they are specifically designed to see and hear. They are deaf and blind to all else. Hence, when we design them, willy-nilly we decide to see and hear some things and not others, in ways that will be useful for some purposes and quite useless for others. Merely upgrading a machine's technology leaves intact the virtues and vices inherent in its design. Alas, we tend to imagine otherwise.

Consider, for example, imaging satellites. Beginning in the early 1960s, the presence in orbit of one or two KH-9s (wide-angle photos) and KH-8s (close-ups) provided glimpses of the Soviet heartland. Glimpses: because low-orbit satellites speed around the globe in ninety minutes and, since the earth rotates underneath them, they revisit any given spot only every eighteen hours. When they do, it may be nighttime or cloudy. They cannot stare at any spot and, at best, could photograph anything a few times per month. But since the amount of film they carried was very limited, it was reserved mostly for the few places already known to be interesting. When the KH-11 digital camera satellite replaced them in 1976, it brought better optics, finer imaging resolution, a wider field of view, and online, near-real-time transmission of images. But it did not change the fact that the one or two in orbit could take only glimpses and that its targets knew pretty precisely what it could see, when, and, of course, that it could not penetrate darkness, clouds, or roofs, much less intentions. Nor, of course, could it provide a coherent picture of anything happening quickly or over areas not imaged. Nevertheless, CIA wallpapered its inner lobby with close-ups of downtown Moscow, giving the impression that it "knew."

Knew what? To enable what? The sum of glimpses gave the US government a general idea of the size, quality, and location of the Soviet Union's military forces as well as of its infrastructures. Beyond the wherewithal for playing guessing games among ourselves, that level of knowledge would have sufficed to support the US Strategic Air Command's war plan of the 1950s: disgorging the then-massive US nuclear arsenal on an "optimum mix" of Soviet military and civilian fixed, known targets.

But such satellites are scarcely relevant to military operations. To fight the Gulf War of 1991 (other than bombing infrastructure), the US armed forces needed up-to-the-minute knowledge of the location of mobile forces rather than expensive, high-quality digital images of fixed installations. Even the much greater presence of armed air reconnaissance (4,000 missions over Iraq in January 1991) failed to find even one mobile missile launcher. To keep track of military forces all the time, day or night, rain or shine, would have taken at least two dozen satellites in orbit, equipped for rough visual imaging, infrared sensing, magnetic sensing, passive electronics, and perhaps some radar. Such satellites would have required not so much higher or lower technology than that of the KH series. They would have required using technology differently.

Very different results come even from the same technology when it is applied differently. Thus when US submarines placed recorders astride the Soviet Union's undersea communications cable under the Sea of Okhotsk, the "take" gave us retrospective understanding of how the Soviet military worked. But if the United States had carried through plans to tap the undersea cable near Murmansk, hard-wiring the "take" to Greenland under the ocean floor, America would have had a silent seat at the Soviet military's table. Hence when we build intelligence machines to gather information about, say, missiles or tanks, we must first ask ourselves what we want to know about them. Do we want to copy them, negotiate about them, simply know when they are being used, or to kill them?

But our statesmen did not ask such questions when they ordered the imaging satellites and other sensors that bore on Soviet missiles. To some extent that is understandable: Though the information that these yielded told us very little, it was all we had. Conventional wisdom notwithstanding, no American satellite ever even took a picture of any of the Soviet Union's fearsome fourth-generation missiles—the SS-17s, -18s, and -19s—only of silos and canisters. Nor could the satellites (or any other means) tell us whether any of these were full or empty, how many were manufactured, where they were stored, or in what other ways they might be launched. The satellites only counted the silos and measured them accurately. This served to reassure us that they were no more numerous or wider than those that had housed the third generation, and hence were in compliance with the US-Soviet treaty of 1972. But we also learned that the fourth-generation missiles carried about six times the number of warheads as the third, each of which was orders of magnitude more effective against US forces. That was enough to feed three decades of intramural fights among American policymakers.

Had these systems been intended for another purpose, they would have used technology very differently. Soviet systems were designed to track missiles in flight and convey their data to antimissile interceptors.[2]

But since US national policy was (and remains, rhetoric aside) to give Soviet/Russian/Chinese missiles free rides to American soil, we studiously avoided equipping our systems that bear on missiles to do that. In short, US intelligence would be more useful if policymakers were more serious about what they want from it.

Unseriousness about missions, as well as bureaucratic inertia, is also responsible for the fact that America's communications intelligence is stuck in a mold cast in World War II, even though the technical tools, targets, and environment are unrecognizably different. In a nutshell, whereas in the 1940s the electromagnetic spectrum carried few signals, many of which were relevant to war and statecraft, and even the best encoded of which were subject to decryption, nowadays the electronic environment carries gargantuan amounts of broadcast and beamed material from myriad sources, almost none of which is of interest, while that which is almost always is either unidentifiable (e.g., one-time cell phones) or in unbreakable codes. Technology has decided the old battle between code makers and breakers in favor of encoders and clandestine communicators. Nevertheless, in our time as in World War II, US intelligence puts the bulk of its communications intelligence (COMINT) resources in sorting through electronic haystacks. This laboring elephant brings forth mice.

The alternative to picking conversations out of cyberspace is to pick them up live through remote sensing or as they are being transmitted— more like bugging than wiretapping. It happens that technologies for such things as reading vibrations from windows and emanations from cables have made enormous advances, and though only a small part of the US COMINT budget, they have produced disproportionately big results. But to bug someone is somehow to designate him as an enemy. By contrast, sorting through electronic haystacks is so attractive precisely because it avoids political choices. For example, though US officials wring hands over the fact that financing for much anti-American terror comes from the vast Saudi Arabian royal family and entourage, they have been unwilling to commit emplaced sensors to finding out who is doing what because they would not want to act on the information. They prefer to argue about who our enemies may be, just as they preferred arguing about Soviet intentions. The point in communications intelligence, as in missile intelligence or anything else, is that technology at the service of tergiversation is worse than useless.

How useful communications intelligence can be when it is targeted on known enemies is well illustrated by what happened when an FBI telephone watch on international arms traffickers in Florida turned up a call from someone in Colombia, ordering a set of supplies. She turned out to be Nancy Conde Rubio, alias Doris Adriana, the quartermaster for Colombia's FARC, a terrorist group formerly part of the Soviet entourage that controlled large parts of the country with some 60,000 fighters and profits from cocaine trafficking. With support from Venezuela, the FARC was holding some five hundred hostages, including Americans. The FBI forced the traffickers to put Adriana in contact with its own front company, which then supplied the FARC with its needs, including bugged communications equipment. This let Colombian and American authorities control its communications and enabled them to inflict defeats on the FARC, rescue its highest-profile hostages, and arrest both Adriana and her man, Gerardo Aguilar, alias Cesar, who had been in charge of the hostages.

COMINT that proceeds from ignorance, however, only deepens it. After 9/11 the Defense Department started putting together a computer program it called Total Information Awareness to bring together all publicly available (and some nonpublicly available) information about Americans, such as records of telephone calls, credit card transactions, and Internet and email usage, especially as they concerned "sensitive" subjects and contacts with foreigners. The program would sift these gargantuan records in search of "patterns or associations" that would warrant further investigation. After a public outcry, the program essentially shifted to the National Security Agency (NSA), which was already doing something similar with patterns of communication between phones and computers in America and abroad. NSA called it "Transactional Analysis." But this affection for data mining depends logically on the conviction that no sector of the universe of communications is any more interesting than any other. It is a declaration of intellectual bankruptcy akin to airport screeners paying equal attention to grandmas as to imams.

The one sector of technical collection to which these criticisms do not apply—the roughly half of the US intelligence budget devoted to the armed forces' "intelligence-related activities"—points the US technical collection system in the direction the rest of it should go. Those who design the systems in this category—aircraft for battlefield reconnaissance, various battlefield sensors, and means of communicating data in "bent pipe mode" directly to US weapons systems—do so to find, categorize, and prioritize enemy targets, as well as to anticipate and avoid the enemy's blows in real-world situations. Because they do, the more closely an intelligence device is to firing weapons, the likelier it is actually to serve its intended purpose. The questions these designers ask—beginning with "What activity of ours does this information enable?"—should be incumbent on those responsible for any and all US technical collection.

Men

That question should also guide human collection. Some human individuals can see, hear, and understand things that others cannot, have access to some kinds of people and not to others. Hence when putting together a system of espionage, it behooves you to keep in mind what your plans and policies are and, accordingly, to figure out first what information you need to make your plans go, which foreigners have that info, and then what kinds of people are best suited to elicit it from those who have it. Only then can you build your spy network. And the network that serves one operation will not likely serve another as well.

CIA has gone about this backwards. It began, and has stayed with, the notion that "the best people"—namely, those who most closely approximate its ideal of the "gentleman spy"—are best suited to be "case officers." Stationed at embassies and posing as diplomats or other US government employees, they would do their nominal jobs enough to maintain plausible "cover." Then, so goes the legend, slipping away, they would recruit and direct persons with access to desired information to be "agents"— spies. Thus defining the instrument of human collection has the same effect as defining the instruments of technical collection in terms of "the best technology." Namely, it precludes the question "Best for what?" Precluding that question, and building an espionage system designed for bureaucratic convenience rather than to approach this or that kind of target, is attractive because it permits the illusion that the system is capable of getting at everything and anything. The opposite is true.

You have to be clear about who has the information you need, the kinds of persons with whom he normally shares it, and whether you can either persuade such people to get it out of him for you, or to employ people who can do it. With what kinds of persons did Soviet leaders discuss frankly what they hoped, feared, and did? With some respected foreign Communists. With whom do Saudi royals, big and small, discuss their favorite charities? Surely Sunni pedigree and sympathy with Sunni causes are prerequisites. With whom will Iranians talk about the pieces of their nuclear puzzles? Necessarily, with technology merchants. Can you get such people to ask the right questions for you and send you the answers? If you can't, can you pose questions to them through trusted secondhand sources? Note that secondhand sources who are not wholly trusted, and third-hand ones, such as the intelligence services of governments at odds with us, are a lot worse than nothing.

Well-conceived "cover" serves only secondarily to conceal the collector's mission. Primarily, the "cover job" should enable him to approach the target naturally. Designing cover should be the same thing as designing espionage operations. But since it is impossible for CIA or any agency to keep on the payroll the gamut of persons who are or can pass for all the kinds of people that may be needed to approach dictators and doctors, scientists and soldiers, clerics and courtiers of all races, a competent spy agency must rely on the temporary services of nonemployees who have natural access to the targets. CIA does a token bit of this when it asks the help of prominent Americans who have professional contact with interesting foreigners.

CIA not only fails to engineer its case officers' access to targets. It also does not require that the case officers understand the subject matter they are collecting about. Trying to manipulate the target's motivation— supposedly the essence of the CIA collector's job—is inherently problematic. But trying to do it to people whose life experiences are very different from your own—whether scientists, soldiers, or adventurers—without fluency in their language, familiarity with their subcultures, or knowledge of what they are talking about, guarantees CIA's poor results.

The point here is well known to reporters and scholars: You can neither create sources nor demand information. Since most transfers of
information occur naturally, intelligence collectors should approach
sources with plausible reason for contacting them, and with a depth of
expertise in the subject that commands their respect. This, at any rate, is
what the classics teach.[3] Yet only about 4 percent of CIA case officers (up
from 2 percent historically) are under "nonofficial cover" (NOC), meaning they pretend not to be US government employees.

After 9/11 CIA came under pressure to "get to" terrorists by increasing the number of NOCs. But its plan for doing so produced tiny results
because it varied so slightly from the traditional Agency spy model. The
new NOCs were grouped in specially created American business con-
sulting agencies abroad—effectively unofficial CIA stations—in the
hope that this would lead to contact with people involved in terrorism.
An internal critic called this the "field of dreams" approach: "If you
build it, they will come." They did not. But why should these people,
given their pretend-expertise, have expected access to people involved in
terrorism? In one case, however, one of the NOCs had built up real credentials in nuclear engineering and had got himself invited to a conference in Riyadh where he could meet a potential source. But the CIA
station chief in the Saudi capital refused to let him attend. "No, that's
why we have case officers here," he reportedly said.[4]

Most of the CIA case officers' human sources, other than ordinary
diplomatic contacts, are "walk-ins"—people whom you don't know, but
who know you and are likely trying to manipulate you. That goes doubly for the "take" from "liaison" with foreign countries' intelligence services, whose motivation—serving their governments' interests rather
than ours—is obvious to all but CIA. The worth of walk-ins, liaison services, and interrogations depends substantially on issues of quality control that we will consider under the heading of counterintelligence (see
below). In our time, it also depends on the worth of the CIA's theory of
terrorism, which became official US doctrine in 1993, namely, that terrorists are "rogue" individuals and groups rather than direct or indirect
agents of states.[5] If, on the other hand, as Thomas Friedman has written,
"98% of terrorism is what states want to happen or let happen," then
these sources are a waste of time at best and likely of negative worth.

Logic commands that to organize human collection you must begin by gauging the struggle, the war, the mission, that the espionage is to serve and that you operate on the basis of whatever you may have. If you sit back and wait for intelligence to define your task and deliver the keys to success, intelligence will become an excuse for evading your responsibilities. Intelligence is a tool for success—never an excuse for lack thereof.

COUNTERINTELLIGENCE

But how can you make sure that your intelligence service is depicting reality rather than passing on what your enemies want you to think—or its own prejudices? You should start by realizing that US agencies have conducted counterintelligence in self-indulgent ways. By being skeptical about those ways, you should make them skeptical about themselves.

All intelligence services employ some people who try to understand, manipulate, and control what the other side collects and what conclusions it draws from what it collects—protecting their control of their own channels of information and struggling to master the other side's. This struggle goes by the name *counterintelligence*. The twentieth-century poster-case for its importance is the British-American use of captured German spies as well as of make-believe military units to convince German intelligence that the 1944 Allied invasion of France would take place near Calais rather than in Normandy. Conversely, defending your intelligence consists of pitiless quality control of everything your service does and thinks, watching for what hostile services know and how they are using that knowledge to affect you. If your intelligence service does quality control well, it may gain the chance offensively to manipulate what the other side thinks it knows. But to the extent quality control fails, your intelligence service will end up hurting your country while making a fool of you.

Seldom can your human and electronic spies be wholly invisible. The policies you pursue are always on display, while your analytical prejudices—what you prefer to think—are often too evident, like Hitler's view that the Allies would land at Calais. Your satellites are largely visible, your electronics radiate, and your human collectors ask questions and have meetings. So although counterintelligence must try to minimize what hostile services know about your sources and methods, you must start with what they surely know and ask what they can do with it. Hence to equate counter-intelligence (CI) with "security"—plugging leaks or catching spies—is to get it wrong. Rather, quality control consists of managing your exposure to hostile intelligence, of learning the depth of their knowledge, and then of letting them collect such facts and impressions as you want.

To inject your narrative into the bloodstream of hostile intelligence is to penetrate it. Gaining access to codes by which the hostile services encrypt messages allows deep penetration. In World War II the United States did this to Japan strictly through cryptology, and Britain did it to Germany by combining cryptology with the theft of an encryption machine. The Soviet Union did it to the United States for two decades by purchasing naval codebooks from John Walker. The deepest penetration consists of having an official of the hostile service acting as your agent. When that official is in charge of counterintelligence—as was the CIA's Aldrich Ames when he worked as an agent of the KGB between 1984 and 1994—penetration becomes control: As long as Ames was in place, the KGB controlled the CIA network in its area. Lesser degrees of penetration can be achieved by letting the hostile service recruit agents who are really yours, called "dangles," or by "doubling" captured agents, or by sending false defectors.

QUALITY CONTROL

The most difficult part of any CI case is to know that it exists. The natural path to that knowledge is to imagine how hostile services might be using what they know about our own intelligence. Hypotheses must come first, followed by investigations to check them. So, the true logic of CI runs from facts that raise questions to hypotheses that explain them, to investigations that may point to the people whose actions caused the facts. The key to successful quality control is the organization's willingness to question its own competence.

Consider what happens when the requisite attitude is not present, when questions are not asked. Beginning in the late 1960s, Soviet electronic intelligence ships started showing up outside US Navy ports whenever fleet exercises were to begin. I recall, as a junior officer, the wardroom grousing that "they" always knew because sailors blurt operational schedules to "the whores in the bars." But the Soviet ships had started across the ocean long before sailors had learned of the schedules. Also in those years, naval aviators bombing North Vietnam rued the fact that enemy antiaircraft batteries were always ready for them. "They" knew. But how come their knowledge was up-to-the-minute? Nobody looked into that. Through the 1970s and into the 1980s our ballistic missile submariners lived in fear because Soviet patrol aircraft were flying patterns with magnetic detection devices right over their very secret deployment areas. How did "they" know? Finally, in the 1980s, the Navy, desperate about this, formulated a hypothesis: Perhaps the Soviets' Radar Ocean Reconnaissance Satellite was scanning the world's waters and discerning disturbances on the surface made by submarines a thousand feet below. On the staff of the Senate Intelligence Committee, I helped authorize millions of dollars to check this out by trying to duplicate the feat. We could not, despite superior imaging and data processing. Wrong hypothesis.

But no one had asked the CI question: "What vulnerability of ours might explain the Soviets' timely knowledge of fleet exercises, *and* of bombing schedules, *and* of submarine deployments?" One answer would have been that facts about all these had been transmitted, year in, year out, over several Navy encryption machines, the KWR-37, the KG13, the KL-11, and the KL-47. The hypothesis that perhaps some persons with access to the codebooks and manuals of these machines were spies would have been easily checkable: The number of custodians was seldom over two hundred at any given time, while fewer than a fourth of that number had access from the late 1960s through the early 1980s. Surveillance and investigation would quickly have pointed to Warrant Officer John Walker as the leader of the espionage ring. But since no one asked, the Walker ring would have continued to operate indefinitely had Barbara Walker not turned her husband in to the FBI in 1984.

Quality control of US human intelligence is equally a travesty because CIA is systemically allergic to it. This stems from embarrassment that it never recruited significant sources within the Kremlin despite having employed thousands and spent billions on it. Over a half-century, it received only a handful of bona fide, high-level defectors and just two or three peripheral "defectors in place." While the old OSS had included a small counterintelligence section, X2, which could argue to the Director that certain sources might be enemy-controlled, CIA limited this function to a tiny staff advising the Directorate of Operations, with only such information about any case as the Directorate would allow. Nevertheless, CIA saw the CI staff's raising of questions about the bona fides of sources and defectors as an injurious insult. In 1974, CIA disestablished it and devolved to the collectors the job of auditing themselves. The results were predictable.

In 1979, director Stansfield Turner spelled out for the Senate Intelligence Committee why CIA could never be penetrated: First, any and all recruits, defectors, and information from the USSR had to be for real because the KGB, nuts about security, could be relied on never to let out information even in order to sucker CIA. Second, polygraph examinations of employees and agents guaranteed that everything CIA accepted as true, and everyone it accepted as legitimate, was technically, certifiably so. Hence quality control was a nonproblem.

In fact, the polygraph only validated the polygraphers' prejudices, which reflected the CIA ruling class's attachment to its own social class, reputation, and political preferences—all of which overrode concerns for quality and integrity. This made CIA comfortable for a remarkable number of high-level officers who in fact were working for the KGB. (Aldrich Ames passed his periodic polygraphs.) It made for agent networks in fact controlled by hostile intelligence services and made CIA the dupe in its relationships with foreign liaison services.

When Germany's reunification turned the East German Staatssicherheitdienst (Stasi) over to Bonn in 1990, it turned out that all but three agents that CIA had considered its own were in fact working for the Stasi. When Major Florentino Aspillaga defected from the Cuban DGI in 1988 and gave CIA the names of Castro's agents, CIA found that all of the people it thought it had recruited were in fact working for Castro.[6] And, of course, between 1984 and 1994 all of CIA's agents in and from the USSR/Russia were controlled by the KGB: Aldrich Ames, chief of counterintelligence for CIA's Soviet East European division, had guaranteed that by identifying ours to them and certifying theirs to us. In 2002–2003, as the United States prepared to invade Iraq, it sent a team of hotshot case officers into the Kurdish safe area with suitcases of $100 bills to develop sources inside Iraq. So happy was the Agency with the resulting information that it gave the sources the name ROCKSTARS. Two days before the invasion, one of them said he knew that Saddam Hussein and sons would be spending the night in a bunker outside Baghdad and later radioed that he was watching them go into it. On that basis, George W. Bush started the invasion a day early with what he supposed was a decapitating strike on that bunker by US stealth bombers and cruise missiles. But when US forces got to the site they found no bunker and, of course, no Saddam. Because CIA's appetite for information exceeded its discretion, the ROCKSTARS turned out to have been controlled by Iraqi intelligence.[7] Such are the ordinary consequences of dysfunctional counterintelligence.

That dysfunction's most obvious result was that between 1986 and 1994, as Mikhail Gorbachev's inept attempt to recentralize the Communist Party was destroying the Soviet Union, and later as the character of post-Soviet Russia was up for grabs, the CIA's network of agents, now run by the KGB, was reporting that Gorbachev was a canny liberal reformer worthy of US support, and later that Vladimir Putin's renamed KGB posed no danger to Russia or to the West. CIA did not ask why its reports were so contrary to those of diplomats and journalists.

But even after CIA officials suspected that their agents had come under the KGB's control, they continued to mainline their reports to the White House. They did it because they were embarrassed to admit failure but, most shocking of all, because the reports contained things they believed the Presidents "needed to hear."[8] Because these officials fancied themselves entitled to steer US foreign policy—as Ames himself had—Presidents Reagan, Bush I, and Clinton made some of their most momentous decisions in part on the basis of counsel hostile to America. And George H.W. Bush made a fool of himself in Kiev's central square on July 31, 1991, by telling incredulous Ukrainians (in what became known as the "Chicken Kiev speech") that the Soviet Union had a bright future and that they should stay within it.[9]

CIA's allergy to quality control has affected its performance with regard to Middle Eastern terrorism as it did with regard to the Soviet empire because CIA's human collection has been under even more pressure to do even less quality control than usual and to be less skeptical about defectors, liaison services, and interrogations—above all because CIA officers were even more confident that their judgment on the Middle East was superior to that of President George W. Bush than they were of their judgments' superiority over that of his predecessors.

Among the more important and misrepresented dysfunctions caused by CIA's excessive faith in liaison services concerns one Rafid Ahmed Alwan, an Iraqi who defected to Germany in 1999, who told its intelligence service, the *Bundesnachrichtendienst* (BND), that Saddam Hussein was building weapons of mass destruction. The BND passed reports based on his story to CIA, which never saw him but code-named him "Curveball." After 2003, CIA spread the falsehood—refuted by the Congressionally chartered Robb-Silberman commission in 1995—that Iraqi exile leader Ahmed Chalabi and his Neoconservative friends in Washington had mainlined Curveball and his warnings to a credulous White House. In fact, all of the roughly one hundred Curveball reports had come through CIA, which had passed them on approvingly though it had not done due diligence on them. This was a serious professional lapse, because the BND had refused CIA's request to let its agents interview the source and probe his story. Nevertheless, CIA simply trusted the BND. Then, corruptly, it blamed its domestic political opponents for its own mistakes.

CIA had less excuse to trust the Arab world's intelligence services. Yes, they are well placed to report on terrorist groups. But that is because these intelligence services are *major constituents* of terrorist groups. Prototypically, the PLO (originally Fatah) was a 1950s creature of Gamal Nasser's Egyptian intelligence service. Yasser Arafat, its leader, had been working with the KGB since at least 1957 and his deputy, Mahmoud Abbas, graduated from Moscow's Patrice Lumumba Peoples' Friendship University (with a thesis on why tales of the Holocaust are Zionist fabrications). Jordanian intelligence briefly wielded substantial influence in the PLO in the late 1960s but was overwhelmed by Syrian and Iraqi as well as Egyptian agents. Each of these services used its factions for war against one another, to the point that the one loyal to Egypt murdered Jordan's Prime Minister, Wasfi al-Tal, in 1971. Saudi money was ever present. Similarly, al-Qaeda was originally almost exclusively Saudi. But by the mid-1990s it had been infiltrated massively by Iraqis (using Baluchi agents), as well as by Egyptians, Jordanians, Syrians, and Sudanese as well as by Pakistanis. And whereas prior to 2001 the Taliban were creatures of Pakistani intelligence, thereafter they became beholden to the Saudis. *In the real world, professionals manipulate amateurs—not the other way around.* Alas, CIA officially believes the contrary, disregarding that these services' infiltrators into terrorist groups are spies only incidentally. Primarily, they serve their governments by steering these groups' acts and giving the Americans their favorite version of what is happening.

Preference for confirming prejudices over quality control also underlies the US approach to interrogations. Torture is usually irrelevant to getting anything of value out of prisoners, especially in the "war on terror," primarily because seldom do US interrogators know what the prisoner in question knows or even what his relevance to the problem may be. Consider a contrasting exception. In the 1956 Battle of Algiers, Colonel Jaques Massu's French paratroopers knew that the FLN terrorists were organized in pyramidal three-man cells, in which each man knew only his superior and subordinate. Hence when they caught a terrorist *in flagrante* and rushed him to a torture chamber, they asked only the questions that they knew he could answer and checked the answers instantly by using them. But America's "terror suspects" are either "fingered" by foreign services (or, as in the case of prisoners of war from Afghanistan, sold wholesale by the victorious Northern Alliance), by unreliable informants, or less reliably still by other prisoners under interrogation. So when US interrogators ask prisoners questions to which the prisoners do not know the answers, they reveal their own ignorance. They also reveal what it is they want to hear. This enables the prisoners to control the interrogators by stroking their prejudices. For example, CIA looked none too closely at the 2003 confession that Khalid Sheikh Mohammed gave after being subjected to waterboarding (simulated drowning) to the effect that he had planned 9/11 and most other anti-American outrages under the detailed direction and control of Osama bin Laden, because it neatly confirmed all of its prejudices.[10] Criticism of such confessions that focuses on torture obscures the question of what reasons there are to believe that any item in them is true. By contrast, counterintelligence worthy of the name tries to find out the true reasons behind lies.

True Lies

The reverse, what can happen when intelligence looks skeptically at what it sees or hears, is best illustrated by what a lowly Air Force photo interpreter noticed in 1984 while looking at an old roll of satellite photos of the Moscow suburbs, previously milked of all "positive intelligence." He was part of a brief and rare US effort to ask whether anything in the data raised questions about its authenticity. The airman focused on a building that had been identified as a wind tunnel for testing aircraft. It looked every bit like one. But he concluded that it could not be a wind tunnel because another building stood in the path of what should have been the tunnel's air exhaust. Having discovered a lie, the analysts investigated. Older film showed the site covered by a roof, into which trains had come in empty and left full of dirt. Back-of-the-envelope calculations showed that an enormous amount had been removed. Searches of old film from the area showed other instances—previously unremarked because they were unremarkable by themselves—of trains taking dirt from under covered sites. Research that brought to bear all other intelligence sources ended up showing that the Soviet military had built a deep underground headquarters for nuclear war, impervious to nukes and connected to the Kremlin by subway. "The counterintelligence attitude" can yield far more than proper epistemology.

Unfortunately, US intelligence acquired the habit of accepting lies as part of various "cooperative arrangements" for collecting information. The prototypical argument for what amounts to willful collaboration in deception was made by one Nikolai Brusnitsyn of the USSR Ministry of Defense: "Brusnitsyn defines control as 'obtaining by an agreed procedure authorized data, stipulated by agreements, on the subject of the treaty. . . . ' He then says 'All we have to do is agree on the composition of the national verification facilities, the procedure of the verification, the way we are going to use technical equipment, the degree to which obtained data should be detailed, and the procedure of [sic] exchanging them."[11] US intelligence officials, as I mentioned, had habituated themselves to equate the diameter of launchers with the potency of missiles, to assume that what satellites can see was all there was to see. "Cooperative arrangements"—taking the number of containers coming out of certain exits to certain factories as proof that no more than a certain number of missiles of a particular kind were being manufactured in those factories or anywhere else—were part of the 1987 Intermediate Nuclear Forces Treaty.

The propensity to accept true lies did not die with the Soviet Union but grew into the US (and UN) default mode of "verifying." Beginning in 1994, North Korea agreed to show US inspectors proof that its cessation of operations of the Yongbyon nuclear reactor amounted to "disabling" it (but surely not dismantling it), and the United States agreed to accept this as meaning that North Korea had "given up its nuclear program." But to cooperate with the security services one is trying to learn about is to hand them the keys to your mind.

Why some government officials are amenable to true lies is plain enough: They care about the substance of problems less than they crave domestic credit for having solved them. Thus Paul Nitze once suggested to a Soviet, to whom he was officially communicating the US position that its radar at Krasnoyarsk was an antimissile radar, that the Soviets turn on that radar as the US "Jumpseat" satellite was passing by and that they program the radar to emit signals that officials like himself would then judge to be not optimal for antimissile purposes. Problem solved. Technical intelligence officers also traveled this slippery slope tending to believe, as Vice Admiral Bobby Ray Inman once put it to the Senate Intelligence Committee, that the signals that intelligence gets, and the pictures that satellites take, are real, "pure," or that as a button once worn by CIA's imagery analysts proclaimed: "Seeing is believing."

But since true facts can lie today just as much as they did in 1944 when the Allies used them to deceive the Germans, technical counterintelligence can grasp reality confidently only by hiding or disguising its means of collection. As on the human side, the governing attitude has to combine humility about our own security and aggressive, intellectually agile attempts to penetrate the other side's. Counterintelligence depends on attitude.

ANALYSIS AND PRODUCTION

When, inevitably, intelligence analysts mix their judgment with the "take," they preempt their customers' intellectual authority to some extent. Hence

translating reports into products tempts analysts to erase the distinction between hard facts and (their own) soft judgments. That is why Stalin refused
to look at analyses and told his services not to produce them lest they "ride
straight into self-made traps"—or he ride into theirs.

Facts and Judgments

Inescapably, to answer even the simplest questions about large phenomena one must aggregate small pieces of data according to models and assumptions of one's own making. How many tanks does North Korea
have? Since you can't take a picture of the whole country simultaneously,
and all its tanks are never in plain sight anyway, you can't just count them.
You have to figure out how many are in a typical unit, estimate how many
units there are, what percentage of their complement they have, and what
percentage of that may be in working order. How inherently uncertain
this kind of thing may be was illustrated by a charge made by CBS News
in 1968 that the difference between the US Army's estimate of the number of Vietcong guerrillas and the CIA's estimate showed that General
William Westmoreland had politicized the Army's intelligence. Westmoreland sued for libel. In fact, there was and could not be any "ground
truth" about the number of Vietcong. Both the Army's and CIA's estimates flowed from models based on assumptions, neither set of which
made any more inherent sense than the other. Even mere bean-counting
requires defining the beans: Estimates of Soviet civil defense—or of Iraq's
preparations for biological warfare or of Iran's nuclear program—depend
largely on how one scores "dual-purpose" facilities.

Even what seem to be purely technical models will reflect assumptions
as much as data: The engineers who examine telemetry data radioed
from foreign weapons tests must make educated guesses about which
channel represents which sensor and what the scale of each reading
might be. And the climatologists who discuss changes in the Earth's tem-
perature are not reading a thermometer they've stuck up the planet's
axis. Rather, each report is an aggregation of thousands of readings, from
locations chosen and weighted for time, latitude, altitude, and other
criteria, according to peculiar models. So when you encounter models,
keep your hand on your intellectual wallet.

Intelligence products should be clear about the proportion of data to judgment that they contain, as well as about the data's pedigree. But the most common phrases in US intelligence products—"we believe" and "we have no confirmed evidence that" (longhand for "Yes" and "No") are features of a system that confuses fact and judgment. Because the analysts are "compartmented" from knowing about secret "sources and methods," they can neither evaluate them nor ask them more questions. Working as they do from oracles that have little specific to say, they spout oracular generalities—based substantially on their own biases.

Usefulness and Policy

Analysis should squeeze as much sense out of secret tidbits as they may contain, mix it with relevant facts from the library, and confect products that help statesmen and soldiers to win. That presupposes that the analysts are clear about—and sympathize with—the statesmen's and soldiers' plans. The OSS's biggest contributions to World War II were made by its Research and Analysis section, mostly academics, who scoured libraries to build databases on the places where US troops operated and on foreign forces. That war's inescapable logic focused analysts and operators alike.

Initially, the Cold War's simple logic—repel all attempts to expand the Soviet and Chinese empires—implicitly shaped US intelligence analysts. Arguably CIA's main product in the two decades after 1949 was the National Intelligence Survey (NIS)—a "book" on every country that included information on beaches, airfields, roads, climate, and the population's capacities and attitudes: religion, family customs, political personalities and sects, armed forces, and so on. The NIS narrative format forced analysts to evaluate the relevance of facts, new and old, by the standard of usefulness in anti-Communist warfare. But beginning in the mid-1960s, as the anti-Communist consensus within the US government broke down, as détente, human rights, and other priorities delegitimized its focus, the NIS was abandoned. This should have made clear to all that intelligence products are meaningful only in relation to the purposes they are intended to serve.

CIA's founding generation recognized this—in theory. In 1949, Yale professor Willmoore Kendall debated Sherman Kent, fellow OSS alumnus and the father of CIA analysis, on whether and how intelligence products should take US policy into account.[12] Whereas under Kent CIA policy meant (and nominally still pretends) to produce "objective" pictures of the world, letting the policy chips fall where they may, Kendall argued that what is worthy of the analyst's attention in any situation depends primarily on the objective of the policy. Unless the analyst clearly states that objective and espouses it, unless he looks at the subject matter from the standpoint of one who wants the policy to succeed, his product may reflect other priorities, and protestations of "objectivity" may disguise outright clashes of purpose.

In the 1970s, as computers became the main tool for storage and retrieval of data, US intelligence seemed to have sidestepped this problem. Absent the discipline of fitting facts into narratives, masses of data were simply shoved into categories. This served technical military operations well: "Order of battle" books (compilations of facts about the nature and location of foreign equipment) became readily accessible and were even programmed directly into US weapons systems. But computer storage did not serve strategic analysis well. In 1980, when the United States set out to rescue hostages in Iran, and when it invaded Grenada in 1983 and Panama in 1989—never mind in the Gulf War of 1991 and the Iraq War of 2003 as well as in Afghanistan—it became clear that available facts had not been organized specifically to achieve political objectives.

Official Truths

But CIA's analysts do organize their thoughts around policy objectives: their own. And so CIA's foremost concern, from its inception, has been ensuring that what it considers its premier products, some eighty National Intelligence Estimates (NIEs) per year, and its quotidian "current intelligence" briefings as well as the *National Intelligence Daily,* a classified newspaper, be the US government's official truths. Hence the January 1, 1949, Dulles-Jackson-Correa report, which led to the current analytical system, set as the primary requirement that CIA's products not be merely "competitive with similar products of other agencies."[13]

Senior analysts know that executive officials want bureaucratic bases for decisions more than they want facts, and they are painfully aware that they have never had the facts to answer such questions as "Who is really behind North Korea's invasion of the South?" or "What is Saddam after in Kuwait?" or "How far is China really prepared to go to prevent Taiwan's independence?" or "Where is Putin trying to take Russia?" Analyst Russell Jack Smith was only half kidding when he told Sherman Kent: "There hasn't been a fact in a National Intelligence Estimate in five years."[14]

Estimates, daily briefings, and summaries are drafted rather quickly by persons with some knowledge of the subject, then reworked more slowly at much greater length at ever higher bureaucratic levels by persons with ever less knowledge of substance. The results often contain basic errors (my favorite was mislabeling Syria and Iraq on a map). Why? Because while the higher-ups know less about the world, they are expert in and meticulous about the Agency's political positions. They take longest to work out the executive summaries and argue bitterly over the wording of the "key judgments" because that's all that executives bother to read, and that's what they will mainline to the press. In short, these documents are political acts stemming from political priorities.

Thomas Powers' description of the CIA founding generation's priorities fits a half-century later: "Incoming papers might be a foot deep on his desk in L Building in the morning but [Frank Wisner, one of its founding greats] would neglect it all if he noticed a wrong-headed column by Scotty Reston in the morning *Times*. Nothing took precedence over getting Reston straightened out."[15] Factual scrupulousness was never the point. Rather it was to validate CIA's perennial claim to be Washington's sole arbiter of what the world is really like—that any perception of the outside world that conflicts with CIA's is by definition partial, unprofessional, illegitimate. In our time as in the founding era, it is commonplace at CIA that intelligence analysis "comprises all the major evaluative and predictive functions" of foreign affairs and "leaves the policy maker with little or nothing in the decision making process but the ceremonial finale."[16] This claim became official in 1978 when CIA renamed its analytical shop "The National Foreign Assessment Center."

A generation later, CIA had dropped the name but not the pretense. George Tenet, Director from 1997 to 2004, explained: "Policy makers *are allowed* to come to independent judgments about what the intelligence may mean. . . . What they cannot do is overstate the intelligence itself. . . . They must clearly delineate between what the intelligence says and the conclusions they have reached"[17] (emphasis mine). But CIA willfully confuses "the intelligence itself" and "what the intelligence says" with their own conclusions, while denigrating any facts that lead to contrary conclusions as "cherry-picking" or "fragments" or "their own set of facts." It confuses with facts the opinions that bolster its authority, while trashing inconvenient facts into the category of opinion—often by tailoring standards of significance, as we shall see.

Substantively, CIA officials see themselves as indispensable antidotes to the US government's default simplistic, chauvinistic, militaristic thinking. Without their sophisticated dedication to peace and progress, unwashed Congressmen and reactionary Presidents would barge about on history's wrong side. Hence CIA has written (and leaked) NIEs as crises loomed, precisely to tip balances in Washington. While many if not most of these were incorrect factually about events abroad, they correctly served the authors' political causes in Washington. Thus the 1962 NIE stating that the Soviets had not and would not place nuclear-tipped missiles in Cuba countered growing pressures on the Kennedy Administration to invade Cuba. In 1974, two quick NIEs stating that North Vietnam was not preparing a conventional invasion of the South helped kill Congressional support for the Nixon Administration's last efforts to aid Saigon prior to the North's decisive invasion the following spring. From 1965 to 1977, the yearly NIE 11-3-8 series was a major hurdle for those in Congress and the White House who wanted to counter the Soviet buildup of first-strike missiles. It argued first that the Soviets would not try to match the number of US intercontinental missiles; when they matched it, that they would not exceed it substantially; when they exceeded it substantially, that they would not obtain the combination of yield and accuracy for a first strike; and when they attained it, that it did not matter.[18] In 1990 and 1991, respectively, CIA judged that Saddam Hussein would not invade Kuwait and that he did not have a serious nuclear program. In 1998, CIA denied that India (and, later, Pakistan) would test nuclear weapons, disregarding their governments' expressed intentions in favor of its own prejudice that they should not and hence would not. In sum, incompetent as it may be on intelligence, the CIA-led intelligence community is a competent Washington lobby.

CIA'S WAR

Beginning in 2002, CIA feared that President George W. Bush was inclined to satisfy the American body politic's demand for action against countries involved in terrorism and set about dissuading him. But sensing that Bush did not have it in him to push back, CIA went beyond its usual lobbying and waged open political war, first to detune and detour, and then to discredit and defeat his Administration. It wrote NIEs to contradict basic Administration positions, Agency officials wrote and publicized books that amounted to indictments of the Administration, it turned the Congressionally mandated commission that investigated intelligence performance on 9/11 to its own ends by controlling its working staff's membership list, and it cooperated with and even instigated the media's anti-Bush ventures.[19]

CIA's position, for the sake of which it wrote and fought, was the proposition "Terrorism is a spontaneous reaction by rogue individuals and groups to socioeconomic events, religious phenomena, and US policies. Arab states are not responsible for it. Our principal enemy, almost synonymous with terrorism itself, is al-Qaeda."

But who and what is al-Qaeda? In 1988, Osama bin Laden founded "the base" in Afghanistan with fourteen forlorn Arabs. A decade later, in 1998, when the US government suddenly charged it with having bombed two US embassies in Africa and having tried to bomb twelve US aircraft, US intelligence had taken no notice of it, largely because there had been little evidence that it had done anything remarkable. The little band of amateurs that had moved with bin Laden from Afghanistan to Sudan in 1992 and then back in 1996 had shown no capacity for effective action. Its main recruits, Ayman al-Zawahiri's Egyptian Islamic Jihad, had fumbled attacks. No one suggests that al-Qaeda had been involved in the 1993 World Trade Center bombing. Its mastermind, Ramzi Yousef, never met bin Laden. Only in 1996, back in Afghanistan, did bin Laden meet Yousef's associates, Khalid Sheikh Mohammed and Ammar al-Baluchi—the very people who had bombed the World Trade Center in 1993, who in 1995 planned to bomb twelve US airliners over the Pacific, who then very professionally bombed the US embassies in 1998, and who eventually carried out the September 11 bombings. In short, this group of men that preexisted al-Qaeda and affiliated itself with it *en bloc,* who are in no way bin Laden's creatures or pupils, are the actual persons responsible for the only professional terrorist acts outside Afghanistan that US intelligence imputes to bin Laden, according to the joint Congressional committee that investigated 9/11. They, not bin Laden, are the reason why al-Qaeda became a household word, why CIA director George Tenet said (possibly not realizing what he was saying) that al-Qaeda was connected to the 1993 World Trade Center bombing.

But these people are neither Arabs nor Islamists. They are all ethnic Baluchs who claim to be uncles and cousins. We do not know their real names, since they used as many as sixty aliases. We do know that during the 1980s Saddam Hussein's intelligence service armed and supported some four thousand Baluchs on the border of Iran and Pakistan, and that Yousef as well as the other main author of the 1993 attack, Abdul Rahman Yasin, traveled on an Iraqi passport. But whether these Baluchs were Iraqi agents or not, regardless of whether we call them infiltrators, adjuncts, or whatever, they surely were very different from the original al-Qaeda: Whereas Islamism moved bin Laden and al-Zawahiri, all evidence pointed to Yousef, Khalid Sheikh Mohammed, and such, as being secularists. Whereas others seem to have had lives prior to terrorism, these seem to be professionals. Hence we also know that the line that CIA fed to eager news media after 9/11, to the effect that bin Laden and friends were responsible for much of the terrorism in some fifty countries, controlling it from high-tech caves in Afghanistan's mountains, is nonsense.

But after no such caves had been found, most of Afghanistan's "Afghan Arabs" had been captured or killed, and yet terrorism increased worldwide and especially in Iraq, CIA stated that, but never explained how, al-Qaeda had "metastasized." Willy-nilly, it made al-Qaeda a brand name attractive to any who would frighten America. Eagerly it accepted the claims of various terrorists that they were "al-Qaeda" and attributed to "al-Qaeda" certain kinds of bombings because those were kinds of things al-Qaeda did. But never did it reason that since the real al-Qaeda's roots and money had been Saudi, and since most of the money and suicide bombers expended by those among Iraq's "al-Qaeda" Sunni insurgents, as well as Afghanistan's post-2001 Taliban, was from Saudi Arabia, perhaps that country's regime had a unique relationship with them. Moreover, since most of the acts and plots of terrorism since 2001 that looked professional had taken place in Iraq, where the Sunni insurgency was run by remnants of Saddam Hussein's Ba'ath party and its intelligence service, it would not have been unreasonable for US intelligence to look into the peculiar confluence of Saudi money and Iraqi intelligence expertise. But CIA did all it could to delegitimize such thinking because its principal preoccupation was to restrain the US government from acting against states from which terrorists come and for whose causes terrorists fight.

It has been so since Cold War days. In 1981–1983, CIA looked at the Italian Interior Ministry's evidence that Pope John Paul II's would-be assassin, Mehmet Ali Agca, was acting on Bulgaria's (and hence the KGB's) behalf and concluded there was "no proof."[20] The Agency translated this judgment to the public as "there is proof that the Soviets were not involved, indeed the evidence is that states are not responsible for terrorism." In CIA's corporate view, the most dangerous thing about 9/11 was that it might lead the US government to abandon that position and, as CIA's Richard Clarke suggested in the title of his book, go to war "against all enemies."

To forestall this, the CIA after 9/11 made it job number one to discount facts that linked Saddam Hussein's Iraq to anti-American terrorism and to discredit the facts' bearers. Intellectually, this was not easy: According to CIA, the leader of the 1993 World Trade Center bombing, Ramzi Yousef, who had come from Iraq along with Abdul Rahman Yasin, who returned, remained, and disappeared there, was part of the same family that masterminded 9/11. If that was so, at the very least Iraq had harbored the family that attacked us. Instead, George Tenet writes that he told "Congress and the Administration that the intelligence did not show any Iraqi authority, direction, or control over any of the many specific terrorist acts carried out by al Qa'ida."[21] That is longhand for CIA's substantive message: "Saddam's Iraq was not responsible for terrorism," which CIA did not dare say outright.

But why should anyone care whether Iraq's or any other country's official government bodies exercised "authority, direction, or control" over any given specific act? Why not ask about the many ways in which the regime contributed to those acts? And why smuggle into the judgment that any contributions to terrorism that were not channeled through corporate al-Qaeda—whatever that might mean—are irrelevant? Because crafting your own definition of the question lets you answer it as you wish without dealing with facts and questions that do not suit you. But while the intellectual pretense was thin, the bureaucratic pretense was potent.

It proved potent enough to form a consensus in the government and media that Saddam's Iraq was innocent of anti-American terrorism, a consensus that intimidated President Bush and led to general disinterest in facts that contradict it. But Iraqi intelligence-service documents that survived the invasion confirmed that as early as 1993 it was organizing groups in Somalia to "hunt Americans." The service provided homes, offices, and training for both Palestinian rival groups, Hamas and Arafat's Force 17, as well as for Egypt's Islamic Jihad. The latter is especially noteworthy since its leader, the man who authorized the relationship, was Ayman al-Zawahiri—who began working with Osama bin Laden in 1991, had Osama's original guru killed, and took over his role. There is every reason to believe he became al-Qaeda's real boss. In 2002 the Iraqi service provided 669 false passports to terrorists and held thirteen conferences on Iraqi soil for international terrorist groups. Iraqi intelligence operated units of killers and trained suicide bombers. Even ordinary Iraqi scholarship students were required to have training in "martyrdom operations." And, of course, Iraqi intelligence had liaison with any and all violent groups in the Middle East. In 1994–1995 it offered Osama bin Laden "safe harbor" in Iraq. In 1996 Khalid Sheikh Mohammed offered his services to Osama bin Laden after having worked with Iraq. In 2008 the Pentagon publicly documented many of the details of Iraqi intelligence's fomenting of terrorism—far more extensively than any National Intelligence Estimate I have ever seen—in collaboration with al-Qaeda, concluding that al-Qaeda was for Iraq's intelligence service "a formal instrument of state power."[22] But by then CIA had long since won the battle for our statesmen's hearts and minds.

Tenet's memoir treats as attempted usurpation that the Vice President's staff disagreed with CIA on the basis of "such detailed knowledge of people, sources, and timelines that the senior CIA analytic manager doing the briefing that day simply could not compete." But CIA trumped intellectual challenge by asserting bureaucratic authority. Tenet tells us that CIA properly discounted facts "that suggested a deeper relationship" between Saddam and al-Qaeda because CIA's "regional analysts who focus on geographic areas believed that fundamental distrust stemming from stark ideological differences . . . significantly limited the cooperation that was suggested by the reporting."[23] Note: Facts that displease CIA are opinion no matter how specific they are, while CIA's favorite dogmas are facts.

Keep in mind, however, that this sort of thing can happen only by default. Presidents have it in their power ex officio to challenge such assertions intellectually or to dismiss them (and those who make them). Bush did neither.[24]

This war's end is worth remembering: In September 2004, after having borne CIA's attacks for over two years, President Bush appointed Congressman Porter Goss—Chairman of the House Intelligence Committee and a former CIA career officer who had criticized CIA's political attacks—as Director of Central Intelligence. Goss told the staff he took to the Agency that the President had appointed him to stop those attacks, told Agency personnel to stop them, and removed a few of those most responsible for them. To no one's surprise, this displeased the Agency. But surprising some, George W. Bush preferred to please it and fired Goss in May 2006. And the anti-Bush warriors returned, triumphant.

To what extent this poses a problem for all future Presidents—and for democracy—may be seen in a special NIE titled "Iran: Nuclear Intentions and Capabilities"; CIA released its "key judgments" to the press on December 3, 2007. The first of these was: "We judge with high confidence that in fall 2003, Tehran halted its nuclear weapons program." Those fifteen words, which the President did not contradict and did not let anyone in the Executive Branch contradict, officially dismissed the existence of Iran's nuclear weapons program and discredited his Administration's efforts to squeeze it.

Intellectually, the NIE was risible, its analytical basis hidden in a footnote: "By 'nuclear weapons program' we mean Iran's nuclear weapons design and weaponization work and covert uranium enrichment-related work; we do not mean Iran's declared civil work related to uranium conversion and enrichment." English translation: We choose not to care about

Iran's major program that produces weapons-grade uranium, the most essential and difficult part of building nukes. Nor do we know or care to what extent Iran had engineered the nonnuclear components of nuclear weapons prior to fall 2003. Having made their point, the authors covered themselves at the end of the text as follows: "We assess with high confidence that Iran has the scientific, technical, and industrial capacity eventually to produce nuclear weapons if it chooses to do so." And two months later, Director of National Intelligence Admiral Michael McConnell testified to the Senate that what the NIE had defined as the "nuclear weapons program" was really "the least significant portion" of nuclear weapons development, one that it is "very difficult" to know about.

Why, then, the headline? Ostensibly because a defector had provided notes on a meeting of Iranian authorities that suggested that some activities had stopped in 2003. Were the notes so indisputably authentic, and were the activities that allegedly stopped so important as to outweigh the ones continuing, as to compel overturning the Agency's own judgment of 2005 that Iran was building nukes? Considering that the UN's Mohamed ElBaradei, as well as the intelligence services of France and Israel, put no stock in that defector's veracity, and that the NIE did not compare the significance of the several sets of activities, you can bet that its "high confidence" did not flow from intellectual rigor.

Rather, it was the confidence of bureaucrats who had turned the tables on their internal rivals and expected no challenges from the outside. The *Wall Street Journal*'s news story told the tale: "U-Turn on Iran Reflects Iraq Rivalries."[25] Charles Thomas Fingar, who directed the NIE and who had led a faction of analysts who had fought against the Iraq War, explained that his team not only put great weight on new information but reevaluated "the judgments and sourcing used in previous estimates." In other words, having conquered the bureaucracy's commanding heights, the new team replayed the corridor games it had lost in the previous round. Significant for all future presidents is that Fingar, his colleague Vann Van Diepen, and others asserted that their judgments are authoritative because *they* are the professionals.

Endowing bureaucrats with power over truth transforms them into mandarins, neuters Presidents, Congresses, and citizens regardless of political leanings, and subverts democracy.

SUBVERSION AND COVERT ACTION

All operations of politics and war involve mixtures of forthrightness and deception. Subversion means turning parts of foreign bodies politic to your use. But implying that hiding your hand is the key to it hides the essence of subversion: appealing to their hopes, fears, pride, resentments. Thus to co-opt another's will is also called seduction. Note that nobody has ever been co-opted, seduced, or subverted without his knowledge. Mighty powers that cannot and will not be denied draw others to themselves through hope and fear. Convincing your target that resistance is futile is very subversive. Moreover, though subversive operations themselves may require hiding your relationships for a while, subversion itself eventuates in actions that cannot be secret.

Pretending that you are not involved in events that are forcing another's hand serves by not adding insult to injury. Thus in the 1980s the US government refrained only from declaring officially the obvious fact that it was funding Afghanistan's anti-Soviet resistance. The Soviet Union took even less care to cover its sponsorship of its proxies' wars in Nicaragua and Angola. By the same token, Iran makes no secret that Hezbollah is its tool in Lebanon, and neither the Lebanese nor anyone else doubts that Syria is the author of the murders that physically whittle down Lebanon's opposition to Syria. Success in such heavy-handed interference comes not from able pretense but rather from the target's reluctance to answer indirect war with the direct kind. That, in turn, depends on devising the operation to put enough pressure on the target to make the effort worthwhile, but not enough to trigger an unwanted reaction.

Subversion is one of the operations of war. Before Nazi Germany swallowed Austria and attacked Czechoslovakia and Poland, it organized local supporters to weaken their governments from within. The Nazis did this in Switzerland as well—without success before the war because the Swiss government jailed the organizers and held the German embassy responsible—but with considerable success in the two years following June 1940, when Germany was the likely winner. In the Soviets' Cold War, the Foreign Ministry played a supporting and defensive role while the Communist Party's International Department wielded the vast array of parties, contacts, and "mass organizations" that sought to pressure or revolutionize non-Communist societies. Meanwhile, the Soviet armed forces' immensity ensured a warm welcome for Soviet offers of peace. Post-Soviet Russia moved similarly to reabsorb Georgia and Ukraine: In both places it organized local sympathizers. In Georgia it invaded ostensibly to "protect them" so brutally as to send to Ukraine—its main target—the very subversive message that taking whatever deal the Russians might offer is preferable to suffering Georgia's fate. In short, subversion's success is usually proportionate to prospects for overt victory.

US "covert action," which began at the height of America's influence after World War II, mistook the fact that lots of foreigners were bending to America's wishes as evidence that subversive techniques were powerful in themselves. The prototype covert action was the CIA's conveyance in 1947–1948 of suitcases of money to Italy's Socialists and Christian Democrats, intended to prevent the Communists from winning that country's 1948 elections. As things turned out, the Communist coalition got only 34 percent of the vote. Did the dollars do that? In fact the Communists had not expected more, and never got much more in later years. The 1948 result was due to the fact that Stalin had forced the Communists to run on the choice between "Washington and Moscow" in a country where the word "America" was a synonym for good, whose people envied their American relatives, which was living on food from America, and which was hearing officially from America that the aid and relationship would have to stop if the Communists took power. But CIA attributed the result to its little tricks, not to the big realities.

The covert action myth grew in 1953, when Iranian generals who had received money from CIA as well as open encouragement from the rest of the US government overthrew a prime minister unfriendly to America and installed the friendly Shah. But note: If the money had been offered really secretly, on a "whatever happens, you're on your own" basis, it is doubtful that the generals would have bet their lives on the venture. Rather, the money was a token of something more valuable: the presumed commitment of American power.

Presumption is the key concept. The following year, as the US government tried by all means to persuade Guatemala's dictatorial President Jacobo Árbenz Gúzman to leave, CIA mounted a "revolutionary army" in the jungle consisting of radios talking to each other about nonexistent units moving toward the capital with US support. Frightened, the dictator ran. CIA boasted to the press about how its technical virtuosity could unmake governments.[26] Not at all. In fact, a tin-pot dictator had concluded that mighty America would do whatever necessary to remove him. But the incident taught others similarly placed that American statesmen use covert action precisely because they are unwilling to do "whatever it takes." So in 1961, when CIA sent a force to Cuba's Bay of Pigs designed to frighten the island's dictator but not to defeat him, Fidel Castro disregarded the presumption of US commitment and defeated the actual forces sent against him.

Because CIA misunderstood the reasons for its early successes, it has suffered mostly disasters ever since. From Indonesia in 1956, through Kurdistan from 1972 until 2003, and throughout the Middle East, those whom CIA recruited for its operations as well as those at whom the operations were targeted, knew that CIA involvement meant that while America hoped certain things would happen, it was unwilling to make sure they would happen. In Vietnam, the CIA made and unmade officials at every level and prescribed recipes, believing it knew best how to win. But then it was content to lose. Among the Palestinians, it armed and financed Fatah, imagining it was creating a force peaceful toward Israel and potent against Hamas. But Fatah ran away from Hamas and shot at Israel. With few exceptions, like the late Ted Shackley, who organized an army of Hmong tribesmen that kept North Vietnam out of Indochina's northwestern corner throughout the Vietnam war, these "covert warriors" have been sorcerers' apprentices. You would not trust electricians of comparable competence to wire your house.

The promise of covert action continued to let policymakers imagine they can do big things with small tools. Thus in 2008, as some bemoaned that the Iraqi people had voted to affirm their separate ethnic and sectarian identities, they proposed using the US-created Sunni militias to bring about "positive change" in the way Iraqis of different sects feel about each other. Doing this, so went the argument, "may require covert help from the United States, given how well financed the incumbent parties are. The United States played this sort of role during the

Cold War when the CIA heavily subsidized Italy's Christian Democrats and other anti-Communist parties."[27]

People who think this way seem really to think that they can divest some foreigners of their own goals and get them to embrace ours by bribing, tricking, and sermonizing them. People who think this way may never have learned that most of the parties and movements that US covert action funded turned against us. But common sense makes clear enough that transplanting your purposes into other people is impossible because they naturally put their own purposes ahead of yours, and hence that the art of coalitions consists of riding ever-shifting convergences and divergences.

US covert activities have been small in comparison to the goals they were expected to achieve, and often carried a disproportionate part of the burden of overt policy. Because our statesmen regarded covert operations as a "third option" between doing nothing and "sending the Marines," they ended up as the alternative to doing nothing and admitting that one is doing nothing. Worse, sometimes "third options" have been attempts to hedge policies by choosing opposing options but doing one covertly, in minor key. This amounts to subverting yourself.

MISSION IMPOSSIBLE

Nevertheless, all factions in American politics share the notion that intelligence should be and can be the key element in the "war on terrorism." That is because the desire to achieve much on the cheap is so widespread.

Beware of the temptation to spare yourself the responsibility of making decisions on policy because you cannot get access to the sources you want. For example, you may not have secret sources that tell you precisely what role Syria played in the assassination of pro-American politicians in Beirut after 2003. But you cannot pretend you don't know the essentials of the matter. What are you going to do about it?

Today, plenty of information is available to any newspaper reader about leaders of states and movements who advocate terrorizing Americans and without whose inspiration, propaganda, money, and protection terrorists could not operate. However, "Liberal Internationalists," "Neoconservatives," and "Realists" vie to demand that US intelligence supply information about the names, movements, and intentions of all small fry who are preparing to commit terrorist acts—information about acts that have not happened—that would have to stand up in courts of law and public opinion. That mission is impossible.

First, unless it were accomplished more thoroughly than imaginable, it would not stop terrorism. Second, since conspiracy is rightly difficult to prove in civilized courts, the kind of intelligence needed to convict persons preparing to commit terrorism would have to be of the kind that police forces within countries run against criminals and subversives—vastly different from that which countries run against one another or that occupying forces can run. Such intelligence would have to be pervasive and intrusive into society's nooks and crannies, able to compel persons to become and remain faithful informants. In short, it would have to be like the Second Chief Directorate of the old KGB, or the East German Stasi. The notion of America tightening such a grip on itself, never mind on mankind, need not detain us. Moreover, civilized societies would demand real evidence. The Bush Administration's proposal to bring terror suspects to trial but not to reveal the evidence against them is a foredoomed attempt to meld the totalitarian square with the civilized circle.

Intelligence is an instrument of war, not law. Distinguishing between friend and foe is fundamental to any organism's life and seldom requires more than ordinary perspicacity. The precise relationship between any person and event is only tangential to the only question that matters in war: Is this person an enemy, an obstacle to my peace, or not? Nevertheless, our statesmen impose on our intelligence services the task of searching out insignificant persons they not know—precisely because they disagree among themselves about whether to wage war on the significant ones they do know about.

CHAPTER 8
///////////////////

SECURITY FOR
OUR SIDE

The prince who is more afraid of the people than of foreigners must make fortresses; but the one who is more afraid of foreigners than of the people must leave them out.

There never was any reason why a prince should disarm his subjects; on the contrary, when he finds them disarmed he should always arm them; because by arming them those arms become yours . . . and the subjects make themselves partisans. And because one cannot arm all subjects, if you benefit those whom you arm you can do [what you like] to the others more securely; and that difference which they recognize in their own regard makes them obliged to you. . . . But when you disarm them you begin to offend them; you show you distrust them either out of vileness or out of little faith: and both these opinions generate hate against you.
　—MACHIAVELLI, *THE PRINCE*

Treason doth never prosper. What's the reason? Why, if it prosper none dare call it treason.
　—OVID, SHAKESPEARE: *THE TEMPEST*

War's most important front is at home. Defeats at home are less redeemable than ones abroad. The home front's cohesion, its faith in the regime's competence and capacity to protect, is always the king of the chessboard. When Carthage's emissaries congratulated Hannibal on having beaten Rome's armies again and again after his triumph at Cannae (216 BC), he cautioned them that nothing he had done had broken the Roman people's spirit.[1] No Roman faction clamored for concessions to Carthage. No temple resounded with cries that the gods damn Rome. But in the ultimate election that is war, some do vote for the enemy, while others already disaffected from the regime may find further reason to despise it. For a people embattled to tolerate internal opposition violates the law of self-preservation. Securing the home front's safety and cohesion against what the American oath of office calls "enemies foreign and domestic" is arguably more vital than winning foreign battles.

It is also more difficult and fraught with greater danger. Governments that feel threatened tend to "clamp down" on the population indiscriminately. But security measures applied to all are worse than impotent because they are inherently harsh on those who pose no threat and too permissive of those who do. By their nature, most of the people they touch feel they are affected unfairly. To them, they make a lively case that the government is incompetent and not on the people's side. On the other hand, trying to cleanse society of dissidents means endless purges, and attempts to eliminate dissidence amount to civil war—the most insecure condition of all.

Just as important, if a regime is under attack from foreigners whose sympathizers have any kind of presence within its borders and that regime's performance in war does not augur victory, its efforts to maintain internal security are doomed. Fortresses without hope fall, regardless of what else they may have going for them. In the short run, even when security measures are rigorous and well targeted, they merely reduce internal strife. In the long run, they face diminishing returns.

The state of Israel is a cautionary example. Under siege since before its birth in 1948, Israel has fought for its life against Arab states and against Arabs in its midst. Some of the latter are citizens, while others are sojourners. But Israel is on guard against all of them because it assumes, reasonably, that their sympathies are with the Arab world and that many will act on those sympathies. Hence Israeli security measures restrict Arabs far more than others. Also, Israel's police and intelligence services blanket the country with every kind of surveillance. Checkpoints are everywhere. The authorities search at will. They penalize even speech that they deem "incitement." If anything about a person raises a gate-keeper's suspicion, that person will be barred from the bus or the building and taken in. Nevertheless, Arab terrorists terrorize Israel, surely less than they would absent the security, but enough to feed substantial political movements among Israelis that urge concessions to the Arab states in the hope of obtaining "peace now." Overlapping this "peace constituency" is a body of Israeli opinion that holds other Israelis responsible for the Arabs' hostility. Over a half-century, during which the state of Israel fought battles with the Arab states for survival but without aiming at any kind of decisive victory, terrorism has combined with politics to dispirit the country. Against that deadly combination, security measures are powerless.

Internal security must be understood as a part of war and as sharing the problems and characteristics of war. Just as there is no such thing as peace for all, there is no such thing as security for all. Just as you must ask "Whose peace? Despite who?" you must ask "Whose security? Against whom?" *Wisely choosing those against whom we are to secure ourselves at home is as essential as is identifying enemies in war. In fact it is the same thing.* Statesmen are tempted to avoid clarity about enemies and what is to be done about them even more when facing domestic than when facing foreign problems. Reticence to deal with the fact that not all the regime's citizens feel the same way about it is understandable but pregnant with trouble.

At home as well as abroad, politics is the art of choosing sides. Because it is, one person's security is often the reverse of someone else's insecurity. Because some people are the pillars of our order while others are indifferent to it or aspire to another, the wise regime secures itself by treating these different people differently. Conversely, regimes that refuse to distinguish domestic friends and enemies, that fail to enlist the ones against the others, end up neutralizing the friends and emboldening the enemies. Security, then, is not about administrative arrangements, much less about fences and badges and screaming sirens. *It is intensely political and social.*

It is all about discrimination. It is by, of, and for fellow combatants. It is against thoughts, words, and deeds that give aid and comfort to the enemy. It happens when peoples mobilize against anyone in their midst whom they suspect of insufficient devotion to the common cause. It is the body politic's immunological rejection of foreign bodies. The now common notion that freedom hampers security, and that if you want security you must sacrifice some freedoms, is the reverse of a truth only recently forgotten: The greatest security exists among peoples who are freely committed to each other against common enemies.

The art of statesmanship consists of treating as enemies as few as possible and—if possible—only those who *insist* on placing themselves in that category. During the Revolutionary War, George Washington offered full citizenship to those Americans who preferred King George, coupling insistence on allegiance to the United States with freedom to leave it. In sum, the essence of domestic security is to empower and encourage the regime's partisans to act as owners of society and to encourage those who might be on the wrong side to get on the right side. By contrast, to pretend in wartime that all domestic political and social tendencies are equally worthy of respect and freedom is suicidally to abdicate statesmanship.

Only in the short run, however, can suppression of civil conflict substitute for real civil peace. Hence this kind of tyranny of the majority makes sense only as *a tool of foreign war,* as part of *an exceptional event* to the end of which all can look forward, and the *foreign focus* of which limits the tyranny. Moreover, because not even social mobilization and draconian police can stop individuals from despising your cause or (and) taking up the enemy's causes, *waging war indefinitely and emphasizing homeland security guarantees internal strife.* By contrast, defeating foreign enemies and their causes quickly is the main way, the surest way, of securing domestic peace because victory encourages support and discourages dissent. Hence wisely, America defines treason not by mere statute, but in the Constitution, and strictly in terms of war, duly voted. In traditional American statesmanship, war is an exceptional event meant to restore a normalcy in which domestic security and treason are irrelevant.

Domestic security, then, is naturally a part of war's effort for victory. Most emphatically, it cannot substitute for such an effort. Unfortunately,

America's experience with Homeland Security after 9/11 is paradigmatic of what happens when people try to do just that. Our statesmen focused less on how to eliminate enemies and too much on the extent to which the government ought to restrict and surveil Americans in general, as well as on how harsh the government should be to those it deems to be "enemy combatants." Whether and to what extent American arms and foreign policy changed the world after 9/11, how long such changes might endure, is less clear than that the US government changed life at home in ways not meant to be reversed. Unserious about waging war abroad, our statesmen tried to secure the home front by politically blind security measures.

Debate about what we Americans should do to others that would secure our peace degenerated into stylized clashes in the halls of Congress and the media about what the government should do to us, between some on the Right who want to give the government more power to be used more harshly, and others on the Left who want to reduce the government's power and harshness. For the Left, government power is the problem. For the Right, it is the solution. The former position leads Americans to treat the US government as the enemy while tolerating foreign ones; the latter leads Americans to accept despotism in the name of security. One position seemingly discounts the fact that America is at war, while the other aims more at giving the government "war powers" than at how, even whether, they are used to win the war. Both sets of positions are irrelevant to victory, and both evade the political question: Who are the people whose restriction will give us safety?

The American experience with Homeland Security should reinforce for future generations the old Machiavellian maxims: First, only the people, not the police, can ensure security. Second, mixing law and war perverts both. Having established that, we can consider the problem's true nature and its solution.

HOMELAND SECURITY IS FUTILE

A moment's reflection is enough to realize that securing America through police, locks, badges, and procedures is impossible. All but a few American homes can be entered with a hammer, or less. Daily, we are all vulnerable to anyone driving by or lurking by the roadside. In 2002 it took weeks and an alert citizen to catch one John Allen Muhammad, who had paralyzed the Washington, DC, area with a rifle fired from the trunk of his car. Our borders, crossed by tons of illegal drugs, can be crossed just as easily by tons of explosives or toxins. Almost a decade after six letters containing Anthrax spores went through the US postal system, the US government has made no official decision about who sent them and has no way of preventing similar events. Hijacking tanker trucks (or trains) filled with the most flammable, explosive, and toxic materials is child's play. Buying crop-dusting aircraft and filling them with toxins is straightforward. Entering public buildings with fake credentials or forcibly with armed units that impersonate antiterrorist forces is even easier.

So what might reasonably be expected of the US government's venture into Homeland Security? This security complex, which also includes the Federal Bureau of Investigation, the Department of Defense, and the State Department's visa program, bought nearly $100 billion per year of physical force. But force combined with political agnosticism is sham at best. Most of "Homeland Security" is either what one might call "honest man fences," effective only against those who aren't set on crossing them, or pretense, or theater—or pork. The latter—for example, the city of Newark got $250,000 to buy air-conditioned garbage trucks, and the Massachusetts agency that runs ferries to Martha's Vineyard got $900,000—only wastes money. But the pretense of security transformed the face of American life.

According to *The National Strategy for the Physical Protection of Critical Infrastructures and Key Assets,* the "insider problem"—a terrorist gaining access to critical locations and positions—is the most serious of all problems. The document promises uniform standards for clearances, and organizations to screen and clear all for the codes and badges that grant access to countless critical places. Its treatment of America's infrastructures—food, water, energy, transportation, public places—says a lot about many of American society's vulnerabilities. But what it promises to do about them—convene conferences and foster coordination of conversations about them among all the public and private parties that are involved in them—is no strategy: Doing all it recommends would scarcely cause anyone intent on wreaking havoc to break stride. That is because passive security might hamper a serious terrorist *only* if it were based on stringent sociopolitical screening of the population. But the US government eliminated serious security clearances in the 1970s.

At that time, precisely to avoid confronting the fact that some Americans were trying to defeat their country in the Vietnam War, our statesmen ordered personnel security investigators not to ask for, listen to, much less consider any information about a person's religion or politics (as well as about his or her ideas or sexual practices). So, because neither sadomasochism nor Wahabism nor believing that America is the bane of the world now disqualifies any US citizen from a security clearance, the clearance badge around the neck of the FBI agent or of the guy in the power dam's control room will reassure only the ignorant. You should not imagine that the US government's security criteria for access to America's most sensitive positions are qualitatively different from the ones by which it hires the sometimes menacing-looking Middle Easterners who search *you* at the airport.[2] Note also that the badges or (and) the documents by which they were procured may be counterfeit.

The US General Accounting Office's report on how easy it is to fake IDs will not surprise millions of underage drinkers and illegal workers:

Tests we have performed over the past 3 years have shown that counterfeit identification can be used to

- enter the United States
- purchase firearms
- gain access to buildings and other facilities
- obtain genuine identification for both fictitious and stolen identities, and
- obtain social security numbers for fictitious identities . . .

We counterfeited state drivers' licenses and birth certificates, and social security cards and used them to enter the United States . . . used counterfeit drivers licenses to purchase firearms. . . . If the prospective purchaser is using a fictitious identity, as we did, an instant background check is not effective. . . . We breached the security of four federal buildings and other facilities in the Atlanta area using counterfeit law enforcement credentials to obtain genuine building passes, which we then counterfeited. . . . Several investigators, including one carrying a briefcase suitable for carrying firearms, bypassed the magnetometers and x ray machines using the counterfeit building passes. . . . We similarly gained access to numerous federal buildings in Washington DC that contained the offices of cabinet secretaries or agency heads. We easily obtained social security numbers for fictitious names.[3]

Nor will its report on how easy it is to pass explosives and the components thereof through airport security onto airliners surprise sentient airline passengers: *"Our investigators succeeded in passing through TSA [Transportation Security Administration] security screening checkpoints undetected with components for several IEDs and an improvised incendiary device. The components for these devices and the items used to conceal the components were commercially available."* They cost $150. Moreover, the investigators got themselves selected for extra screening by leaving coins in their pockets. The pat-downs did not detect the bomb components. Nor did the X-ray machines detect pounds of materials hidden in carry-on baggage that had all the properties of plastic explosives. But the screeners did confiscate a bottle of medicated shampoo that one of the investigators was carrying for personal use.[4] A year after 9/11 the *New York Daily News* sent two reporters through the TSA checkpoints of the same airports that the hijackers had used, carrying box cutters and pepper spray. "Not a single airport security checkpoint spotted or confiscated any of the dangerous items. . . . [The security] amounted to nothing more than a big show."[5] Despite constant refinements in airport screening procedures, tests of airport security over the years have shown that about 90 percent of attempts to smuggle guns onto aircraft succeed, according to Bogdan Dzakovic, who served as a Red Team security tester for the Federal Aviation Administration (FAA) and later for the TSA: "There is very little substance to security. . . . It's really all window dressing that we're doing, it's big security theater on TV, and when you go to the airport it's security theater."[6] The US government empowered its personnel to get anybody they please delayed or arrested for criminal "interference" with this theater, for any expression of displeasure, assertion of rights, or even humor. But this protects only absurdity.

Not surprisingly, secrecy about the rest of Homeland Security similarly shields corruption born of unseriousness. The following is typical:

An exercise to test preparedness against a terrorist attack at a nuclear
weapons plant in Oak Ridge, Tennessee, was compromised last summer
when guards got a peek at the plans, according to a report by the Department of Energy's inspector general. The report . . . further said there was
"compelling" evidence that security tests have been manipulated since the
mid-1980s. The site was being tested to see if it could defend against potential security incidents. But the exercise was compromised when personnel
were shown computer simulations of the attack in advance. . . . The test
manager became suspicious after guards at the Y-12 complex fended off all
four simulated attacks, each involving a different scenario, Inspector General
Gregory H. Friedman wrote. . . . The manager investigated and found that
shortly before the June 26 test, two security workers employed by Wacken-
hut Services Inc. were inappropriately allowed to view the computer simulations of the four scenarios. . . . Among the reported abuses . . . Security
personnel would be assigned to "tail" those acting as aggressors . . . security
managers told security officers "the building and target to be attacked, the
exact number of adversaries, and the location where a diversion would
occur." . . . Where security personnel wore gear to determine whether they
had received a simulated fatal gunshot, participants at times removed the
batteries from the gear, put the batteries in backward, or placed tape, mud or
Vaseline over the sensors so they would not operate properly.[7]

Alas, because looking good tends to be more important than doing a
good job, secrecy in government tends to cover incompetence.

Homeland Security proved to be much more efficacious in putting
new twists and taboos into the lives of ordinary Americans. The young do
not know and may never know, as their parents knew, what it feels like to
walk into any public area as a matter of right, trusting and trusted, not
having to identify yourself, not having your ordinary transactions subject
to some guard deciding whether to call "security" on you and having you
"processed." Once upon a time not so long ago Presidents and high officials walked the streets like human beings. Now they have less contact

with humanity than the Chinese emperors of old, and inaugural parades look like armored columns moving through enemy territory. Major events feature lines of armed men facing the crowd, and even small-town parades include police roaring up and down as if they knew who they were after. They don't. Once, government employees were just ordinary folks. Now, a caste apart in pass-only buildings or behind bulletproof glass, they deal with you when and as they please. To the young, this is America. To those of a certain age it feels like a banana republic.

FORCE AND HABIT

The US government took to Homeland Security with the naturalness of a duck to water because it had habituated itself over the previous generation to applying ever more force, ever less discriminately, for ends ever less well defined.

The tools of Homeland Security and the American people's habituation to them grew apace: In the 1960s' riots in New York, Detroit, and Los Angeles, confrontations between police and murderous Leftist gangs with names like "Symbionese Liberation Army" and "Black Panthers," and the police's attempt to capture a man who had shot people from the University of Texas library tower in 1975—all televised—led to the formation and popularity of Special Weapons and Tactics (SWAT) teams—militarized police. Second, beginning in the 1970s, trying to deal with American society's increasing taste for mind-altering drugs by pursuing armed drug traffickers, the "war on drugs" spread SWAT far and wide and made it part of popular culture. Third, in 1972 the Nixon Administration decided to deal with aircraft hijackings by forbidding passengers from carrying weapons, criminalizing attempts by airline passengers to interfere with hijackings, and forcing passengers to pass through magnetometers. This got Americans used to being distrusted, searched, and ordered around.

Instruments of police violence are accepted in twenty-first-century America to an extent that none I know imagined. Whereas in the early 1960s Alabama Sheriff "Bull" Connor's use of a mere cattle prod to disperse a crowd was scandalous news, forty years later the use of electron beam "Tasers" and pepper spray by police around the country to convulse and subdue (and occasionally kill) individuals even outside crowds was routine, quotidian, and unremarkable. In 2008 the New York Police Department made "Tasers" standard equipment for some 3,000 sergeants. Shooting to death innocent persons because they *might* have "had a gun" came to be seen as understandable. But police violence can kill terrorists and disrupt the social strata that spawn them only if the authorities aim it appropriately. Force undirected or badly directed is worse than useless.

SWAT teams, invented in 1966, remained curiosities into the 1970s. But by 1980 there were some 3,000 SWAT team deployments per year, and by 1997 the number had jumped to 40,000 per year.[8] Thereafter, as they became increasingly indistinguishable from other police operations, they could no longer be counted accurately. By 1997, 90 percent of US cities with a population over 50,000 had a SWAT team, as did various agencies and college campuses. Soon, so did countless small towns and suburbs, and even national parks. They rode in armored vehicles, dressed in military garb, carried the same submachine guns as navy SEALS. They trained to knock down doors, wreck the premises, subdue, or shoot to kill. Most of all, they treated people as hindrances or enemies. Whereas the policeman's traditional motto "to protect and to serve" assumes that the person he meets is his client unless there is "probable cause" to believe otherwise—and even then that the person is innocent until judged guilty—SWAT teams assume that "it's a war out there." Whereas Sergeant Joe Friday, in the 1950s popular TV show "Dragnet," wore jacket and tie and said, "Yes ma'am, no ma'am," "Dallas SWAT"'s turn-of-the-century heroes shout obscenities, shove, and shoot.

And since SWAT teams don't know who the enemy is, their working assumption is that you are an enemy unless proven otherwise. The FAA has this advice for passengers escaping from a hostage situation: "Expect to be handled roughly." Quite so. Few deny, and older policemen are aghast, that so many young cops are attracted to SWAT by the thrills of using cool guns and military operations—but only against people who let themselves be herded, who don't shoot back. "Officer safety" comes first. And indeed the contribution of the SWAT teams from five jurisdictions, totaling eight hundred men, who went to Columbine High School in Littleton, Colorado, on April 20, 1999, as two students were killing twelve others and a teacher, was to force the frightened students fleeing the school to put their hands on their heads and to frisk them. Whereas a sheriff's deputy was exchanging fire with the killers—at least preventing them from killing more—and other local police wanted to go get them, the SWAT teams set up a four-hour siege, even ignoring a sign that students had put in a window: "1 bleeding to death." The shooting stopped at noon, and the SWAT walked in on the corpses at 3:30 P.M. The victim had bled to death. SWAT may provide "safety" to officers, but not to the general public.

The War on Drugs was the occasion for arming and training police on armored personnel carriers, M-16s, grenade launchers, helicopters, and attitude. The Military Cooperation With Law Enforcement Act of 1981 first directed the Pentagon to make equipment useful for drug interdiction available to police forces at all levels. Congress and the President ordered more help in 1986 and 1989. In 1994 President Clinton ordered the military simply to turn over equipment to police forces, and Congress legislated the "reutilization program" that paid for the military to dispose of older equipment to police. In 1997 CBS's "60 Minutes" showed a rural Florida sheriff with twenty-three helicopters, a tank, and an arsenal of assault weapons. Beginning in 1993 the military began teaching urban combat to SWATs. The SWAT subculture—possessed of its own magazines, suppliers, and Olympics—revels in the image of itself at war. But against whom?

Our statesmen's response to aircraft hijackings combined political agnosticism, disempowerment of citizens, and military might. Forcing passengers to pass through magnetometers prevented law-abiding citizens from carrying weapons to protect themselves and others. The ostensible reason for this—in addition to the naive belief that hijackers would be disarmed as well—was the government's calculation that resisting hijackers would endanger passengers more than complying with their demands. So just to make sure that passengers would not resist even with their bare hands, the FAA adopted the rule most fully explained on State Department Publication 10214, "Hijacking Survival Guidelines." This states in part: "Stay calm and encourage others around you to do the same. . . . Do not challenge the hijackers physically or verbally. . . . Comply with their instructions. Do not struggle or try to escape unless you are absolutely certain of success. . . . If you are told to keep your head down or maintain another body position, talk yourself into relaxing into the position. You may need to stay that way for some time. . . . Prepare yourself mentally and emotionally for a long ordeal with possible verbal or physical abuse, lack of food and drink, and unsanitary conditions." None of this prevented further hijackings.

But instead of reversing the policy, our statesmen put their faith in the Army's newly created "Delta Force," expert marksmen trained to rescue passengers. But Yasser Arafat's disciple Imad Mughniyah had no trouble slipping arms aboard TWA flight 847 in 1985, hijacking it, taking it out of Delta Force's reach, and torturing and killing a US sailor on board. Because our statesmen's policy was in force on 9/11, when the hijackers told their victims to keep quiet and they wouldn't get hurt, they were echoing US government policy. Passengers may also have dreamed that the US government would rescue them. And when the passengers of United 93 fought the hijackers, they violated US government policy.

After 9/11's deadly lesson, American airline passengers took it upon themselves to smother with sheer weight any disturbance that might develop into a hijacking. But the US government continued to expand Homeland Security on the basis of a failed model. The point of all this is that massive increases in the size, equipment, and prerogatives of American security forces produced a parody of security. When heavily armed police swarm and clunk menacingly onto places where criminals, terrorists, or deranged persons have slaughtered victims, they advertise pathetic impotence.

In sum, nothing in Homeland Security's ponderous apparatus would stop any ten people from shutting down our school system by throwing bottles of flaming gasoline into ten school buses in ten states at the same time, from crippling public assembly by detonating ten suicide vests among crowds at ten football stadia, or from bringing down airliners with bombs in carry-on luggage—or even with tampons made of *plastique*. Nor do fences, concrete barriers, or entry codes, much less SWAT teams, reduce the likelihood that a squad of terrorists clothed, fake-credentialed, armed, vehicled, and shouting "go, go, go," like the paramilitaries of any federal, state, or local agency, might enter a nuclear installation, a dam, the New York Stock Exchange, or any place they wished, to do what they wish.

WAR AND LAW DON'T MIX

Who are America's enemies at home and abroad? What should we do about them? Too typically, our statesmen have answered with what seem legal arguments. Pseudolegal is more accurate, because when persons in public life talk about what *the law* allows or disallows with regard to domestic security, when they force the judicial system to arbitrate disputes over policy (or to hide the lack thereof), they are really beating around the bush of what they propose doing to whom, and what good that might accomplish. The legalisms divert from the substantive issues. This parallels our statesmen's attempts to slip responsibility for judgment about foreign problems onto intelligence agencies: "I acted according to intelligence." Ill-using law became just another way of evading political issues. This is even more harmful to battles on the home front than on foreign ones.

How to treat prisoners—some of whom are US citizens—whom the US government designates as terrorists has been one of the top topics of national debate—as if the outcome of the war or even America's short-term security depended on that treatment. Nevertheless, the topic is "hot" because concentrating on individuals lets all sides skirt political choices.

Should they be tortured? Should they be tried at all and, if so, should ordinary rules of evidence apply? One side, typically on the Right, argues that because the prisoners currently held (and by logical extension any others who may be taken in the future) are *enemies* who intend us grievous harm, we may rightly subject them to whatever procedures will get them to "talk." Because they are enemies in war, so goes the argument, the government may hold them without trial, for as long as it chooses. And if it does try them, it should do so without subjecting evidence to ordinary scrutiny. America does not owe its enemies that. The other side, typically on the Left, argues that the US Constitution as well as the Geneva Conventions prohibit torture, that war does not negate the principle that no person should be imprisoned without some account of the reasons for the imprisonment that he may challenge, and that trials that do not observe proper rules of evidence are shams. America owes it to itself to follow proper procedure.

While both sets of arguments contain truths, those who make them agree more than they realize because both *choose to confuse* the laws that govern war with the ones that govern peace. Under the laws of war—the Hague Convention of 1907 and the Geneva Convention of 1929—the armed forces may kill at their discretion anyone they deem an enemy combatant. And when they capture one who is not wearing proper military insignia, they may execute him summarily or after a summary trial to ascertain that he was not wearing proper insignia. Since none of the prisoners in US custody in the "war on terror" were captured in uniform, any who were caught arms in hand may be lawfully executed on that basis alone. But torture? Domestic as well as international law forbids it, as does common sense: The notion that forcing a prisoner to "talk" months or years after his capture may tell you anything useful, much less prevent a terrorist attack is the sort of stupidity peddled on the TV drama "24," in which the hero US agent "saves lives" by brutalizing prisoners. As for trials, the laws of war mandate them only for such individuals who stand accused of specific crimes. But the trials must be for real.

If the purpose were to punish criminals, or just to rid the world of them, why hold trials under American rules for persons who, whatever else they may or may not have done, have undeniably committed what the laws of war deem the capital crime of making war out of uniform? Our statesmen, Right and Left, seem intent on bringing these individuals to the bar of American justice to demonstrate, respectively, its harshness and its fairness. But note: This has little to do with establishing internal security or winning any war. Moreover, while the Left impugns the process for its harshness and the Right insists on even more, neither seems terribly concerned with the only question that real trials address: Regardless of what any of these people might say about themselves, or what their prosecutors or defenders say, *what is the substance of the evidence* against them? Are they the ones who animate the movement that is at war with us? And if these are not, who might such people be?

The contrast between Left and Right is sharpest and arguably least enlightening on the issue of what *extraordinary* powers does the fact that the US government has invoked "war" give the government? On one side is John Yoo, Professor of Law at UC-Berkeley's Boalt Hall law school. On the other side is the American Civil Liberties Union (ACLU).

Yoo wrote that "the days . . . when our forces against terrorism were limited to the Federal Bureau of Investigation, federal prosecutors, and the criminal justice system will not return."[9] They will not, he wrote, because a four-judge plurality of the Supreme Court agreed that Congress' authorization of "all necessary and appropriate force" against all who may have been involved in the 9/11 attacks instituted a state of war. This, he argued, meant that henceforth, *implicitly forever,* the President, in the exercise of his war power, could imprison as a prisoner of war anyone he deemed an "enemy combatant" without justifying it to anybody. Yoo argued against any limits on such detention: "[While the Court] acknowledged the 'unconventional nature' of the war on terrorism and suggested that if hostilities continued 'for two generations,' [the defendant] Hamdi's detention might indeed exceed the government's war powers. . . . The court did not provide any reason why after two generations it may be necessary to reconsider the laws of war. If American troops remain engaged in combat in Afghanistan in 2040, the laws of war do not require the United States to release Hamdi or other Taliban detainees."[10] Or anybody else for that matter, or to justify it to anyone.

Yoo has also argued that *because* surveillance of enemies and potential enemies is an inherent part of the power to command in war, neither the 1978 Foreign Intelligence Surveillance Act that requires judicial warrants for surveillance of "non-US persons"—a law suggested by the intelligence agencies, asked for by President Carter, passed by Congress, and observed by Presidents thereafter—nor any statute, can trammel it. That argument implies, absurdly, that Presidents don't have to "faithfully execute" the laws that they have signed. This amounts to claiming that Presidents may legitimately pretend to enforce, but actually disregard, any law duly enacted and legitimized by usage and that, when their ruse is discovered, they may argue that it really was never valid. This is law?

Yoo claims that this position is none other than Lincoln's in the Civil War: We may rightly set aside any one of America's precious laws to preserve all the other, equally precious ones. But whereas Lincoln exercised exceptional powers only at an exceptional time, Yoo's argument—the Bush Administration's argument, accepted by many on the Right—is that the US government may do anything it thinks proper in the name of war *indefinitely.* But *if war, once exceptional, is now normal and henceforth forever,* our complex of laws boils down to the Roman dictatorial formula *salus populi suprema lex*—a frighteningly short Constitution.

Note that republican Rome's "dictators" were appointed for brief emergencies and could not extend their terms. For many on the Right, however, increasing Presidential war powers in perpetuity seemed to be an end in itself, apart from how, when, or even whether those powers should be exercised unto victory. In this regard, it is important to repeat that our statesmen on the Left largely agree that terrorism is coterminous with modernity and hold even more vigorously than does John Yoo the notion that victory is *passé* and that greater regimentation of society in perpetuity is inevitable. In sum, there is less fundamental difference between Right and Left than meets the eye.

This may stem from our statesmen's childish ideas about history and international affairs. Thus, Yoo cites conventional wisdom: *"One of the few facts considered to be close to an empirical truth in international relations: democracies do not tend to go to war with each other"* and concludes that

> if the United States were involved in a dispute with another democracy, the President ought to involve Congress because a dual branch process would help facilitate a peaceful resolution to the dispute by allowing the United States to signal more effectively its intentions. If, however, the United States were involved in a dispute with a non-democracy or a terrorist organization, a unilateral presidential approach might make much more sense because a non-democratic regime or terrorist organization is unlikely to appreciate the value of congressional participation.[11]

Whatever the logic here, it is not that of war. Yoo also cites Alexander Hamilton's remark that "secrecy and dispatch" make Presidents better managers of foreign affairs than assemblies. But, like some others on the Right, he ignores Hamilton, who wrote in *Federalist #25* that the people's representatives must vote any major military action other than repelling aggression, in *Federalist #6* that democracies are as warlike as any other states, and that those who believe otherwise "must be far gone in speculation."[12] A substantial part of the American body politic's Right side, it seems, is "far gone" in substituting faith in government power for reason about war.

Faith in government power—except for military power—is even more common on America's Left than on its Right. Hence the ACLU and the Left reduced reasoning about war to minimizing the US government's war powers while expanding power in general.

For instance, the ACLU filed suit in 2004 claiming that *if* the President had ever had Constitutional power as commander in chief of the armed forces to surveil whomever he thinks fit, that power was eclipsed when Congress passed and the President signed the 1978 Foreign Intelligence Surveillance Act. But in so claiming, the ACLU ignored that the President's Constitutional responsibility for commanding the armed forces really does imply the power to do it effectively, that this includes surveillance, and that the Constitution cannot be changed by statute. More important, that position prefers process to results: If persons who should have been surveilled and were not end up causing disasters, the ACLU position seems content to chalk it up to the greater good of having gone through the proper process.

The ACLU claimed that it was trying to restrict the government's war powers out of concern for the rights of "ordinary Americans." In fact, however, with regard to "war powers," as to other matters, the ACLU battled for constituencies quite at odds with ordinary Americans. One illustration of this was its 2006 lawsuit to stop the US government's warrantless interception of electronic communications between persons abroad who may be associated with terrorism and persons in the United States.[13] In response to the ACLU's claim that it was advocating the privacy of innocent, ordinary persons, the 6th Circuit Court wrote:

> Implicit in each of the plaintiffs' alleged injuries is the underlying possibility—which the plaintiffs label a "well founded belief" and seek to treat as a probability or even a certainty—that the NSA is presently intercepting, or will eventually intercept, communications to or from one or more of these particular plaintiffs, and that such interception would be detrimental to the plaintiffs' clients, sources, or overseas contacts. This is the premise upon which the plaintiffs' entire theory is built. But even though the plaintiffs' beliefs—based on their superior knowledge of their contacts' activities—may be reasonable, the alternative possibility remains that the NSA might not be intercepting, and might never actually intercept, any communication by any of the plaintiffs named in this lawsuit." (emphasis mine)

The Court's ironic point was that if in fact the plaintiffs' communications were scrutinized, there would be *prima facie* reason to do it and, above all, that the plaintiffs feared scrutiny precisely because they knew that their overseas friends *are* America's enemies, and that it was suing to shield America's enemies from America's defenders.

And indeed the ACLU filed many of its suits against US security measures in conjunction or in parallel with organizations that aimed precisely to make life easier for America's enemies and harder for its defenders: American Muslim Union, Islamic Society of North America, Council on American-Islamic Relations (CAIR), Nation of Islam, Muslim Students' Association, Middle East Children's Alliance.[14] The ACLU provided legal services to men over sixteen from Arab and Muslim countries to resist the Justice Department's post-9/11 order that they register or be deported, arguing that such discrimination was unreasonable. By the same argument it opposed the FBI's plan to catalog mosques in America. It sued to stop the US government from using information about the International Institute of Islamic Thought, which indicated it was helping to fund Palestinian Islamic Jihad, arguing that the search warrant under which the information was obtained was overly broad. And it championed legally Sami Al-Arian, convicted of conspiracy to aid a terrorist organization. And it sued for the "right" of noncitizens to work as airport screeners.

Why? Not because of blind impartiality. You may see its partiality as regards security in how it deceived donors and the US government who might have supposed that it was really just after civil liberties. The federal government lets employees contribute to their favorite organizations through payroll deductions. The government grants such access to its employees' donations on condition that the organizations certify that they do not knowingly employ or fund terrorists whose names appear on its "watch lists." The ACLU certified and got access. But its executive director, Anthony Romero, explained later that ACLU officials never had any intention of even looking at the watch lists, thus taking advantage of the law while intending to frustrate its objective—the very definition of subversion.

Also, when *The New York Times* revealed that the US government was tracking terrorist finances in cooperation with the international SWIFT financial transfer network, Romero demanded not just that the program "be stopped now," but also "a full accounting of what information has been demanded by the U.S. government, how they have used it, with whom it was shared."[15] To whom and for what purpose, do you imagine, might such an account be useful? Is it likely Mr. Romero did not ask that question before making his demand?

The notion that the ACLU's shrewd operatives are just impartial libertarians who minimize the government's security efforts and divert them from America's enemies ignorant or careless of what they do, is not worth a second thought. The ACLU's efforts to diminish the US government's capacity to defend America flow naturally from its political preferences for the causes it takes up. By contrast, the Right is willing to trade generic increases in government power and information for fuzzying the focus of security. Alas, these vectors' convergence decreases American officials' focus and competence against enemies and makes them dangerous to us. It decreases freedom *and* security.

WHY NO LINE?

In short, our statesmen refuse to acknowledge that there is not a unity of purpose among us and to draw public lines between what is permissible and not because they refuse to take war seriously. They prefer the aimless force and sterile arguments of Homeland Security in part because they believe, as the Department of Homeland Security's 2002 founding charter, signed by President George W. Bush, asserts: "The terrorist threat to America . . . is an unavoidable byproduct of the technological, educational, economic and social progress" of our time. "It is a permanent condition to which America and the entire world must adjust."

Hence the burdens, expenses, and restrictions that Homeland Security imposes on the American people are not the domestic sector of a war against particular enemies, victory in which would end them. Rather, they are permanent, apolitical changes in America's way of life desirable in and of themselves. Force will be needed to police Americans because they are inherently disunited, since disunity is another word for pluralism and freedom. Trying to return to America's old, free, and trusting ways is not just unrealistic. It is wrong. Defenders of "Homeland Security" such as the Naval Postgraduate School's David Tucker label the aim of returning to America's former way of life "bombast," "unattainable," and suggest that the program's skeptics are the real threat.[16] "Get used to it!" might well be the "Homeland Security" motto.

Pretending political neutrality, the Charter characterizes "terrorism" as "invisible," that is, impersonal and not coming from any particular political direction, race, or religion—don't even mention "our Arab friends" or the "religion of peace," Islam. It is even more politically incorrect to mention that Islamists and Marxists from Havana to Teheran to the Ivy League and Dupont Circle share philosophical roots and work together against "imperialism and Zionism," or to quote prominent American Leftists' praise that some prominent Leftists have converted to Islam.

But why avoid the obvious foreign and domestic political points of contention? The answer is that our statesmen are trying to avoid political divisions within America itself by acting as if they did not matter. Thus President George W. Bush declared that "racial profiling is wrong, and we will end it in America," and US Immigration, Border Patrol, and Customs agents were told that "preventing racial profiling is a priority mission." Hence also, the Transportation Security Administration arranged and re-arranged its airport screening procedures to make sure that Middle Easterners are scrutinized in no greater proportion than the rest of the population.

Note, however, that this position itself is not politically neutral. The proposition that Muslims in general and Arabs in particular are responsible for most terrorism and that America needs to secure itself against them is far more widespread among the American people than the Charter's position. Most obviously, it is not the position of any person I know on the political Right. It is a position found only on the political Left. When Heather MacDonald asked prominent Leftists whether the FBI should investigate Middle Eastern students at US flight schools or all students, they answered that the FBI should make no distinction based on race, religion, or national origin.[17] In short, the US government's official refusal to aim Homeland Security at those most likely to threaten it is a political choice to defer to the prejudices and predilections of one side of America's political spectrum over another's.

Similarly, although most Muslims in America are not anti-American, our statesmen chose to court the ones that are. The US government treats as Islam's chief representative in America something that calls itself the Council on American-Islamic Relations (CAIR), founded in 1994 by former officials of the Islamic Association of Palestine, which was cited by a federal judge for complicity with Hamas in the murder of an American. CAIR also raised funds in America for the Holy Land Foundation, which is linked to Hamas. Along with Hamas, CAIR is funded by Saudi Arabia's Islamic Development Bank. Nevertheless, the White House invited it and lesser organizations to advise it on how to do right by Muslims. One Hersham Islam, an Islamist counselor to Gordon England, George Bush's Deputy Secretary of Defense, vetted the US armed forces' Muslim chaplains, as a result of which many are Wahabis. Nor do our statesmen object to the Saudi Wahabi movement building and financing the majority of new mosques in the United States. In the Washington, DC, area, the Dar Al Hijra mosque that reportedly dealt with some of the 9/11 hijackers is Saudi-funded. The ADAMS Center is paid for by Egypt's Muslim Brotherhood.[18]

One practical consequence of our statesmen's choice of a bogus sociopolitical neutrality is that the US government has had little success in prosecuting persons it believes are terrorists. After 9/11 the FBI recruited informants in America's Muslim communities, resulting in the prosecution of semiserious young Muslims for incipient, bush-league terror plots in California, North Carolina, and New Jersey that might or might not have existed except for the FBI informants among them. Such prosecutions surely put small-fry similarly lightly inclined on guard against getting mixed up in such things. But prosecutions of serious people engaged in serious support of terrorism have had difficulty convincing juries precisely because they have been based on political equivocation.

The US government's premier antiterrorist case, against the Holy Land Foundation and seven men—some prominent in CAIR—for sending $12.4 million to the Palestinian terrorist group Hamas, ended in a mistrial on October 22, 2007, because our statesmen could not bring themselves to argue that the defendants were aiding and abetting war against the American people. The defendants admitted financing Hamas but pointed out truly that Hamas does things other than murder. The government could hardly prove that the men *intended* the money for murder rather than for those other things. After all, money is fungible. The defense also argued that American Jews as well as the US government send money to Israel while Israel kills people too. Is this not also terrorism?

The government lost the case because it was unwilling to explain the political difference between America and Israel on one side and our enemies on the other, and as well that, given the fungibility of resources, anyone aiding any part of any enterprise aids all of it. Having failed to do that, it showed what little suffices to secure terrorist operators *within the United States itself* under Homeland Security.[19] Thus one Khalil Jassem, founder of Life for Relief and Development, wrote and distributed a "Comprehensive Guide to Running a Muslim Non Profit in the US."[20]

But on November 24, 2008, a federal jury convicted all the defendants after prosecutors argued, as Judge Richard Posner of the seventh Circuit Court wrote in a separate case imposing a $156 million fine on related organizations, "If you give money to an organization that you know to be engaged in terrorism the fact that you earmark it for the organization's nonterrorist activities does not get you off the liability hook." Prosecutors also introduced documents from the Palestinian Authority, an enemy of Hamas and allied (dubiously at best) with the US, that claimed Hamas is America's enemy. The point here is that focusing on political intentions rather than on specific acts is the key to placing serious obstacles in the way of terrorists in America.

LINES DRAWN, LINES BLURRED

The US government did not always so accommodate its enemies. During the Civil War President Lincoln's Provost Marshals arrested people who discouraged enlistment or opposed the draft. The Lincoln Administration imprisoned over 10,000 people without charges for opposing Union war aims, including a congressman from Ohio. Federal troops even prevented anti-Union Maryland state legislators from voting. During World Wars I and II, the US government mobilized the public preemptively against anyone who might hinder the war effort. In 1917 and 1918 the vast German-speaking communities of the upper Midwest came under great pressure to speak English. And Socialist union organizers were stigmatized as presumed hindrances to war production. The 1918 Sedition Act made it a crime to express "disloyal, profane, scurrilous, or abusive" opinions. The Justice Department worked with the American Protective League—deputized civilians who reported and sometimes arrested persons they thought might be disloyal. A generation later, German Americans—a big part of society and one of whose number, named Eisenhower, was America's commander in Europe—suppressed their *"Bund"* and made sure to be on their best patriotic behavior. And, of course, Japanese Americans were removed from the West Coast, though very few sympathized with Japan after Pearl Harbor. On the one hand, countless injustices pressed the target populations to preclude the rise among themselves of movements that might have dragged them into serious conflicts with the rest of society. On the other, the majority's involvement in and responsibility for internal security contributed to the feeling of unity and confidence that characterized mainstream American society during these great wars.

Due to the majority's remarkable sociopolitical unity, the American people fought two hot world wars and a cold one against great powers without wrapping themselves in razor wire, and maintained freedom such as peoples in war have seldom if ever maintained, freedom such as contemporary Americans may never experience.

The Cold War broke that unity along preexisting fault lines between the political Left and Right. While anti-Communist Americans opposed Soviet causes, the anti-anti-Communists advocated that we join Soviet causes, not oppose them.[21] Our statesmen tried to abstract from this by pretending that political differences "stopped at the waters' edge." They did not. Nor did the statesmen's own prejudices: Robert McNamara tells us that during that war he regarded American conservatives as bigger threats to world peace than North Vietnam.[22] As we have seen, Anthony Lake's *The Vietnam Legacy* and William Appleman Williams's *The Tragedy of American Diplomacy*—icons for a substantial part of our foreign policy Establishment—argued that America was the greatest danger to the world's peace and progress.[23]

America's domestic factions took up toward terrorism roughly the same positions they had held during the Cold War, while our statesmen tried to deal with the divisions by faux neutrality as they had a generation earlier—and with similar results.[24] From terrorism's irruption upon America in the 1960s our statesmen sought to avoid dealing with the primordial fact that some Americans support the states whence the terrorists come, and some the causes for which the terrorists act. Not to displease such people, our statesmen neither made war on the Cuban, Algerian, and Ugandan regimes that made hijacking possible, nor allowed American society to put pressure on their sympathizers. Rather, they tried to establish security by applying police measures indiscriminately, as if they did not know whence the threat was coming, or friend from enemy.

This synthetic ignorance had consequences. Gradually, support for "the Palestinians"—increasing tolerance of their terrorism or simply endorsing it as "resistance"—became part of Progressive Americans' creed.[25] Some Progressives came to damn Israel, once their beloved, for being on America's side, to see America as the world's oppressor, and to imagine that the oppressed are justified in doing violence to us too. Whistling past this reality, our statesmen pretended to presume that there is equal probability that any given American will be loyal, and that the real problem is non-Progressive Americans' bigoted refusal to admit it.

This results in Homeland Security empowerment of police. But since police deal with behavior, not objectives, they do not draw lines between the people who share your cause and those who oppose it. Nor can policing push to your side those who might be inclined against it. *Apolitical policing of political strife ends up as impotent, random harassment at best. Too often, the pretense of political neutrality hides indefensible political choices.*

CHOOSING SIDES

Wisdom about domestic security begins with the fact that no society, including our own, is homogeneous; that although our population is not essentially at odds with itself, not everyone among us is a friend; that the negative laws that frame our civic freedoms make sense, are operable, only among friends, and that we neither can close down our open society— "Israelize" it—nor desire to. That is why preserving the framework or our civic freedoms in the face of war depends so much on forging unity of purpose.

But since absolute unity of purpose cannot exist, it is better to admit that there cannot be the same freedoms for those with sympathy for the enemy as for friends. Civic freedoms in wartime can exist fully only among fellow combatants. Hence drawing the line between friends and enemies is the prerequisite for preserving freedom among friends. Drawing that line is a matter of political choice. Because political choice is inevitable, it is better for all concerned that it be made explicitly, publicly, and responsibly.

One example of the opposite, of political choice under cover of neutrality, was the Federal Bureau of Investigation's handling of the five letters that entered the US postal system in the weeks after 9/11 bearing Anthrax spores, killing five people and temporarily shutting down the US Senate. On June 27, 2008, the Justice Department paid Dr. Stephen Hatfill $4.6 million, plus attorneys' fees, to settle his suit for defamation and violation of privacy. The US government had named Hatfill to the press as the sole "Person of Interest" (it dared not say "suspect") in the Anthrax case and had otherwise harassed him. The case is interesting for our purpose because the FBI pursued Hatfill despite *zero* evidence that he had "done it," while going to some lengths to avoid taking seriously *some hard* evidence that the 9/11 hijackers had been involved, and that the deadliest of the Anthrax had come from Iraq's biological warfare laboratories.

The FBI would not take the evidence seriously. Confirming an October 29, 2001, White House briefing by Major General John Parker, the Army Institute of Pathology stated that the deadliest samples had been professionally coated with silica: "Significantly, we noted the absence of aluminum with the silica. This combination had previously been found in anthrax produced by Iraq." Thereafter, ABC News interviewed former UN weapons inspectors familiar with Iraq's biological weapons, who confirmed that this particular technique for aerosolizing Anthrax was peculiarly Iraqi. But the FBI denied that. On August 26, 2002, Douglas Beecher of the FBI wrote in the journal *Applied Environmental Microbiology* that reports about the Anthrax spores being coated with silica were baseless. But he gave no evidence, and the FBI never replied to challenges in the same journal to produce it. Moreover, the FBI ignored the fact that Dr. Christos Tsonas in Fort Lauderdale, Florida, treated Ahmed al-Haznawi, one of the 9/11 hijackers, for skin ulcers he thought "consistent with cutaneous anthrax" and that in nearby Delray Beach pharmacist

Greg Chatterton recalled chief hijacker Mohamed Atta asking for medication for his very itchy hands. Also, not incidentally, the first victim of the Anthrax letters worked at American Media International, right near where the hijackers lived and had sought medical treatment for the kinds of symptoms that would result from handling Anthrax. Finally, the FBI also refused to take *the fact* that the Anthrax letters had been mailed on Nassau Street across from Princeton University as a basis for looking into the possibility that some persons on that campus were part of the operation.

Then in August 2008 the FBI announced that it was about to arrest Bruce Ivins, another scientist at the US Army Medical Research Institute of Infectious Diseases whom it had been harassing for years, for having manufactured and mailed the Anthrax. The FBI argued that Ivins was mentally unstable, to which Ivins gave credence by committing suicide forthwith. But the FBI neglected the massive fact that the Anthrax spores of 2001 had been milled to 1.5 to 3 microns and coated with silica, and that no equipment for doing that existed at Ivins's laboratory. Moreover, as Laurie Mylroie pointed out, the FBI's contention that Ivins took off from work in Maryland on September 17 to place the letters in a Princeton mailbox which were postmarked on the 18th is implausible. Letters thus postmarked had to be deposited between 5 P.M. on the 17th and noon the following day. Ivins was at work for a meeting at 4 P.M. on the 17th. In short, believing the FBI's case takes effort. Alas Ivins's suicide, if the strongest evidence for his guilt, is all too easily explained by years of harassment.

Why did the FBI focus on these men while not even confronting evidence that points in other directions? Because it had drawn a line, made a judgment, according to which "right-wing elements" within the United States are the likeliest sources of high-tech terrorism. Drs. Hatfill and Ivins fit its profile and were persecuted. But they were never prosecuted, *logically, presumably because the evidence for doing so was not there.* That profile's reverse side was our statesmen's political prejudice to the effect that Iraq must not be named as a major source of terrorism, much less as having contributed to 9/11, and that places like Princeton would never, ever produce or harbor sympathizers, much less collaborators with terrorism.

The FBI drew a line, chose sides. Wrong line. Wrong sides. It did it by following the US government's logic with regard to Homeland Security.

Wrong logic. We can take a small amount of comfort from the fact that our statesmen developed this logic largely *in pectore* and explained it in public hypocritically, that is, unsustainably. It would not be easy to make a public case that America must be at least as much on guard against right-wing elements in league with Zionists intent on mass slaughter to impose their foreign and domestic policies as against Islamists whose anti-Western agenda finds echoes in America's far Left.

Our point here is that the choice of against whom the country should secure itself, of what the logic of Homeland Security should be, is quintessentially *the public's business, to be decided by open debates and votes*—not by officials who make political choices under pretense of political neutrality or of technical expertise.

THE SALIENT QUESTIONS

The Islamists are pressing American society to meet their demands. Is meeting them consistent with domestic security or not? How may the American people behave and how must they not behave with regard to persons whom they regard as sympathetic to terrorists? Which forms of cultural affirmation are permissible and which not? In December 2004 CAIR sued to force an Ohio school to ban students from wearing explicitly Christian T-shirts. With the support of the ACLU, it has also sued schools to accommodate Muslim minorities' wearing of distinctive clothes though they are offensive to others. Islamists agitate for prayer facilities in schools and airports to be run by them but paid for by the public. They lobby to increase the Muslim population through special immigration quotas, as well as for "affirmative action" to increase Muslim representation in universities and in management positions. And, of course, they have used the influence of the oil states' sovereign wealth funds to compel US financial institutions to adopt "Sharia-compliant" procedures.

They seek to send a message to Americans: "Thou shalt not displease Muslims, even if by so doing you displease yourselves." Daniel Pipes writes: "While seeking wide latitude for themselves, for instance when it comes to expressing disrespect for American national symbols, they would penalize expressions of disrespect for religious figures whom Islam deems holy, especially the prophet Muhammad; punish criticism of Islam, Islamism, or Islamists; and close down critical analysis of Islam."[26] To this end, CAIR sued, for example, the San Francisco talk-show host Michael Savage for defamation of Muslims. Regardless of their prospects in court, and given that unsuccessful plaintiffs in the United States are not normally assessed legal fees, people try to avoid the expense of such suits. Savage, however, countersued, charging CAIR with extortion, wire fraud, and supporting al-Qaeda.[27] But though CAIR lost the public relations battle and of course did not win in court, it succeeded in making Savage's show "controversial," which was enough for J.C. Penney and Wal-Mart to cease advertising on it. CAIR also protested the sale by chain stores of video games that depict Muslim terrorists. Its explicit threat of boycott by Muslims was less powerful than the implicit one of violence. In a small but significant victory, CAIR succeeded in getting Wal-Mart to "sensitivity-train" a cash register operator who asked a veiled customer "You're not going to hold me up, are you?" and to issue a public apology. The message of such things to the American people and corporations is that you are not allowed to displease the Muslim Establishment.

But the Islamists' intimidation of the private sector is small compared with its successes in persuading public officials to carve out special privileges and exemptions for Muslims in the law. Thus, in plain violation of the Public Accommodations section of the 1964 Civil Rights Act, the Minneapolis airport commission allowed the two-thirds of its cab drivers who are Muslim to refuse to carry passengers who have alcoholic beverages with them.[28] The Islamists' objective is to accustom America to accommodation of Muslim tastes as in Britain, where the government recognizes polygamous marriages as valid if contracted in foreign countries (and pays welfare benefits to multiple wives), or in Ontario, Canada's biggest province, where family law recognizes such marriages explicitly.[29]

The partiality of the impartiality that our statesmen advertise is no secret. Thus in December 2007 the State Department agreed to Arab demands that a conference it was holding on US soil be organized so that Arabs would never occupy the same space as Jews, or even walk where Jews had walked. In February 2008 the Department chose one Muqtedar Khan to administer a half-million dollar grant "to initiate a dialogue on religion and politics between key members of religious and community organizations in the Middle East and the United States," even though Khan had refused to sit on a panel because one of its members, Asaf Romirowsky, had served in the Israeli armed forces.[30] Can you imagine any public agency in America, or any university, paying anybody—except a Muslim—who acts in such a discriminatory fashion? And whereas the National Endowment for the Arts defended paying $15,000 to produce a picture of a crucifix in a glass of urine, can anyone imagine the US government paying for, or any gallery displaying, one of Muhammad buggering a pig? Why? What are the implications for security at home?

On November 30, 2006, aware of our statesmen's preference for avoiding discrimination over security, six imams staged an incident to leverage those preferences against the airline industry and the public. They called attention to themselves outside a boarding gate of the Minneapolis airport by praying loudly and ostentatiously, they refused to take their assigned seats and instead sat together in exit rows, they demanded heavy seat belt extenders, and spoke of Osama bin Laden. Passengers raised alarm, and the pilot had them taken off the plane by the police. CAIR, joined by the NAACP, mounted protests, demanded a consent agreement that would bind the airline (and implicitly all airlines) to disregard such complaints in the future. Above all, they sought damages from the passengers who had complained. Thus merely by presenting individuals with the prospect of having to defend well-financed lawsuits, they hoped thenceforth to discourage citizens even from warning the police of dangerous behavior—much less dealing with it.

The outcomes of these and similar trials of moral and physical force determine what society will and will not accept, what it will and will not stand for, what is permissible, even "cool," and what is out-of-bounds. They set the ever-changing balance between different conceptions of what society will be. By determining whose peace will prevail, they change its character. In sum, our statesmen's understanding of domestic security has set that character flowing in the wrong direction.

Thus in California a twenty-something daughter of prosperous, patriotic, and secular Afghan immigrants starts affecting Middle Eastern clothing, manners, and anti-American attitudes—without adopting Islam. It's cool. Such coolness, it seems, was the reason why a mild-mannered

British-born Muslim in her teens put on the *burqa* and became a phenom by writing poems with lines such as: "For the living martyrs are awakening / And kuffars [non-believers] world soon to be shaking." And: "Let us make jihad / Move to the front line / To chop chop head of kuffar swine." Her most famous work, "How to Behead," reads in part: "It's not as messy or as hard as some may think / It's all about the flow of the wrist." And: "No doubt that the punk will twitch and scream / But ignore the donkey's ass / And continue to slice back and forth / You'll feel the knife hit the wind and food pipe / But don't stop / Continue with all your might."[31] A British judge sentenced her to probation. America's laws preclude charges for such things. Hence America's security must depend less on criminal penalties than on attitudes.

Alexis de Tocqueville explained why life in the America of his time was far more secure than in Europe—why in Europe homes and public buildings were unsafe though like fortresses, while in America they were unguarded and safe: In Europe, he wrote, the criminal is a luckless man trying to save his head from the authorities as the people look on. But in America, he is hunted by every man. In Europe, the government owned the state. In America, the people owned it, and acted like it. The point is straightforward: Police forces are poor, and often counterproductive substitutes for the population's immunological reaction—pervasive and preclusive—against those they recognize as not on their side. Governments cannot bring it forth. They can only suppress or pervert it. This natural function of living bodies politic is the basis of foreign war and the essence of domestic security.

DRAWING LINES

At least in America, Lincoln's dictum applies: "Public sentiment is everything. With public sentiment nothing can fail. Without it, nothing can succeed." As regards internal security even more than anything else, the statesman's paramount job is to be a good steward of the American people's innate good sense. Internal security against the German and Japanese empires was no problem despite the fact that both had natural ethnic constituencies among us that numbered in the millions—constituencies that were considerably more resourceful than the populations from which today's terrorists come—because the Americans of those generations made some clear political choices. But since World War II the US government has done more to fuzz than to draw the political lines between who is with us and who is against us.

Internal security against the Soviet Union was problematic because Franklin Roosevelt and a substantial wing of his party in the 1940s misled many Americans into thinking that the Soviet Union was no problem. And when it turned out to be a problem, and lots and lots of evidence surfaced that many influential Americans had followed Roosevelt's lead to give aid and comfort to the enemy, our statesmen reacted defensively: There never was Communist infiltration, or any such thing as Communist sympathizers. Correct as any fact to the contrary might be, talking about it was incorrect politically and put you Beyond The Pale.[32] And when one Lee Harvey Oswald killed President John F. Kennedy, our mainstream statesmen, backed by the prestige press, indicted America's "climate of hatred"—that is, the fact that Kennedy and his party were unpopular in conservative Texas. That Oswald was a Communist with privileged relations with the Soviet Union was no less politically incorrect for being indisputable. And after Saudis and Egyptians had killed some 3,000 Americans on 9/11, after the US government had hurriedly flown the bin Laden family out of the country, our statesmen continued to accept Saudi criticism about American intolerance of Islam, echoed by the Muslims our government chooses as interlocutors.[33]

Few American people have any difficulty regarding as monstrous Saudi Wahabism and its funding of suicide bombing. Few Americans feel the slightest sympathy for the various Palestinian potentates' raising of a generation to get up in the morning asking themselves what they are going to do to kill Americans this day. Nor do Americans have any problem ostracizing, pressuring, restricting, delegitimizing, or making uncool anybody who looks or sounds even vaguely as if he might not be entirely against such monsters. The biggest barrier to our dealing with the foreign and domestic manifestations of these monstrosities is our statesmen's sleepy confidence in apolitical obfuscation.

The statesman's task is to focus the war as precisely as possible, leaving no doubt as to the enemy, and as little as possible about what is and is not permissible domestically. To declare war, to declare the enemy, is to draw the line between our society on one side, and anyone who might give "aid and comfort" to the other side. That must be done with proper, not abstract nouns. *Our civil freedoms, our wonderful American negative laws, can exist only on the friendly side of this divide.* Aiding the enemy, or even sympathizing with him, is not good sport. Nor is it innocuous to damn America, to suffer it to be damned, or to rejoice in its sorrows. On the other hand, pseudocriminal prosecutions in lieu of social and political line-drawing feed a spiral of personal vengeance that can only destroy the mutual friendship that is the condition of freedom.

So it is self evident—to those who understand the meaning of the terms—that freedom and internal security will take care of themselves to the extent that war on foreign enemies is taken seriously.

CHAPTER 9
/////////////////////

KEEP IT SIMPLE

Speak softly and carry a big stick.
— THEODORE ROOSEVELT

A merica's situation in our time is no more unprecedented than ours or any other nation's ever was. For statesmen to argue that novelty wipes out all previous rules is to claim that they can make up their own, exempt from questioning. But though all international interactions were, are, and will be singular, none is exempt from the rules of common sense, accessible to all who read history. Only principles that are the very opposite of complex and peculiar make it possible to make sense of peculiarly complex choices.

The first of these simple, general rules, from which all others follow, is that any country's statesmen must represent its people in all its peculiarities—their geographic position, their culture and capacities, their interests and proclivities. Americans are peculiar. While Poles, for example, must worry about Germans on one side and Russians on the other, Americans must deal with oceans. While Chinese call themselves *Zung Guo,* theoretically central to the world but racially defined, America continues to draw all the world's races to itself. While Western Europeans are content to live highly regulated lives, have followed Nietzsche "beyond good and evil," and will not fight, Americans are jealous of private life, keen to better it, preoccupied with moral right, and willing to fight when right and interest coincide. While even tiny Switzerland has interests all over the globe but no capacity to defend them, the Americans have global interests and the capacity to defend them. And for better or worse, America has become a byword, an issue for all mankind. Yet great as America is, its concerns—just like those of any other country—are limited by character and interest, by right and power.

Our focus must be on the United States of America. It is false and dangerous to suppose any universal convergence of interests or regimes, any sort of universal harmony—or universal strife. Rather, all peoples, including Americans, are endowed inalienably with the will to decide on the business of the day on whatever basis they choose. Our twentieth-century statesmen's basic mistake has been to confuse America with the world. By imagining America responsible for others, they also imagined that America is subject to something like a grand jury of mankind—of which they fancy themselves the *rapporteurs*. But we are not the world, there is no such grand jury, and our statesmen are responsible to us. Hence competent statesmanship's prerequisite is to forswear hubris, to focus America's foreign relations in our time as they were focused in the eighteenth and nineteenth: on the American people's peculiar wants and needs. Though less ambitious than world-keeping, minding one country's business calls upon the limits of the statesman's art. If our statesmen prove good and prudent at it, and if we are lucky, we may maintain ourselves.

This will require transcending Liberal Internationalism, Neoconservatism, and Realism—all variations of an ideology that assumes America's objectives and powers are essentially limitless, and that what happens in other countries is chiefly related, respectively, to human progress, to democratic progress, or to progress in the orderly adjustment of interests. Each from its own angle, these schools look for opportunities to manipulate foreigners for their own good, which they assume to be common or compatible with our good, rather than to assert and look out for America's good. The proper questions, which all the components of our foreign policy establishment neglect, are, "What business of ours does *this* involve?" "Where in this does America's interest lie?" Only by answering them can one understand individual choices and apply statecraft's instruments properly.

AMERICA

The only bones in America's body politic that yearn to shape mankind belong to those Americans who fancy themselves the world's leaders—who like Woodrow Wilson feel more comfortable among the foreign potentates they imagine to be their peers, pretending that their agendas represent their countrymen's commitment, than they do at home dealing with their equals' concerns, which they deem parochial and low. Thus like Wilson do they represent only themselves. Nor are these Americans a true imperial class. Spain's sixteenth-century Conquistadores, the British colonial administrators on whom the sun did not set from the seventeenth through the first half of the twentieth century, and the French who ruled Africa and Southeast Asia for a hundred years, lent their bodies to discomfort and their lives to danger. Forcing what had to be forced, their moral and physical means were equal to their ends. By contrast, our Liberals, Neoconservatives, and Realists fancy themselves shaping the planet from climate-controlled conference rooms, within bubbles that eliminate physical risk by precluding contact with unauthorized persons. Expecting to manage passions they cannot feel, they leave the dirty work to the armed forces but restrict what those forces may do. Though the meetings be in Ruritania, they might as well be in Washington, DC, or on the moon. Disagree as they might on details, our Liberals, Neoconservatives, and Realists agree on the essential: The American people suffer from "isolationism." In fact, the American people embody common sense.

The American people are chiefly concerned with bettering their lives—a concern not necessarily less worthy than those of the people who run our foreign policy. More to the point, anyone who purports to represent his country had better guard against the temptation to believe that he and his friends know better. In America, foreign affairs are as much the people's business as any, especially as they touch war and peace. Therefore it was fitting that during the eighteenth and nineteenth centuries America's foreign relations depended on the government's political branches for conception as well as conduct. But any historian who traces US foreign affairs into our century finds that the intellectual substance of American statesmanship has come from persons outside any process responsible to the voters. Whereas once "the national interest" was the things that the country was interested in, its latter-day version amounts to the preferences of a self-selected, self-perpetuating Establishment whose language and interests seem to be on a planet other than the American people's.

What the American people want from the rest of the world is peace. The few bands of exiles who have come to America intending to gather strength so as to return to their homelands in triumph have found mostly indifference, and a life that beguiled them to become Americans.[1] None of the nineteenth-century Americans who mounted "filibustering" expeditions, chiefly to Central America, found that their government would back them up. America's one imperial venture, in the Philippines, quickly purged imperialism from the body politic. The American people agreed to enter World War I only after Germany had let it slip that it would underwrite Mexico's *reconquista* of the American Southwest and had sunk American ships (whose neutrality Wilson had mendaciously compromised). Though danger had loomed for some years, they entered World War II only after Japan had attacked and Hitler had declared war. They fought the Cold War all over the globe because the Soviets trumpeted their intention to use every part of it to undo our way of life. Fighting the Soviet Union while avoiding major military actions required mixing the tools of war and of peace. But while the American people valued the Cold War's political-military apparatus as an exceptional instrument, our statesmen got used to using it as a peacetime tool.

Dismissing the American people's desire for the "normalcy" of peace has been common currency among our statesmen since Wilson. There is satisfaction, even joy, in countless statements to the effect that the American people's dreams of freedom from others' quarrels are illusions. When John F. Kennedy spoke in 1961 of a "twilight struggle," neither peace nor war, of indefinite duration, there was much head-nodding at Harvard. Criticism in those very quarters of George W. Bush's similar commitment in 2005 to the "concentrated work of generations"—neither war nor peace or rather both at the same time in every land, forever—was more partisan than substantive. By contrast, the sharp distinction between peace and war so dear to the American people is essential to any statesmanship worthy of the name. It certainly was characteristic of American statesmanship during the eighteenth and nineteenth centuries. George Washington's twin maxims, to "observe good faith and justice toward all nations . . . cultivate peace and harmony with all," and to "prepare for war" in order to earn peace, are perennial common sense.

Blurring that distinction really does run against common sense. As Machiavelli counseled, people in general and enemies in particular are to be "caressed or extinguished."[2] Never do anybody a little harm. The American people's preference for tolerating inconveniences, but then ridding themselves of enemies by short, decisive wars, is a mark of sophistication, not of immaturity. Nor does our presumptive preference for peace amount to pacifism. On the contrary, it means recognizing that peace is the result of dealing with enemies successfully, and it concentrates the mind on what is needed to do so—including war.

THE GOLDEN RULE

Our Founding Generation's message to Europe, formulated by John Quincy Adams as President James Monroe's famous "doctrine" of 1823, boils down to: "We leave you to mind your business, you leave us to mind ours." Peace was the rule's purpose. Its force, however, flowed less from its logic than from the subtlety and, above all, the power by which statesmen applied it. We are concerned here not with the confluence of interests with Britain that made this rule work for America in the nineteenth century but rather with the rule's logic. That rests on the recognition that *their* business really is theirs—that we can neither know nor control what happens in or to Europe, China, Russia, Persia, or any other part of the world. We can be sure only that, absent war, the locals, not we, will decide such things. Much as we may wish that any country's internal order were different, or opine unofficially about what any foreign country's way of life should be, the US government should forswear interference, by word or deed, in the internal affairs of other countries.

But we alone get to decide what *our* business is, what anything that happens abroad may be worth to us. Since we want peace, we should be willing to give it—unless we see that some foreigners are interfering with our business intolerably, are waging or may be about to wage war on us.

When words and forbearance fail to dissuade foreigners from minding what we consider our business, only war can stop them. That means interfering with the enemy's affairs, external and internal, in whatever way and to whatever extent may be required to secure our peace.

Our interest in any foreign country's political order is secondary, as is our interest in its welfare. Our primary interest is to protect our peace, our lives and vital interests, from any country's government that endangers them by omission or commission. The offending country's government will have brought America's wrath upon itself. War almost always ends up making changes in the enemy's internal order, and often aims at doing so as part of what may be needed to win. But generally, it is nonsense to hope that promoting some kind of political change will defeat the enemy. Military victory is the horse that draws the cart of political change. Unless the rare circumstances that followed World War II repeat themselves, the United American people should not try to repair the broken crockery.

BACK TO BASICS

The image of America as a corrupt, impotent empire that our twentieth-century statesmen earned for us is not easily shed. More people hate us more and fear us less. *We had better reverse that.* To do that, we must talk less, act in fewer instances—obviously in our interest—and much more decisively. The alternatives are, on the one hand, to try dominating the globe and, on the other, to sacrifice our judgment to that of "the jury of mankind." But seriousness about world domination is patently unserious. As well, consider the jury. In 2008 the United Nations General Assembly chose as its President one Miguel d'Escoto Brockmann, winner of the 1985 Lenin Prize. That Americans should choose their policies and officials so as to be acceptable to such foreigners is surely the most wrongheaded of notions. Moreover, the American people will no more support serious imperialism than they will support serious groveling. The real choice for America is between continuing to bluster and pander halfheartedly in pursuit of universal dreams, or to get back to the basics of national, rational statecraft.

We need neither dwell on how incompatible those fundamentals are with the beliefs and moods of our dominant social class, nor speculate on the circumstances that might eclipse its dysfunctional ideas and habits. Nor do we prescribe a regimen for detoxifying it. We only describe sobriety.

WORDS AND REALITY

Being sober starts with using words according to their ordinary meaning. Bandying words crafted or altered to suppose that the world is as you prefer does not magically change it. By contrast, calling things by their name can bring reality into focus, as a cold shower does for a hangover. Consider, for example, the US embassy in Iraq, and to a lesser extent any number of other US embassies in our time. *"Embass?"* These structures are not embassies but fortresses, and the people who work in them do not live and work as diplomats in the dictionary and historic sense of the word. What, then, are they? Look closely. The first rule of diplomacy, from time immemorial, is diplomatic immunity. The *sine qua non* for sending an envoy is that the foreign host guarantees the envoy's safety. But many of the governments that host US embassies do not want to guarantee our diplomats' safety, and some, like Iraq's, cannot. Often, parts of the foreign body politic use physical pressure on the embassy as leverage on the US government or on other parts of their own body politic. Sometimes, as in Iraq, the contending parts are armed against one another and against us. Our diplomats end up living in a bubble and move among the locals guarded by Americans who shoot on the slightest suspicion. What do these supposed diplomats do? Not negotiation with a sovereign. Rather, they superintend local government ministries and manipulate local politics. This is meddling, not diplomacy. And because meddling is inherently partisan, it makes us allies of some and enemies of others in foreign civil strife. We may wish to be parties to such strife. But we should not confuse it with diplomacy.

Grasping the reality of the word "war" is even more important. Our statesmen have declared "war" on poverty and on illegal drugs, promising middle-class life and sobriety for all. Many have also suggested declaring "coordinated war on climate change."[3] Such a war, they say, would give mankind no less than a 50-50 chance of surviving the twenty-first century![4] Countless people have built careers and fortunes on the two former "wars," and more are sure to do the same on the next.[5] But apply to these "wars" the criteria by which to judge any human enterprise: Is the objective reasonable? Is it achievable? Are the means proposed such as may reasonably be expected to achieve it? Poverty and drug abuse result from human weaknesses. The drug and poverty warriors did not argue it is possible to cancel those weaknesses. Nor did the warriors define victory. They seemed less concerned with the consequences of what they did—outlawing drug use while giving a pass to users, and pouring hundreds of billions of dollars' profit into the pockets of drug traffickers—less concerned with what actually happened to "the poor" than with building and running and profiting from the vast infrastructure of these so-called wars. Any "war" on "climate change" would have the same characteristics. Why, then, call these enterprises "war"? Because "war" has come to mean giving powerful people even more power to deal with a problem as they define it, with means convenient to them, to satisfy the contradictory urge to do something while not doing it. But that is not what "war" means.

The problem gets really serious when we apply the word "war" in this contemporary meaning to campaigns that involve massive killing and dying. Wage "war on terror"? By all means, we must do something. But though we know that the terrorists fight for causes espoused and financed by Arab countries, we must not wage war on those countries. Our Department of Homeland Security advised Americans not even to use words that point to the Islamic or Arab origins of the terrorists. Rather, the Department bids us refer to the enemy as an anonymous, apolitical "murder cult" and to the war as "a global struggle for security and progress."[6] Security against whom? Progress toward what? With guidance like that, our statesmen can do whatever they please in the name of something they are wholly free to define, and as convenient to them as they can manage. *Cui bono?*

Cynical officials may use loose talk as a tool for self-empowerment. But obfuscation is especially dangerous because it also obfuscates the obfuscators. Officials whose own convenience is their the sole point of reference quickly end up disoriented about the substance of what they are doing. Spinners end up spinning themselves. As Confucius suggested, if there is arbitrariness in what is said, if what is said is not what is meant, confusion reigns because there can be no intelligible relationship between what is expected to happen and what happens. Discussion does not benefit a nation of loose talkers. Is it too much to demand of those in public life to use words according to dictionary meanings, to exchange sentences full of proper nouns and transitive verbs?

IDEAS AND POWER

To understand the role of ideas in international affairs you must straightaway dismiss the notion that, somehow, talk can substitute for the traditionally "hard" disciplines of military strategy and diplomacy, that America can be made so attractive to foreigners as to lessen the need for harsh measures. Statesmen who countenance this notion are like doctors who prefer miracle cures to medicine and surgery. In our time, newspapers report the reactions of their foreign friends to candidates and issues on the American political scene, tacitly suggesting that pleasing them is America's best defense.[7] But ideas cannot be reduced to polls indicating like and dislike, and these say nothing about what people will do for or against you in particular circumstances. Consider, then, what thoughts may move foreigners, what thoughts should move America, and of what the battleground for the human mind may consist.

Since the human mind is moved by fear, interest, and honor as well as by reason about truth, goodness, and beauty, power exerts an elemental grip on it. Winners inspire praise. Losers get shunned. The old saying "He who has good arms will always have good friends" means that, if your armed forces are successful, if they are reassuring to friends and feared by foes, more people will be attracted to you and fewer repelled by you. Just as victory and success are attractive, failure and defeat are repulsive. The difference between the two is self-evident. If a nation is victorious, praise will come unsolicited. But trying to spin a favorable image of defeat only makes things worse. Whether others like us or not is their business. Whether they respect us is ours. If you want America to be loved, win. Then many will profess to love it, and you will be free to ask them to prove it.

What America is, says, or does is a minuscule part of why foreigners think and act as they do. The only reason foreigners care about you at all is that you may do something to them or for them. The only opinions they have about you that have a chance of moving them concern matters that, as Jefferson used to say, "pick the pocket or break the leg"—their pockets, their legs. Their opinions about how Americans live, what Americans should do or not do, all rolled together, will never keep them from sitting down to dinner. Conversely, each piece of foreign opinion matters to Americans only insofar as it can pick our pockets, break our legs, or safeguard them. So when matters of war and peace, of large national interest are contested, respect naturally flows to people who take war seriously, who radiate gravitas. The first half of Theodore Roosevelt's dictum, "speak softly," defined gravitas for our time: "Speak courteously and respectfully," avoid "loose-tongued denunciations of other peoples." But take yourself seriously, and take no guff.

Taking America seriously means above all taking seriously the ideas on which it is founded. Foreigners in our time have taken America less seriously in part because leading Americans have acted as if America's moral-intellectual core were as Chief Justice William Rehnquist described it: "At the heart of liberty is the right to define one's own concept of existence, of meaning, of the universe, and of the mystery of human life"[8]—that is to say, America means whatever anybody feels like.

By contrast, according to America's Founders, that core consisted of "self-evident" truths about "inalienable rights" with which our "Creator" endowed us. Human equality, the foremost of these truths and endowments, means that we to whom it is self-evident are obliged to deal with others to whom it is equally self-evident, through reason. Equality *requires* the politics of persuasion. But the politics of persuasion is possible only because all sides may, indeed should, refer to common, objective standards of true and false, good and evil, better and worse. These are the standards—again using the Founders' language—"of Nature and Nature's God." Because America's core consists of these ideas, because they became habitual, the American people uniquely speak the language of right and wrong. Though reason does not simply rule in American councils, it holds an endowed place.

Because doing the right thing is important to Americans as to no other people, American politics is like politics nowhere else, and to count on the American people's backing our statesmen must show that they have taken up a just cause. Alas, the essence of twentieth-century American statecraft has been to confuse justice with what Walter McDougall calls "global meliorism." But because the American people are a practical lot, eventually they see through mere motivational rhetoric. Basing statecraft on the American people's penchant for trying to do the right thing, as did Lincoln and Theodore Roosevelt, brings forth awesome energy. So do attacks such as those of December 7, 1941, and September 11, 2001, that are obvious negations of right. But using the American people's righteousness as a propellant for private dreams, as did Wilson, or as cover for tergiversation, as did George W. Bush, is ruinous. In the end, to compete successfully in the *American* marketplace of ideas it is necessary to marshal reason about right and wrong, as well as about interest, fear, and honor.

Most of mankind, however, is not ruled by reason, and may never be. Our Founders premised their foreign relations on *the rule of reason insofar as possible, and on the interplay of interest, fear, and honor insofar as necessary.* Indeed the assumption of our twentieth-century statesmen that international affairs are between men who share the same moral and intellectual horizon is contrary not just to America's heritage and to reality but to modernist ideology itself: If indeed, as Justice Rehnquist wrote, "concept[s] of existence, of meaning, of the universe" are purely subjective, then reason is useless.

But it is not. The battleground for the human mind is as diverse as mankind. But reason is never wholly absent. As Pope Benedict XVI reminded his former university colleagues at Regensburg, certain truths about human life are accessible to ordinary human reason regardless of civilization or religion.[9] Reason, the human mind's essential constituent, is not essentially what Thomas Hobbes called it—"a scout for the passions"—though there is no shortage of examples of its being used just so. Each civilization, each religion, has its own logic, its own *logos,* its own reason. But all have in common some reference to truth, acknowledge some relation between cause and effect. It is incumbent on practitioners of international relations to learn foreign *logi* as they learn foreign languages and, insofar as possible, to contend with foreigners for right as we understand it in terms of their own logic.[10] We should realize, however, that whatever we say to foreigners we are saying even more loudly to ourselves and that the beliefs most important for the peace and prosperity of our country are the ones in our own heads. We ourselves are the most important front in the battle for the mind.

And since the human mind is usually influenced if not ruled by the logics of interest, fear, and honor, we must conclude that a good argument combined with a stick is usually more effective than a good argument alone.

DIPLOMACY

The compelling reality that diplomacy conveys verbally includes both reason and the stick—interest, fear, and honor. Your words must be softer and less demanding than one might imagine given your stick's hardness and size, and the offers you make should be such that compliance with them would be much less onerous than refusal would be painful. In short, good diplomacy means making offers they can't refuse and with which they may comply, even gratefully. Diplomatic solvency is an excess of power over demands, while bankruptcy consists of demands in excess of the power to compel compliance.

The purpose is persuasion by reason insofar as possible and, insofar as necessary, by bringing to bear verbally those features of reality that argue compellingly for the outcome you desire. Axiomatically, diplomatic offers and demands should proceed from and reflect the balance of the factors influencing both sides. Insisting on much less or on much more than the balance indicates runs against the grain of the art. It follows, then, that effective diplomacy begins with an accurate assessment of what the balance dictates to both sides. Given their governments' proper understanding of reality, diplomats then become its executors.

But US diplomacy has consisted too heavily of offers easy to refuse and of deals profitably reneged precisely because our statesmen's grip on reality has been tenuous. On the one hand, unlimited ends guarantee in-

solvent diplomacy: The US government has set objectives such as reme-
dying deep cultural hostilities that are not reachable by any means. On
the other hand, our statesmen have been loath to use the tools reality
does provide. In short, US diplomacy has failed to coerce because its
words have overshot or undershot compelling reality.

For example, after the 2003 US invasion of Iraq, US troops were on
Syria's border. As arguably the world's biggest supporter of terrorist groups,
many of which have offices in downtown Damascus, Syria had been a
thorn in America's side. Weapons from Syria had killed Americans in Iraq.
Surrounded by countries hostile to it and hostage to the US military next
door, Syria was in no position to resist serious diplomatic pressure. In the
summer of 2003 Syria's regime would have had no choice but to pay whatever price the Americans might demand for their forbearance. But the
Bush team began by assuring the Syrians that the US government looked
forward to a long and useful relationship, that it was urging its allies, including Israel, to have the very best relationship with Syria, and that US
troops would not be used against it. Having thus removed any negative incentive for complying, the United States made minimal demands. At the
same time, the Bush team also gave verbal support to the Lebanese resistance against Syria but made no attempt to stop Syria's killing of anyone
who took America's supporting words seriously. Syria promised Secretary
of State Colin Powell that it would close down terrorist offices and then
reneged publicly, insulting him and America. Adding injury to insult, it
intensified its support for Iraqi insurgents killing American soldiers and
authorized and supplied its Lebanese agents' war against Israel.

Secretary of State Condoleezza Rice called this intercourse "coercive
diplomacy." And so it was. But Syria was the coercer and America the
coercee. The Americans telegraphed diplomatic incompetence by making
requests that were too small in proportion to the real balance of power and
interest. Thus having discredited their own superior assets, they left no
doubt about their incompetence by not matching their words with deeds
and then by suffering insult. By contrast, once the Americans' puny deeds
had discredited their big words, the Syrians' deadly deeds sealed their own
diplomatic success. Unburdened by American PhDs, the Syrian statesmen
understood the Americans better than the Americans understood them,

and their words and deeds matched each other as well as they matched the balance of power created by the Americans' incompetence.

This typical failure points to the root cause of American diplomacy's problems, namely, the fatal supposition that the purpose of international intercourse is "good relations," understood generically and apolitically, just as "peace" is often misunderstood generically and apolitically. But just as you must ask of any existing or proposed state of peace: "Whose peace is it? "To whose advantage?" "What does it mean for us?" so you must ask of any international relationship: "Good? For whom? For what? What does it mean for us?" To pursue "good relations" without due attention to such questions is to surrender the substance of those relations to the side that does consider them. By the same token, if you neglect what the balance of power, interest, fear, and honor suggests is rightly yours, you may be sure that the other side will notice and conclude reasonably that you are incompetent.

Diplomacy is not the art of "conflict resolution." It cannot satisfy all sides' real needs through "win-win" arrangements. It could do so if all governments' interests, fears, and sense of honor matched. They do not. Diplomacy is just a means of communication, and its essence lies in the substance of what is communicated. If American statesmen communicate their own disregard for the instruments and balance of power, or greater concern for pleasing foreigners than for pleasing the American people, they have no reason to be surprised at the results. What could US diplomacy say that might cause European states to incur the Muslim world's displeasure for an America that courts Arab favor? What words might persuade Arab rulers to risk their lives by shutting down anti-American agitation within their ruling class? Diplomacy cannot endow unserious policy with seriousness.

For American diplomats, "good relations" with a foreign country should mean above all that it not trouble us. If the things our government does in America's interest please foreigners, so much the better. But nothing is more contrary to the nature of diplomacy or to America's interest than to suppose that "good relations" mean accommodating the desires, much less adopting the standards, of other nations or groups of nations. If the millions who emigrated to America had wanted to live by "world standards" they would not have bothered becoming Americans.

VICTORY, OR WHAT?

Because actions are more convincing than words, weight in diplomatic commerce comes from the very fact that a people are willing to back their diplomats' reasoning with "carrots and sticks." And though few international requests or objections are such as to require being backed by willingness to shed blood, nevertheless when statesmen consider remonstrating with foreigners about what is most important to their peoples, about their biggest fears and most vital interests, they must first be sure that their country is ready, willing, and able to resort to the ultimate persuasion: war. If either statesmen or peoples are not willing to back these important things with blood, then perhaps they are not so important. But very surely it is most imprudent for any statesman even to "take note" of any matter's vital importance, much less to make requests, even less public demands about it, unless he is willing to lead his country (and it is willing to follow) into war. If they are not so willing, "taking note" of the matter's importance and then standing by as your requests are denied or ignored is almost like having fought a war and lost. Better to pretend there is no trouble, that what is happening does not concern you. But if you intend to press vital matters, you must do so with a strategy for forcing the issue unto victory.

President George W. Bush's trips to Saudi Arabia in January and May 2008 to ask for help in reducing oil prices are among the more pathetic examples of how not to handle vital matters. Before the President's meetings, the White House had stated officially that the current prices were intolerable for Americans because "we have not enough supply and too much demand." The President asked the Saudis to increase supply, to make money by selling more at lower prices. But after the meetings, the Saudi oil minister slapped down the Americans: "Demand and supply are in balance today."[11] The Saudis preferred to make more money by selling less at higher prices, and the Americans smiled.

What, one wonders, led them to imagine that such a request would be honored? The Americans offered neither positive nor negative incentives—especially not such negative incentives as might have balanced the Saudi royals' deepest fear, namely, that factions among themselves would use accommodation of the Americans as a lever by which to raise support from the general population—long inured to anti-American Wahabi preaching—for some kind of intradynastic civil war. The Americans could have supplied two fears to trump that: either removing any shield to whatever bellicose plans Iran might have for the Persian Gulf, or else making war on the Saudis directly. The point is simply that the tool you choose to demolish resistance to your demands must be proportionate to that resistance.

When gauging what it might take to overcome any given resistance, it is essential to identify the human beings and institutions of which it consists. Who, or whose will, is to be broken? In life as in math, one judges the importance of any factor by factoring it out. Remove *this*. If the equation still works or the problem persists, the factor or enemy you chose is insignificant. Then you must figure out what will actually cause the enemy or factor to go away. It is no good to say that this measure "will contribute" to doing away with the enemy. You must reasonably calculate that the complex of measures you propose *will* actually cause the effect you want. Executing that complex of coercive measures is war. This chain of reasoning's very simplicity makes it morally demanding and hence difficult to follow.

Who is the enemy? Against whom do we direct deadly pressure? The information available to any newspaper reader about which leaders of states and movements advocate terrorizing Americans, and about who provides inspiration, propaganda, money, and protection to terrorists, is quite enough to make basic decisions on peace and war. But because our statesmen are of opposite minds simultaneously, they seek relief from hard decisions by relying on intelligence—as if we could learn things about foreign leaders and peoples that would make them different from what they are, as if there were a magic key that would let us have the fruits of war without the inconveniences. But while more information serves those already committed to a reasonable course of action, it further confuses those who are trying to evade hard choices: How badly do we want this? Who stands in the way? Will we get our way, our peace, or not? Are we winners or losers?

Our statesmen have found it more comfortable to imagine themselves as the world's teachers, physicians, or even policemen. Because they suppose that foreign peoples and leaders cannot be enemies, that it is unthinkable to pursue our peace by waging war in the massive, frightening, semidiscriminate sense that the word implies. Rather, our leaders have preferred "engagement" at various levels of depth and violence, believing against the weight of experience that we can get our peace, our interests, from antagonists by teaching, buying, even policing them. But armed forces can neither police nor transform foreign lands because they are essentially negative instruments. The natural function of armies is to deal death to foreign lands' ruling classes. This serves the very positive function of clearing the way for new ruling classes who, to avoid their predecessors' fate, would be solicitous of our interests and police their own society accordingly. If armed forces are used in this natural way, they can inspire fear so healthy as to deter opposition. Alas, by using our armed forces unnaturally as constabularies, our statesmen have caused actual and potential enemies to lose fear of them. We will pay heavily for having lost it and more heavily to regain it.

The fundamental reason for this misuse of war's instruments is our statesmen's reluctance to be clear about America's purposes and America's enemies. This befouls domestic even more than it does foreign affairs. Unwilling clearly to designate foreign enemies, our statesmen closed off Pennsylvania Avenue, wrapped America in razor wire, and subjected us all to security measures that habituated Americans to herd one another and to be herded. Suppressing the American people's sense that we have the right to treat presumed enemies as such has had a narcotic effect.

IN SUM

The foreign relations of the United States should be conducted in ways that maximize the American people's allegiance to the United States. That most precious allegiance has waned in our time because our statesmen have worked in a language and with assumptions that have excluded the common sense of the ages and of the American people. For America to live in a peace secured by popular support requires above all that the American people discuss what that peace might be, what enemies stand in its way, and that they vote whether to undo them. Whenever the choice arises between restricting the American people's freedoms at home or waging decisive war abroad, the latter is always advisable.

Our statesmen and the academic, social *milieux* whence they come and return have presided over too much fighting that has brought us too little peace. Thus they have forfeited their claims to places and honors. America needs to replace them. But even more, it needs to understand and hence to immunize itself against the intellectual viruses that vitiated their minds.

NOTES

PREFACE

1. There is no truth in the commonly held opinion that Neoconservatism and Neoconservatives were primarily or even substantially responsible for the G. W. Bush Administration's foreign policy, especially its venture in Iraq. The occupation of Iraq was urged by Secretary of State Colin Powell using arguments both Realist (the Saudis demand it) and Liberal Internationalist (since we broke it we've got to fix it). The occupation's political policy was set by Robert Blackwill, a Realist from the Council on Foreign Relations, and military policy by Walter Slocombe, a Liberal Internationalist from the Carter and Clinton Administrations. The intellectual architect of the Administration's 2007–2008 political military strategy was Stephen Biddle, another Realist from the Council. National Security Adviser and (later) Secretary of State Condoleezza Rice—the person closest to the President—either enabled whatever tendency in the Administration was strongest at any given time or just amalgamated the factions' contrasting recipes into "bridging documents." Yet she herself had risen through Realist ranks under the patronage of former National Security Adviser Brent Scowcroft. As we will see, Iraq was no different from many other twentieth-century US foreign policy ventures in that it was a vessel in which the several tendencies of contemporary American statecraft mixed like oil and water.

2. Stanley Hoffman, "What Should American Foreign Policy Be?" *Dissent,* Fall 1994, p. 498.

3. Steven Holmes, "Choice for National Security Adviser Has Long Waited Chance to Lead," *The New York Times,* January 3, 1993, p. 1.

4. See Joshua Muravchik and Stephen M. Walt, "The Neocons vs. The Realists," *The National Interest,* Fall 2008.

INTRODUCTION

1. Boston University College of Arts and Sciences, Department of International Relations (CAS/IR 345, The Role of Force).

CHAPTER ONE

1. The principle here is that new names preclude the memory of old things, and a new language makes it impossible even to know the past, much less to regret it. Cf. Niccoló Machiavelli, *Treatise Upon Our Language, Discourses II,* 5 and *The Prince,* Chs. 3–5.

2. "The Other Worldliness of Wilson," *The New Republic,* Vol. II, March 27, 1915, p. 195.

3. Nicholas Murray Butler, *The International Mind,* New York, 1912, pp. 49–50. This was originally part of Butler's opening speech to the 1910 Lake Mohonk conference.

4. Woodrow Wilson, speech in Los Angeles, September 20, 1919, reproduced in Norman Graebner, *Ideas and Diplomacy,* Oxford, 1964, pp. 457–462. "The heart of [the Treaty] is that every great fighting nation . . . solemnly engages that it will never resort to war. . . . I think that you will agree with me that you have got ninety-nine percent insurance."

5. Harold Nicolson, *Peacemaking 1919,* Boston, Houghton Mifflin, 1933. There is nothing new or unusual about the tendency to make verbal commitments bigger as the real collateral for them is shrinking. Thucydides relates that during the interval between the Peloponnesian war's two halves, as Athens and Sparta were reneging on promise after promise, they negotiated two peace treaties, for progressively longer terms and involving ever bigger promises that neither intended to keep. Thucydides, Bk. V, 18–19 and 47–48. Nor was this mere cynicism. More generally, we see that the need to "protest too much" flows from the absence of the very thing protested.

6. "Defining Deviancy Down," *The American Scholar,* Winter 1993. All are indebted to Daniel Patrick Moynihan for encapsulating in this phrase the penchant of American elites to channel humanity's gutters into the mainstream.

7. See Paul Johnson, *Modern Times,* NY, Harper, 1985, Ch. 15, "Caliban's Kingdoms."

8. Thus, for example, between 1939 and 1991 the US government recognized the governments of Estonia, Latvia, and Lithuania de jure because it refused to recognize the legitimacy of the Stalin-Hitler pact that had incorporated them into the Soviet Union. Accordingly, they maintained pro forma embassies in Washington. But de facto, the United States treated these countries as part of the Soviet Union.

9. George F. Kennan once held this view: "On many occasions, both before and after this Greek-Turkish episode, I have been struck by the congenital aversion of Americans to taking specific decisions on specific problems, and by their persistent urge to seek universal formulae or doctrines to clothe and justify particular actions." *Memoirs, 1925–1950.* Boston, Little, Brown, 1967, p. 322.

10. Dean Acheson, *Present at the Creation,* New York, 1955. Acheson claims that he spoke to the universalist prejudices of Senators Arthur Vandenberg (R-MI) and Tom Connoly (D-TX) in favor of the UN and collective security, and that those prejudices were widespread. On the Marshall Plan: "Our policy is directed not against any country or doctrine but against hunger, poverty, desperation, and chaos," p. 233. On aiding Greece and Turkey to resist Soviet aggression, "[Vandenberg charged that the Adminstration had made] a colossal blunder in ignoring the UN. He proposed to correct it and, as corrected, to adopt our fumbling efforts. Like Mr. Jorrock's foxes, I cried, *'peccavi!'* and offered to make amends," pp. 223–224. But, in fact, long before 1947 there had been a bipartisan majority in Congress for acting against the Soviet Union. It would have been more accurate for Acheson to have written that he and the Truman Administration were accommodating the prejudices of unreconstructed Wilsonians, as well as of the Democratic Party's extreme Wallaceite Left.

11. There is, in fact, an art to managing the forces of subject nations. The Roman republic practiced it as did Napoleon, who led a *grande armee* into Russia in 1812 composed mostly of non-Frenchmen. The Soviet Union's plans for war in Europe involved the armies of Poland, Hungary, and Czechoslovakia. But it is always an open question whether such forced forces are more dangerous than helpful because they tend to abandon the fight, or even to switch sides at the worst moments.

12. David Starr Jordan, *The Friendship of Nations,* New York, 1913.

13. Thomas Schelling, *The Strategy of Conflict,* Harvard University Press, 1960, p. 102.

14. Ibid., p. 3.

15. Ibid., p. 6.

16. Henry Kissinger, *The Necessity for Choice,* 1960.

17. The PBS News Hour's video of the landing showed US Marines swimming onto the beach ahead of the landing craft and aiming rifles inland to protect the main body of troops in full battle gear. Presumably, they were not armed against natural phenomena.

CHAPTER TWO

1. William McKinley, Message to Congress, April 18, 1898, *Messages and Papers of the Presidents,* Washington, 1899, Vol. X, pp. 139–150.

2. *The New York Times,* October 13, 1898.

3. Albert Beveridge, *Congressional Record,* January 9, 1900, 56th Congress, 1st Session, pp. 704–712.

4. *Time,* March 31, 2008, p. 42.

5. John Quincy Adams to Alexander Hill, December 29, 1817, *Writings of John Quincy Adams,* Vol. VI, pp. 281–283.

6. For a discussion of this point see Samuel P. Huntington, *Who Are We?,* NY, 2004. Huntington describes three visions of America's international role: National, in which statesmen seek to deepen and strengthen America itself; Imperial, in which they try to adjust the rest of the world to what they think America is; and Cosmopolitan, in which they try to adjust America to what they think the world (of which they see themselves as spokesmen) demands of America.

7. John Quincy Adams to Hugh Nelson, April 28, 1823, *Writings of John Quincy Adams,* Vol. VII, pp. 370–381.

8. Woodrow Wilson, Address to the Senate, January 22, 1917, *The Public Papers of Woodrow Wilson: The New Democracy,* Vol. II, pp. 407–414, Ray Stannart Baker and William E. Dodd, eds., New York, 1926. Famously, Wilson told European audiences that the American people demanded the League of Nations and told the American people that "the world will be absolutely in despair if America deserts it." Speech in Los Angeles, September 20, 1919, *The Public Papers of Woodrow Wilson: War and Peace,* Vol. II, pp. 304–310.

9. *The New York Times,* March 29, 2008.

10. W. H. Seward to Marquis de Montholon, February 12, 1866.

11. Theodore Roosevelt's Secretary of State, Elihu Root, won the 1912 Nobel Peace Prize for his organization of the Hague Conferences of 1899 and 1907 that established the world court and international standards for arbitration and the conduct of war. His Nobel lecture is perhaps the finest example of what the twentieth century expected from public opinion. www.nobel.se/peace/laureates/1912/root-lecture.html.

12. William H. Seward (with revisions from A. Lincoln) to Charles Francis Adams, May 21, 1861, *The Works of Abraham Lincoln,* Rutgers University Press, Vol. VI, pp. 376–380.

13. See, for example, William Odom and Robert Dujarric, *America's Inadvertent Empire,* Yale University Press, 2006.

14. John McCain Speech on March 18, 2008, www.JohnMcCain.com.

15. Cf. John L. Esposito and Dalia Mogahed, *Who Speaks for Islam,* Gallup Press, 2008.

16. The May/June 2003 issue of *Foreign Affairs* ran as its lead item, "The U.N. vs. U.S. Power: Michael Glennon on the End of a Grand Experiment."

CHAPTER THREE

1. Chalmers Johnson, "The Pentagon's Ossified Strategy," *Foreign Affairs,* July/August 1995.

2. Thomas Friedman, *The Lexus and the Olive Tree,* Farrar Straus, 2000.

3. Joseph Nye and Eric Alterman, *Bound to Lead the Changing Nature of American Power,* Basic Books, 1990.

4. Joseph Nye, *Soft Power: The Means of Success in World Politics,* Perseus Books, 2004, p. x.

5. Ibid., p. 3.

6. Ibid., p. 17.

7. Ibid., p. 75.

8. Ibid., p. 73. Nye writes that the Soviet Union "attracted many in Europe because of its resistance to Hitler." But most Europeans' historical memory, unlike that of Nye's Harvard colleagues, includes knowledge that World War II started when the Soviet Union *and* Hitler made a deal to divvy up the continent, that the Soviets kept the deal, and that while Hitler kept it, until the very day and hour he invaded the Soviet Union, Liberals the world over defended Hitler because he was on Stalin's side. This lapse in the collective memory of American academics is evidence of Soviet Soft Power.

9. Compare, for example, the speech of Senator John Kerry to the 2007 World Economic Forum, January 27, 2007 (www.weforum.org), with Osama bin Laden's purported videotaped statement of September 7, 2007. The reader may wish to compare the statement's substance, if not its tone, with the editorial positions of *The New York Times.*

10. Arthur Schlesinger Jr., "Back to the Womb," *Foreign Affairs,* September 1995.

11. Henry Kissinger, *Diplomacy,* Simon & Schuster, 1994.

12. See Norman Podhoretz, *World War IV,* Doubleday, 2007. See also "A Masterpiece of American Oratory," *The American Spectator,* February 2007.

13. Schlesinger, "Back to the Womb."

14. Delivered March 15, 2007 (distributed by the Bureau of International Information Programs, U.S. Department of State, http://usinfo.state.gov).

15. The tone of Media mogul Ted Turner's remarks to TV host Charlie Rose gives a hint. Having said that, as a consequence of "global warming," "none of the crops will grow. Most of the people will have died, and the rest of us will be cannibals," Turner concluded: "We're too many people. That's why we have global warming . . . too many people using too much stuff. If there were less people, they'd be using less stuff . . . everybody in the world has got to pledge to themselves that one or two children is it" [sic.], Charlierose.com/shows/2008/04/01/1. What would such psychologically empowered people feel entitled to do to save the planet from surplus folk or violators of rules deemed necessary for planetary survival?

16. E.g., Khaled Khalefa, *In Praise of Hatred,* Beirut, Emissa, 2006. "Hatred possessed me. I was excited by it, I felt it was saving me; it gave me a sense of superiority I had been seeking for a long time."

17. *Machiavelli's Prince,* translated and edited by Angelo M. Codevilla, Yale University Press, 1997.

18. Most interesting is the lack of condemnation that Multiculturalists show for Islamic customs such as polygamy and restrictions on women because Islam has become, in their eyes, the chief vehicle for opposition to Western civilization. That explains not just events such as one Ann Holmes Redding, an Episcopal priest, announcing she was Muslim as well as Episcopalian (*Seattle Times,* July 5, 2007). Hundreds of other conversions seem motivated far less by spiritual than by temporal causes. See Wikipedia, "List of Converts to Islam."

19. James Kurth, "The Adolescent Empire," *The National Interest,* Summer 1997, p. 6.

20. Peter Berger, "Secularism in Retreat," *The National Interest,* Winter 1996–1997, pp. 6–12.

21. Robert Kagan, *Dangerous Nation,* Knopf, 2006.

22. In *Gulliver's Travels,* Jonathan Swift describes the intractable strife between Lilliput's parties, the Tramecksan and the Slameckslan, based on the different heights of their shoes' heels.

23. *The New York Times,* March 31, 2004, December 1, 2005.

24. The formulation is that of Sayyid Qtb's 1964 book *Milestones,* a fundamental text of the Muslim Brotherhood and of modern political Islam.

25. *The New York Times,* February 16, 1979.

26. *Time,* cover story, February 12, 1979.

27. Karl Marx had formed the International Workingmen's Association, the first international, in 1864. Between 1889 and 1914 a second socialist international was formed whose brightest lights were the social democrats Edward Bernstein and Karl Kautsky. V. I. Lenin's Bolshevik faction of the Russian Socialist Party led factions from most member parties of the second international to form a third, Communist, international thoroughly dominated by the Soviet Union and known first as the Comintern then as the Cominform, and finally to exist informally as an emanation of the International Department of the Communist Party of the Soviet Union.

28. Antonio Gramsci, *Prison Notebooks, 1929–1935,* Joseph A. Buttigieg, ed., Columbia University Press, 1992.

29. Each year between 1966 and 1991 Stanford University's Hoover Institution published a thick *Yearbook of International Communist Affairs.* Each country's section detailed the massive organizational efforts of the Party in that country to do just that.

30. Strobe Talbott, *The Russians and Reagan,* Vintage, 1984, also "Behind the Bear's Angry Growl," *Time,* May 21, 1984. *The New York Times's* Anthony Lewis called it "simplistic theology" (March 10, 1983). For *The Times's* Tom Wicker it was "a near proclamation of holy war," (March 15, 1983), while for *The Washington Post's* Richard Cohen, Reagan had proved himself "a religious bigot" (May 26, 1983). Note the predominant accusation of religiosity—the unpardonable sin.

31. Joseph Nye, *Soft Power,* pp. 73–75.

32. The best account of Pope John Paul II's campaign, including a memorable chapter on his 1979 epochal visit to Poland, is in George Weigel, *Witness to Hope,* HarperCollins, 1999.

CHAPTER FOUR

1. See below, Chapter 6.

2. Henry Kissinger, *Diplomacy,* Simon & Schuster, 1994.

3. That squadron's commander was none other than Thucydides himself.

4. Hans Morgenthau, *Politics Among Nations,* NY, McGraw Hill, 1948. The book's central point is that all men always and everywhere pursue "interest defined in terms of power." Successive editions have continued to qualify this point by broadening the definitions of "interest." This is reminiscent of modern

economic theorists' attempts to squeeze mankind's pesky diversity into the ideological construct of *"homo economicus."* But the closer one gets to defining "interest" as anything in which anyone may be interested, the closer to saying that people seek power to do what they want. Tautologically true. But it adds nothing to common sense.

5. *The New York Times,* January 18, 2007.

6. This question was posed in its definitive form at the outset of the post–World War II era of Arms Control by Fred Iklé in "After Detection, What?" *Foreign Affairs,* January 1961. Then as later, such questions have defined bad taste for Liberal Internationalists.

7. Thomas Schelling, *The Strategy of Conflict,* Galaxy Books, 1960.

8. Michael Spence, Interview with Thomas Schelling, *Wall Street Journal,* February 17, 2007, p. A9.

9. *Wall Street Journal,* February 14, 2007.

10. Henry L. Stimson and McGeorge Bundy, *On Active Service in Peace and War,* NY, Harper, 1947.

11. Henry Kissinger, *Nuclear Weapons and Foreign Policy,* Harper, 1957; *The Necessity for Choice,* Harper, 1961.

12. Henry Kissinger, *A World Restored,* Houghton Mifflin, 1957; *Diplomacy,* Simon & Schuster, 1994. But note that the first book argues that statesmen such as Castlereagh really identified their national interests with the balance of power, whereas the second book states that the balance of power resulted from rival efforts to upset it.

13. Henry Kissinger, *Diplomacy,* p. 669.

14. Ibid., p. 670.

15. William Odom and Robert Dujarric, *America's Inadvertent Empire,* Yale University Press, 2004.

16. Robert Kagan, *Dangerous Nation,* Knopf, 2006.

17. See General Maxwell Taylor, *The Uncertain Trumpet,* Harper, 1960.

18. *Wall Street Journal,* February 20, 2007, p. A16. The figures come from the annual report on export guarantees for 2004 of the Economics Ministry of Germany.

19. Gratefully, I acknowledge my intellectual debt to Fred Iklé's classic *How Nations Negotiate,* Harper & Row, 1964. To this book and to Iklé's wise counsel over many years I owe many of the insights in the next pages—insights that I have shared with innumerable students and that I regard as essential to diplomacy.

20. *The New York Times,* November 6, 1998.

21. Secretery of State Condoleezza Rice at the American University of Cairo, US Department of State, bulletin, June 20, 2005.

CHAPTER FIVE

1. Herodotus, *The Histories*. See Solon with the Lydian King Croesus, Bk. I, and the Spartan Demaratus with the Persian Xerxes, Bk. VII: "The Lacedaemonians, when they fight singly, are as good men as any in the world, and when they fight in a body, are the bravest of all. For though they be free-men, they are not in all respects free; law is the master whom they own, and this master they fear more than thy subjects fear thee. Whatever he commands they do, and his commandment is always the same: it forbids them to flee in battle, whatever the number of their foes, and requires them to stand firm and either to conquer or die."

2. Livy, *History of Rome*, Bk. III. The event took place in 366 BC. But the dialogue is surely legend.

3. Paul Kennedy, *The Rise and Fall of the Great Powers*, Knopf, 1989. The concept of per capita industrialization is developed on page 149. Kennedy's book was primarily an argument that empires fell when their military commitments exceeded their economic capacities—"imperial overstretch" he called it. The Soviet Union's collapse vitiated Kennedy's main point, that the United States was dooming itself vis-à-vis the Soviet Union by spending some 6 percent of GDP on its military. But Kennedy and others held on to the principle, this time arguing that the Soviet Union had simply collapsed first. This "economism" simply refuses to consider that noneconomic factors exist independently.

4. In this Hamilton simply followed Adam Smith. See Edward Mead Earle, "Adam Smith, Alexander Hamilton, Friedrich List: The Economic Foundations of Military Power," in Peter Paret, ed., *Makers of Modern Strategy*, Princeton, 1986.

5. The emperor Gallienus (AD 253–268) issued an edict banning members of the Senatorial class from military rank. This culminated a long divorce between patricians and power and cut the final link between society and the legions, which thenceforth became the sole source of power. See Edward Gibbon, *The Decline and Fall of the Roman Empire*, Chapter X.

6. On the absurdity of lending money to pay interest on previous loans, see *The New York Times*, June 23, 1988, and *Wall Street Journal*, August 25, 1988.

7. Leonid Brezhnev, *Journal of the US USSR Trade and Economic Council*, October/November 1977. Also see *Red Carpet*, by Joseph Finder, A New Republic Book/Holt Rinehart & Winston, NY, 1983.

8. The following reports tell the tale: Joseph A. Christoff, Director International Affairs and Trade, United States General Accounting Office, Testimony Before the Committee on Foreign Relations, US Senate, United Nations Oil

For Food Program, April 7, 2004; 2006 Essential Guide to the Oil-For-Food Iraq and United Nations (UN) Scandal, Saddam Hussein, and International Criminals, Senate and Volcker Investigation Reports, US government, CD-ROM, 2006.

9. David L. Gordon, Royden Dangerfield, *The Hidden Weapon: The Story of Economic Warfare,* Harper, 1947. Gordon and Dangerfield, who had been US government economic warfare officials in World War II, write of how they chose to blacklist the Sulzer company, whose politically potent owner was known as pro-American. This made the point that if the Americans were willing to hurt even Sulzer, they would do worse to others. The Swiss government scrambled to get Sulzer off the list.

10. See Hilton Root, *Institutional Foundations for a Market Economy in Africa,* Stanford University, Hoover Institution, March 1994, Chapter 1. And Hilton Root, "What Democracy Can Do for East Asia," *Journal of Democracy,* January 2002, pp. 113–126.

11. Millennium Challenge is a US government corporation funded by US taxpayers, foreign governments, and private corporations, and managed semiprivately to channel aid to the world's poorest governments, mostly African, supposedly mindful that aid to them in the past through governments has empowered despots, enriched those through whom the aid was delivered, and further impoverished the rest. In this regard, see Hilton Root, *Capital and Collusion: The Political Logic of Economic Development,* Princeton University Press, 2006.

12. Developed by economists Paul Prebisch and Hans Singer in 1950 and dispensed by the UN with the help of the United States in the 1960s as the preferred path to industrializing underdeveloped countries, this approach is basically protectionism—namely, the reverse on the international level of the basic economic concepts of division of labor and comparative advantage. Perhaps its most complete trial was given in Chile between 1964 and 1973 when, after the economy collapsed, the dictatorial government of Augusto Pinochet dropped tariffs. Economic logic wiped away uncompetitive industries, reoriented Chileans' energies, and turned Chile into Latin America's most prosperous country. See James Whelan, *Out of the Ashes,* Regnery, 1989.

13. George Perkovich, director of the Carnegie Endowment project on nonproliferation, wrote that no reasonable person can expect a North Korean dictator to give up a program that has yielded such great benefits to the regime. "Imperfect Progress," *Wall Street Journal,* February 14, 2007.

14. Signed by the President on March 12, 1996, and titled the Cuban Democracy and Solidarity Act. See Ernest Luciano, *New England International and Comparative Law Journal,* 1997.

15. "Iraq's Insurgency Runs on Stolen Oil Profits," *The New York Times,* March 16, 2008.

16. "All creditable reports on the subject strike the same note: The problem is beyond our grasp." Maurice Greenberg, Chair, *Terrorist Financing,* Report of a Special Task Force sponsored by the Council on Foreign Relations, 2002. The US government's *Terrorist Financing Archive* contains report after report of individual successes and exhortations to effort, but no claim that the US government can contain the problem of unofficial terrorist financing, much less solve it.

17. "Aid to Palestinians Rose in '06 Despite International Embargo," *The New York Times,* March 21, 2007, p. 1.

CHAPTER SIX

1. In Chapter 4 we showed, following Fred Iklé, that the diplomat's "perpetual threefold choice" between negotiating on the basis of available terms, walking away, and negotiating for side effects is in a sense the basis of his art. But the art of war is framed by the *twofold* choice—victory or defeat. Thucydides' account of Pericles' last oration makes arguably the most eloquent case for the proposition that, once war starts, walking away is no longer possible.

2. In 1897, Theodore Roosevelt could look back over a century of American history and write confidently, "In this country there is not the slightest danger of an overdevelopment of warlike spirit, and there never has been any such danger." See "Washington's Forgotten Maxim," Address of Theodore Roosevelt before the Naval War College, June 1897, *American Ideals,* G. P. Putnam's Sons, 1898, p. 240. It is difficult to imagine such a claim a century later.

3. Charles de Gaulle, *Memoires de Guerre,* Vol. I, p. 10, Paris, Plon, 1954.

4. As our discussion of strategy will show, "net assessment" is the analysis of asymmetric strengths and weaknesses. In the US Department of Defense one Andrew Marshall has embodied the concept of "net assessment" since 1973.

5. The book most fundamental in shaping American elites' minds on nuclear matters is Bernard Brodie, *The Absolute Weapon,* 1946. Tom Lehrer taught math at Harvard. The satirical ditties he sang at faculty parties became best sellers that amused his generation.

6. Robert Kleiman, *Atlantic Crisis,* Norton, 1964.

7. Henry Kissinger typically argues this. *Diplomacy,* 1994.

8. Morton Halperin's point in Anthony Lake, ed., *The Viet Nam Legacy,* NYU Press, 1976, was that the logic of America's "hard line" opposition to the Soviet Union led to nuclear war, and hence that America's defeat in Vietnam

saved the world from this danger. Anthony Lake also authored the passage in President Jimmy Carter's 1977 Notre Dame speech that celebrated America's defeat in Vietnam as having led America back to its own values.

9. In *The Russians and Reagan,* Vintage Books, 1984, Strobe Talbott wrote that President Reagan's judgment that the Soviet Union was a sad chapter in history whose last pages were now being written was a personal judgment, not the policy of the US government. Talbott was factually correct. Reagan was so out of line with the prevailing view that the Soviet Union was eternal and to be propitiated as to render irrelevant the legal fact that, as President, he was the sole repository of the Constitution's Article II power over foreign affairs, and the political fact that he had been elected in a landslide. So unusual even within the Reagan Administration was the view that US policy should aim to end the Soviet Union that when Secretary of State–designate Alexander Haig read that recommendation in the report of the 1980 State Department transition team he fired its authors, Richard Pipes and Angelo Codevilla.

10. Abraham Lincoln, Chicago, July 10, 1858, *Works,* Vol. II, pp. 499–500.

11. Ibid., "Address to the Young Men's Lyceum," Springfield, Illinois, January 27, 1838, *Works,* Vol. I, pp. 108–115.

12. Thucydides I:140.

13. Cicero, "Speech in the Defense of the Proposed Manilian Law," www/4literature.net.

14. Thucydides I:76.

15. John Winthrop's speech, before disembarking his band from the *Arabella* to found Boston in 1630, paraphrased and referenced Moses' farewell to the Children of Israel (Deuteronomy 28–30), reminding them that because "the eyes of the world" were upon them, their behavior would lead others to God, or away from Him. This "city on a hill" speech has proved to be the template of the most powerful American political rhetoric. John Quincy Adams's famous address of July 4, 1821, ends with the words "go now and do likewise."

16. Thomas Paine, *Common Sense,* 1776; Samuel Cooper Sermon on the inauguration of the Massachusetts Constitution, 1780, in Ellis Sandoz, ed., *Political Sermons of the American Founding Era, 1730–1805,* Liberty Fund, 1998. Human equality is bedrock Christianity. Lincoln called it "the father of moral principle among us." It is the biblical major premise of Winthrop's *Arabella* speech, of Paine's *Common Sense,* of the Declaration of Independence, as well as of other major American documents. Any deviation from it is heretical on its face both to Christianity and to American politics.

17. Alexander Hamilton to George Washington, *The Papers of Alexander Hamilton,* Harold C. Syrett, ed., New York, 1961, Vol. 7, pp. 36–57.

18. For a definitive exposition of the diametrically opposite proposition, namely, that the US armed forces should be a vast "constabulary" trained to police the globe, see Philip Bobbitt, *Terror and Consent,* NY, Knopf, 2008.

19. John Quincy Adams, letter to William Plummer, July 6, 1818. James D. Richardson, ed., *Messages and Papers of the Presidents,* Vol. II, p. 17.

20. In his Farewell Address, Washington enjoined his countrymen to "just pride" in "the name of American, which belongs to all of you." The phrase "we have a National Character to establish" was among George Washington's most common expressions. By it he meant that Americans should cease looking at world affairs as British colonists, and rather regard them from their own nation's standpoint—as well as that they should build good character through virtuous behavior. See, for example, his letter to Lafayette of April 5, 1783, and his "Circular Letter to the States," June 24, 1783.

21. Cf. Bruce B. Lawrence, ed., *Messages to the World: The Statements of Osama bin Laden,* Verso, 2005. Note that Lawrence, professor of religion at Duke, argues persuasively on the basis of the messages' increasingly scarce religious content, as well as of their context, that none of the messages after October 2001 is genuine. Regardless of that, the messages complement the Western Left's critique of America. See also Bernard Lewis, "The Roots of Muslim Rage," *The Atlantic Monthly,* September 1990. It argues in part that the Muslim world has adopted many of the concepts developed by Western detractors of Western civilization.

22. I am indebted for insights into Chinese strategic thought over many years to Dr. Michael Pillsbury of the US Department of Defense, lifelong student of Chinese military matters. His paper "Possible Lessons from China on Teaching Strategy" (US Army War College, April 11, 2008) emphasizes the great emphasis (possibly overemphasis) that Chinese political-military strategy places on setting up mismatches over the long run. That, of course, is the primary teaching of Sun Tzu, *The Art of War.* The art's peak is to prepare battles so advantageously that they are won without fighting.

23. AEGIS radars on destroyers in the Sea of Japan would see the missiles on their way up once they came over the horizon. Originally the idea was to hit them during boost phase, when their speed is low and their visibility high. But surface-based, boost-phase missile defense works only in the *exceptional* case where the interceptors can be located close to the point of launch. It turns out that not even North Korea is such a case, because the launch sites for its missiles are far enough from the coast so that boost phase is finished before sea-based interceptors can get to them. Hence the US-Japanese system has to do the much more difficult job of hitting warheads—faster, harder, and less visible than missiles. This is especially

poignant and telling because the United States has chosen not to use available technology for boost-phase defense to place antimissile devices (lasers or interceptors) in orbits with rolling coverage of missile launches anywhere, or to use the same technology that it uses for spot coverage of North Korean launches to defend whole areas (the Japanese islands or the US mainland) against missiles launched from anywhere. That is precisely because it is US policy, unchanged since 1969, rhetoric notwithstanding, not to interfere with whatever damage Russia or China may choose to wreak anywhere, for any reason.

24. America is about freedom. But whose? To do what? How do you justify protecting those who urge others to kill you?

25. See Richard Pipes, "Why the Soviet Union Thinks It Could Fight, Survive, and Win a Nuclear War," *Commentary*, September 1977.

26. The great exception in our time was North Vietnam's decision to send its entire Vietcong force on a frontal assault on US forces in January 1968's Tet offensive. Militarily, it was an unmitigated disaster for North Vietnam. The Vietcong were slaughtered and ceased to exist as a significant part of its force. But those Americans who were arguing that North Vietnam should win the war seized on the offensive as proof. Some postwar North Vietnamese accounts claim that the high command acted as it did only because it was confident that the American Left would react as it did. The truth of the matter may never be known. See Peter Braestrup, *Big Story*, 1978.

27. See William Broad, "Space Based Laser Almost Ready to Fly," *The New York Times*, science section, January 28, 1995.

28. Francis Fukuyama, "The End of History?" *The National Interest*, Summer 1989; Martin van Creveld, *The Transformation of War*, Simon & Schuster, 1991.

29. See especially Alissa Rubin and Damien Cave, "In a Force for Iraqi Calm, Seeds of Conflict," *The New York Times*, December 23, 2007. Sunni groups compete in calling one another "al-Qaeda" to divert US payments to themselves while turning US forces to attack their enemies. Regarding US knowledge of al-Qaeda, see Michael Gordon, *The New York Times*, July 19, 2007. It turned out that a major leader of al-Qaeda whom the United States had been seeking for years never existed, and was merely a figment of US intelligence created by a senior insurgent who had made his career in Saddam's Republican Guard.

30. Ibid.

31. See Erica Goode, "On Safer Baghdad Streets Friction Infiltrates Sunni Patrols," *The New York Times*, September 22, 2008.

32. Michael Rubin testimony before the House Foreign Relations Committee, July 12, 2008. American Enterprise Institute, Short Publications, July 12, 2008.

CHAPTER SEVEN

1. Quoted in Tim Weiner, *A Legacy of Ashes: The History of the CIA,* Double-day, 2007, p. 6. CIA kept this embarrassing judgment secret for a half-century.

2. When foreign nations want details on how many of what kinds of missiles the United States builds, they look in the government documents section of any major US library. When they want technical details, they may be able to buy the production machinery, as the Soviet Union bought the means of manufacturing our accurate guidance systems in 1973. Or they may buy entire factories, as China bought the McDonnell Douglas Plant 85 in Columbus, Ohio, with the machine tools that had manufactured the MX missiles in 1994.

3. Cf. *The Arthasastra* and the *The Shah Nameh,* the books of statecraft of Hindu and Persian civilizations, respectively.

4. Greg Miller, "CIA's Ambitious Post 9/11 Spy Plan Crumbles," *Los Angeles Times,* February 17, 2008.

5. See Laurie Mylroie, *The War Against America,* HarperCollins, 2001. As Bill Clinton's adviser on Iraq, Mylroie was on the opposing side in the Clinton Administration's intramural battles that resulted in its adoption of the State-CIA thesis that terrorism is the work of rogue groups, despite the states whence they operate. I am indebted to her for many insights herein.

6. These matters are discussed at length in my *Informing Statecraft,* Free Press, 1992, pp. 166–173.

7. Bob Woodward, *Plan of Attack,* Simon & Schuster, 2004, pp. 398–399.

8. Interview with Fred Hitz, the CIA inspector general, who investigated the Ames case. *Weiner,* p. 450.

9. William Safire coined the term and pinned it on Bush. *New York Times Magazine,* August 29, 1991. The speech had been drafted by a junior staffer at the NSC named Condoleezza Rice.

10. *The New York Times,* March 16, 2008, reports that in his statement to the Military Commission Khalid Sheikh Mohammed retracted that confession. Edward Jay Epstein, writing in the March 21 *Wall Street Journal,* notes that Khalid Sheikh Mohammed's March 2007 statement to the effect that he planned both the 1993 and the 2001 bombings of the World Trade Center contradicts what CIA told the 9/11 commission that they had got from him in 2003, namely, that he had not even known about the target of the 1993 attack.

11. Nikolai Brusnitsyn, *Openness and Espionage,* Moscow Military Publishing House, 1990, pp. 4–5, quoted in Angelo Codevilla, *Informing Statecraft,* p. 335.

12. Willmoore Kendall, "The Functions of Intelligence," *World Politics,* July 1949, pp. 450–552.

13. William M. Leary, ed., *The Central Intelligence Agency: History and Documents*, University of Alabama Press, 1984, p. 137.

14. Russel Jack Smith, *The Unknown CIA*, Washington, Brasseys, 1989, p. 77.

15. Thomas Powers, *The Man Who Kept the Secrets*, NY, Knopf, 1978, p. 73.

16. Thomas Hughes, *The Fate of Facts in a World of Men: Foreign Policy and Intelligence-Making*, Headline Series No. 233, New York, NY: Foreign Policy Association, 1976, pp. 36–52.

17. George Tenet, *At the Center of the Storm*, HarperCollins, 2007.

18. See 95th Congress, 2nd session, Report of the Senate Select Committee on Intelligence, Subcommittee on Collection, Production, and Quality, February 16, 1978, esp. pp. 9–14.

19. See Richard Clarke, *Against All Enemies*.

20. I was present in October 1982 as CIA's deputy station chief in Rome said this to Italy's Interior Minister, Virginio Rognoni, who answered: "What proof do you want?" Italy had evidence. CIA discounted it.

21. George Tenet, *At the Center of the Storm*.

22. Kevin M. Woods with James Lacy, *Iraqi Perspectives Project, Saddam and Terrorism: Emerging Insights from Captured Iraqi Documents*, Institute for Defense Analysis, Paper 4287, March 2008. But note: On the one hand CIA attributes *both* World Trade Center bombings to the "family" of Khalid Sheikh Mohammed; on the other, it attributes the second bombing just to "al-Qaeda."

23. Tenet, *At the Center*.

24. Tenet makes one unassailable point. Taunting his rivals, he writes: "And [Undersecretary of Defense Douglas] Feith should have had the courage to tell us that his opening slide, shown to the White House, said in essence that CIA analysis stinks." In fact *though the Pentagon's leadership had built the case* that CIA analysis stinks, they *never had the courage to make that charge* explicitly. They did not because they knew that the President, George W. Bush, would not listen. His ignorant faith in CIA made it possible for such as Tenet to trump fact and reason with prestige and pretense. As a result, the US government affirmed the existence of weapons of mass destruction that did not exist, while denying the cooperation between secular and religious anti-Americans who have been killing us all over the globe.

25. *Wall Street Journal*, January 14, 2008, p. A1.

26. *Time*, July 26, 1954; *The Saturday Evening Post*, November 6, 1954.

27. Max Boot, "We Are Winning We Haven't Won," *The Weekly Standard*, February 4, 2008.

CHAPTER EIGHT

1. Livy, Book XXIII.

2. James Bovard, *Terrorism and Tyranny: Trampling Freedom, Justice, and Peace to Rid the World of Evil*, MacMillan, 2003, reports that the TSA had failed to check the fingerprints of hundreds of its screeners against national criminal databases and hence had hired many criminals.

3. Statement of Ronald D. Malfi, Director, Office of Special Investigations, US General Accounting Office, before US Congress Committee on Homeland Security, October 1, 2003.

4. Statement of Gregory D. Kutz, Managing Director, Forensic Audits and Special Services, US General Accounting Office, November 15, 2007, to the Committee on Oversight and Government Reform, House of Representatives.

5. *New York Daily News,* September 12, 2002.

6. "Undercover Agents Slip Bombs Past DIA Screeners," reported by Deborah Sherman, 9News.com, Colorado's News Leader, March 20, 2007.

7. "Preview Spoils Nuclear Plant Security Test," reported by Mike Ahlers, CNN, Washington, January 26, 2004.

8. Peter B. Kraska and Victor E. Kappler, "Militarizing American Police: The Rise and Normalization of Paramilitary Units," *Social Problems,* February 1997.

9. John Yoo, "Courts at War," *Cornell Law Review,* Vol. 91, p. 574.

10. Ibid., p. 583.

11. Jide Nzelibe and John C. Yoo, "Rational War and Constitutional Design," *Yale Law Journal,* Vol. 115, 2006, p. 1. This notion of democracy is as widespread as Yoo says. But it is no less mistaken for being so widespread.

12. Hamilton, *Federalist #6.* In #25, Hamilton shows that the Constitution places the decision to be in a state of war with the legislative branch. In #41, Madison seconds the point and then makes it powerfully against Hamilton in *Helvidius.*

13. *ACLU v. NSA,* filed January 17, 2006, US District Court, Detroit, decided by Judge Ana Diggs Taylor in favor of the ACLU on August 17, 2006. The case was dismissed by the 6th Circuit Court of Appeals on July 2007 with the language quoted.

14. See David Horowitz and John Perazzo, "Unholy Alliance," *Front Page Magazine,* April 13, 2005, and June 7, 2005.

15. "White House Says Tracking Bank Data Deters Terror," *The New York Times,* June 23, 2006.

298 Notes to Chapter Eight

16. "The Path to Victory: A Symposium on the War," *Claremont Review,* Fall 2002.

17. Heather MacDonald, "Why the FBI Didn't Stop 9/11," *City Journal,* Autumn 2002. "I've been amusing myself recently with the following experiment: I call up the most strident anti-police activists of recent years, including Washington's local police scourge, Georgetown law professor David Cole, who argues that every aspect of the criminal justice system is racist. I ask these police critics the following question: Suppose that in the wake of [the September 11, 2001, terrorist attacks on America] the FBI decides to check out recent graduates of American flight schools to see who else may be plotting to use airplanes as weapons. Which students, I ask, should the FBI investigate—all of the would-be pilots. . . ."

18. According to the "Mapping Sharia" project of the Center for Security Policy, Washington, DC.

19. Ibrahim Warde, *The Price of Fear: The Truth Behind the Financial War on Terror,* University of California Press, 2007. Warde teaches at Tufts University.

20. Glenn R. Simpson, "Islamic Charities Draw More Scrutiny," *Wall Street Journal,* February 23, 2008.

21. That was the thesis of William Appleman Williams's *The Tragedy of American Diplomacy,* Norton, 1972. This book and its author were canonical in the social science curricula of American universities from the 1960s to the 1990s.

22. Robert McNamara, *In Retrospect,* Times Books, 1995, p. 252. "The President, Dean, and I worried far more about the pressure from the Right."

23. See supra.

24. According to Jonathan Rauch, whereas opinion polls showed that Republicans and Democrats differed over the Vietnam War by a maximum of twenty points, they showed that they differed by sixty points over the Iraq War. "Partisan Retreat," *The Atlantic,* January-February 2008, p. 19.

25. See John Mearsheimer and Stephen Walt, "The Israel Lobby," *London Review of Books,* March 23, 2006, and the ensuing debate in the US prestige press.

26. Daniel Pipes, "The Danger Within Militant Islam in America," *Commentary,* November 2001.

27. US District Court, Northern District of California, No. C0706076S1, December 23, 2007 .

28. *The New York Times,* September 30, 2006.

29. Those familiar with American history will recognize in this the logic of slave owners in *Dred Scott v. Sandford* (1857): Since the laws of Southern states secured property in slaves, title to slave property, once vested, rested with the owner wherever he went. The federal government (implicitly, the free states as well) was obliged to respect an owner's exercise of his rights over his slaves when he resided in its jurisdiction. Lincoln's third "Freeport question" in his 1858 debates with Stephen Douglas pointed out that approval of this argument nationalized slavery. See Harry V. Jaffa, *Crisis of the House Divided,* University of Chicago Press, 1958.

30. Winfield Myers, "Coddling Islamists," *Front Page Magazine.com,* February 14, 2008.

31. *The Guardian,* December 6, 2007.

32. See M. Stanton Evans, *Blacklisted by History: The Untold Story of Senator Joe McCarthy,* Crown Forum, 2007.

33. Cf. Craig Unger, *House of Bush, House of Saud,* Gibson Books, 2004.

CHAPTER NINE

1. Robert Kaplan in *Dangerous Nation* disagrees but provides no examples.

2. Machiavelli, *Discourses,* II, Book XXIII.

3. Charles M. Blow, "Farewell Fair Weather," *The New York Times,* May 31, 2008.

4. Dennis Overbye, "'Our Final Hour: Global Warning,'" *The New York Times,* May 18, 2003.

5. Former President Bill Clinton proposed taking part in that war by organizing a $1 billion fund to make buildings more energy efficient. Andrew Rivkin, *The New York Times,* May 17, 2008. As the US Senate considered a "climate change" bill in June 2008 the country's major corporations were lining up to share the proceeds of some $10 *trillion* worth of "carbon credits" that the legislation would have created.

6. Department of Homeland Security, Office of Civil Rights, "Terminology to Define the Terrorist Threat," January 2008.

7. See, for example, Thomas Friedman, "Obama's Image," *The New York Times,* June 11, 2008.

8. *Lawrence v. Texas,* 2005.

9. Benedict XVI, "Faith, Reason, and the University," September 12, 2006, http://www.zenit.org/article-16955?l=english.

10. An imitable practitioner of this principle is the Truespeak Institute (Truespeak.com), which tries to convince Muslims that the Wahabi sect is heretical and killing innocents is wrong by marshaling the logic of the Koran—or at least one of the logics.

11. Reuters, May 16, 2008; Associated Press, May 16, 2008.

INDEX